THE REAL RICHES

A true life story by REBECCA DALUDDUNG

Faith
Love
Hope

And now abideth faith, hope, charity,
but the greatest of these is charity.
(1 Corinthians 13:13)

The Real Riches: A true life story

ISBN 10: 1-933817-71-2
ISBN 13: 978-1-933817-71-2

Published by: Profits Publishing
http://profitspublishing.com

Canadian Address
1265 Charter Hill Drive
Coquitlam, BC, V3E 1P1
Phone: (604) 941-3041
Fax: (604) 944-7993

US Address
1300 Boblett Street
Unit A-218
Blaine, WA 98230
Phone: (866) 492-6623
Fax: (250) 493-6603

Scripture taken from the *King James Version Bible.*

Sell that ye have, and give alms;

provide yourselves bags which wax not old,

*a **treasure in the Heavens** that **faileth not**,*

where no thief approacheth, neither moth corrupteth.

For where your treasure is, there will your heart be also.

(Luke 12: 33)

Who is wise, *and **he shall understand these things?***

Prudent *and he shall **know them?***

*For **the ways of the LORD are right**,*

*and the **just shall walk in them**:*

but the transgressors shall fall therein.

(Hosea 14:9)

A New Life You Gave Me

Oh Lord, never been in my life these happened
For I had found you again, and you take me into your loving
arms
I was lost and weary, and definitely dying
But you came and rescue me, and lifting me up from my
sinking sin.

I was safe and secured again, because you had love me
always
You forgive my sin, and you gave me a new life
A life that is full of Hope, Love, Faith and Peace
A life that no one could ever give, but yours alone: a life
everlasting.

You gave me a **new life** to share
A **new Joy** to face the world again
A new **strength** to tackle the pain and trials and problems
in life
A **love to share** for everyone, especially to the unloved
A **new hope** that no matter what happen, you are always
there for me

A **new Faith** to obey everything you commanded me
A **new peace** like the ocean in my soul
A **new life** that overflows, like a river never stop flowing
And that is your life that you gave me and I received it.

Oh Lord, you are really great and wonderful
I praise you for your goodness and mercy
I thank thee for thy faithfulness
And I worship you for the beauty of thy Holiness.

You renew me day and night
Like a light that shines through the dark
That they may see your life in me
Shining like the stars, that everyone would like to have
Your life that you gave to me.

Oh Lord I love you and I always will
For you had loved me first, before I could ever do
For you had given your life to me and all
You had sacrificed and suffered for me on the cross at
Calvary
That my sin may be wiped out, and maybe white as snow.

Oh Lord I will shout for Joy
And magnify your name forever
For I had know your deepest Love
You are more than anything, anyone else to me.

You are great with power and crown with glory
You are king of Kings and Lord of Lords
Creator of things that is seen and not seen,
You created me and you always will...

For your gentleness and love melts my heart
Your faithfulness and holiness changing my unworthiness
And your **Holy Spirit** will mold me and make me
To become your likeness someday
And to be **ready to meet** you in the air when the time
comes
I magnify your name forever.

Rebecca Daluddung 1995

(First poem I ever wrote)

It was published officially by the Kingdom Publications in
the Philippines.

My Covenant

Heavenly Father,
I commit my life to you today,
I will seek your will,
I want to know your purpose in my life.
In Jesus's name I pray.
Amen

Name:_____

Date:_____

Signature:_____

*And ye shall seek me, and find me, when ye shall
search for me with all your heart.
(Jeremiah 29:13)*

Dedication

This book is dedicated to my loving Heavenly Father, my God and our Lord Jesus Christ, the King of Kings and the Lord of Lords, our soon-coming King.

I am so grateful to our God, for my sister Virgie who is the first seed in our family, and for my parents Teodorico (late) and Carlina Daluddung who were models for me in my life. This book is to my sister Virgie who shares with me the love of God. And this is for all the people God has put in my life, namely (Philippines) Pastor Arlan and Ate Mercy, Brother Awe, Brother Al, Sister Beth, (Singapore) Brother Yeen and his wife, Sister Alice, (Hong Kong) Pastor David, Pastor Apollo, and (Canada) Pastor John. For all the books I read, as well as the songs I sang that have touched and shaped my life. Most of all I dedicate this to the all-knowing God, the omnipotent and ever-present God who revealed to me the Real Riches. And to my Lord, Savior and King Jesus Christ, who gave his life for me and taught me the unconditional love of God, and taught me how to live Holy and acceptable to God. To God be all the honor, majesty, glory, power, and strength, forever and ever. Amen.

HOW TO CONTACT REBECCA DALUDDUNG

Author, speaker, Rebecca is passionately sharing her faith as a prayer warrior. If you have a need and you need someone to pray for you, e-mail us:

info@charisagape.com
realcharisagape@yahoo.com
www.charisagape.com

Donate - Charis Now Foundation
www.charisnow.com
info@charisnow.com
604 719-4187

When you purchase this book, you are helping the work of God in preaching the gospel throughout the world. We are helping missionaries around the world, the poor and the needy, by providing shelter and food to them, and giving witness to the lost. And if you are blessed upon reading this book, please pass it to your friends or to anyone you know. You can reach out to them by giving this book so that they too can be blessed.

What People Are Saying About This Book

The title says it all. Rebecca Daluddung invites her readers to experience firsthand, the riches of Christ's love. By sharing her own life experiences, complete with it's triumphs and failure, Rebecca brings spiritual clarity and understanding on a surprisingly large range of topics. Her story illustrates how one soul, listening to and obeying the Lord, can revel in the abundant life that is available to all.

Rev. Owen Scott
Valley Church
North Vancouver

This book is one of the few that touches a reader's life in its simple, easy to understand and practical messages. You can easily identify yourself with the principles and practicality this book shares. This is can also be considered tool for Christian life and ministry. This book is one of the most important pieces for the believer that I have read in a long time. This book also answers the many questions that many Christians encounter in their everyday life. I hope you will consider reading this book as part of a blessed experience in your Christian life.

Rev. Arlan B. Laroya
Senior Pastor of the Jesus the Rock of Victory
Christian Community

Rebecca's powerful new book is refreshingly relatable. Perhaps even more importantly, it's honest. Truth soars through the pages of The Real Riches, *and Becky's real-life journey as a born-again Christian will inspire any reader. With its well-selected Bible passages and fitting applications,* The Real Riches *can benefit anyone who is lucky enough to discover it, no matter where they fall on the religious spectrum.*

Rebecca Hanna
Executive Editor, Hanna Editing

The Real Riches *is both real in its honesty and rich in inspiration. Rebecca has produced a comprehensive story of her journey through faith that any reader can gain something from.*

Bob Burnham
Author of the # 1 Amazon Best Seller:
101 Reasons Why You Must Write A Book
How To Make A Six Figure Income By Writing & Publishing Your Own Book

Contents

About the Author

I was born in the little town of Paddaya West, Buguey, Cagayan. We are a family of eight and I am the fifth child.

My parents were Catholic. My Dad was a politician, and he was my hero. He became a Captain in our town in 1989 before he passed away.

My Dad was a very good man—all the people in our town had highly respected him, not because of his position, but because he loved the people unconditionally. He was a peace maker; whenever our neighbors quarreled with each other, my Dad talked to them and helped them to make peace with each other in a gentle way. He lived his life in line with the word of God. He knew some of the stories in the Bible. When I was a child, I remember learning the story of Mary and Joseph and how Jesus was born. We loved to hear story upon story before we went to bed. Sometimes I fell asleep before the story was finished.

There was a time when I was in elementary school that I got a stomach ache. My dad would take some gasoline (that's what we used as a lamp because there was no electricity in our town yet) and he asked me to lie down and rubbed my tummy with the gasoline. He said things like, "You, the spirit of stomach ache, I command you to leave right now in Jesus's name, and go to the wall." So in my own mind as a child, I could not comprehend what my Dad was trying to do. All I knew is I trusted him and I would do whatever he asked me to do. Now that I have become a born-again Christian, I know that what my Dad was talking about is faith. He tried to exercise his faith in action.

And Jesus said unto them, Because of your unbelief: for verily I say unto you, If ye have faith as a grain of mustard seed, ye shall say unto this mountain, Remove hence to yonder place; and it shall remove; and nothing shall be impossible unto you.
(Matthew 17:20)

If you have faith as the grain of a mustard seed, you can command.

My Dad also exercised (Proverbs 22:6) **Train up a child in the way he should go: and when he is old, he will not depart from it.**

Foolishness is bound in the heart of a child; but the rod of correction shall drive it far from him.
(Proverbs 22:15)

My Dad always taught us a lesson when we did not obey him. I remember there was a time that we didn't do what he told us to do. We were playing all day and we forget that we had work to do, but it was too late when we finally remembered it. Dad came home and he asked us if we had done it. I remember us children lining up from the oldest to the youngest; Dad would take a stick and hit our buttocks, one time each. It is also written in the Bible that when your father punishes you, it is because you are a legitimate son or daughter, and because he loves you. This taught us a lesson that we would remember all the rest of our lives.

Politicians and teachers would often to our house; it is like our house always had a feast prepared. Our mom and dad taught me hospitality.

My mom is a business woman. She buys and sells fresh fish, dried fish, vegetables, fruit preserves, etc. Whenever she sells all of the fish, she comes home with fresh fruits and vegetables to sell again. I remember our house would smell like fish all the time. My mom is a very hard worker; she is always in and out of the house. Although she was busy, she still found time to cook and wash our clothes. My mom also taught us how to cook simple food. She is loving and compassionate, and she has a quiet spirit. She is the best mom for me and for us.

We may not have riches such as massive houses or cars, but the riches we have are LOVE. Yes, love was the foundation of our family. My dad's love for Mom was indescribable. He was faithful to her and so my mom, even after my dad passed away, was never remarried.

I see how my mom served my dad and how he took care of us seven children. I have never seen them quarrel and yell with each other.

I was so blessed to have parents who truly love me, my brothers, and my sisters unconditionally. I am what I am today because I have role model parents who raised me with so much love and affection.

My sister Glory is already married and has four children. Mel and Peng are both married and have kids (except Boyet). All of my family is still in the Philippines. I am the only one in Canada.

My sister Virgie is a missionary, the first born in our family. She is the first seed (born again) in our family. We are all born-again Christians now. My brother Mel just accepted Jesus last year when I talked to him on the phone. My sister Virgie was the one who brought everyone to Christ except my brother Mel. While I was writing this book, he wasn't a born-again Christian yet. He was the black sheep in our family. Praise God! Before this book came into completion, God had grafted him into the vine. So don't lose heart if one or two of your family have not come to know the Lord yet. Just pray for them and God will move because prayer changes everything.

In 1986 I fell in love with the Lord Jesus Christ. I am so grateful that God called my sister Virgie into our family to be an offering of first fruits. God wants every first born to be used for his Kingdom. My sister was the one who told me about the love of Jesus Christ, how he died on the cross to save me from my sin. Since then, I pray the sinner's prayer every time the preacher invites us to pray with him, because I was not sure if Jesus Christ came into my life. But now, I am fully persuaded that neither life nor death, neither angels, trials, or tribulation, will be able to separate me from the love of God which is in Christ Jesus, to Him be Glory, and honor, forever and ever.

My sister was a worker in the church (Resort Village Christian Church) in 1989, when I was studying in Manila. That is where God taught me about faith. I learned so much about his words. And I was so blessed about the life of our Pastor Arlan and his wife Ate Mercy, Sis, Beth, Brother Awe, and Kuya Al. I was a baby in my faith, but I saw God's love in their hearts and how they cared about me, especially Ate Beth. Whenever we traveled together from Las Pinas to Sampaloc Manila, she always paid for my bus fare, and she made sure I was not hungry by always feeding me. I gained so much weight when I was in Manila!

All of them have a part in my growing spiritually. And I thank God for each and every one of them.

Singapore 1989

I went to Singapore in 1989. I was only twenty years old then, and I had just started my first job as a caregiver. I didn't know how to cook at that point, so I had to learn.

Grand Ma (Popo) taught me and the other caregiver with me, who did the cooking. They had two boys; the first one was only one and a half months old when I came. And I looked after them until the first born was four years old and the other was three years old. I will call them Joe Mun and Joe Hoe (not their real names). I loved them so dearly and treated them as my own brothers. I was so blessed to have the Wong Family. They treated me really well, and they welcomed me as part of their own family. We often dined in very expensive restaurants, and tasted all the most exotic and best foods. Every time we would go out to eat, my employer told me, "Eat this, this is very expensive." So I tasted all the great foods (except for the spicy food). I stayed there for four years. I didn't grow much in my faith, because I didn't have a day off and only went to church twice a year—on my birthday and Christmas. But my employer's brother, Uncle Yeen, and Auntie Alice are born-again Christians, so they gave me a Bible and they loaned me books to read about missionaries and Christian literatures. It was enough for me to feed my spiritual life. I remember reading all night, sometimes, and I could finish a book in a week.

Hong Kong 1993

In 1993, I went to Hong Kong. I attended the Lighthouse Baptist Church and got baptized there and stayed for a year. I then moved to another church where I met sister Heming. I had attended the church and I loved their praises. I joined the choir, because I love to sing to the Lord. It is one of my highest praises to the almighty God—to lift my voice and sing to him. I became a member and got baptized again for the second time.

I was so blessed by the life of Pastor Que (not his real name). I've learned so much about God's word and I grew much in faith, and love to the Lord Jesus Christ. I learned to give my tithes and offering, got involved in the choir, and became one of the Bible Support Group Leaders. God had taught me total commitment in all areas of my life. I was in the church all day Sunday. I was so hungry with the word of God and read my Bible and listened to preaching tapes while I worked. It even seemed that one day a week was not even enough for me to praise God.

I attended the new convert class, Bible Support Leader class, and all the seminars. I had never been so hungry before for the word of God. I read more books and I was constantly learning. My hunger for the word of God was so intense. I remember reading all night and getting so excited with all the revelations in the Bible. And God continued to shower me with more revelations of his word, which are what I am about to tell you in this book. The seed I received, I will sow.

Canada 1997

In 1997 I came to Canada. As the Lord had promised Abraham a Promised Land that is flowing with milk and honey, so the Lord promised to bring me to Canada as my Promised Land. I was with the Cousin family in Saskatchewan in a small town called Carnduff. Again, I was so blessed to have them. They treated me so dearly; they are the best. I learned how to bake cakes there. I watched Paulette and Lisa bake and I learned from them. The little town in Carnduff had a small population. But I am so impressed by the way the town treated me. Even if they didn't know you, they would smile at you and greet you. I also learned the Canadian way of hugging people when you see them. I stayed with this family for less than a year and came to Vancouver in May 1998.

The Church that I attended in Hong Kong had a branch in Canada. I knew the lady who ran the church from my time in Hong Kong, so it was a continuation of my ministry in Hong Kong. During those times, my love for Jesus was so deep that I learned to give my life to God in complete obedience to His will. I learned to live a holy life and to put God first in my life. This is a complete commitment to God—in the areas of my finances, dreams, and my life—to serve him no matter what happens. I was one of the Bible Group Support Leaders, as well as a choir leader, in the church. I love singing very much; it's the expression of my love to God. I use singing to honor him and give him praise.

In 2006, I met the Quins family. They are the first born-again employers I had. They had many Christian movies, which I enjoyed very much. Bernice always gave me books to read and CDs about Christianity to listen to, which was a blessing because I used to buy books to read, so it saved me money when they gave me the books instead. They had blessed me in so many ways, especially with the Charis Now Foundation (the charity that I had started). They gave so many clothes, items, and even money. I am so impressed by Stephen, Bernice's husband. He is a man of dignity, a role model, and business man. Even though he is so busy he still has the time for Bernice, which I really respect a lot. I have seen a lot of business men that often forget their family time. Stephen is one in a million business men who stands in God's standard of a family and a role model. I am so blessed for who they are and how I watched them love each other faithfully. Carol Ann is Bernice's sister, who is also a blessing to the charity. She had so many resources and we never ran out of things to send to the Philippines. She is such a blessing for me and most of all for the charity and for others who are new in Canada.

I thank my God for all the people that he has put in my path to bless my life, to impart knowledge, and to share their faith, love, and obedience to God. But most of all, I want to express my deepest love and grateful thanks to my loving God and Father who taught me everything. I'm going to share with you my experiences with God. To God be all the glory and honor both now and forever. Amen.

Foreword

by Virgie Daluddung

Rebecca is a biblical name chosen by our late father Teodorico Daluddung. We are fond of calling her Beck or Becky. She was a healthy child and gave joy to the family as she learned to walk, talk, and explore things when she was young. She was only four years old when I left my family to continue my studies in Manila. I only saw them all once a year during summer vacation. Mother Carlina said Becky was obedient and enjoyed doing household chores together with our sister Glory, because Mother was always busy buying and selling fish, vegetables, and fruits.

Becky came to know the Lord during her elementary school days. She accepted Jesus Christ as Lord and Savior during one session of our DAILY VACATION BIBLE SCHOOL that I conducted every summer. Our friendship was developed during her teenage years. She started asking questions about God and about the opposite sex, which I explained to her lovingly. This led me to disciple her and teach her the importance of prayer and Bible reading. As a new Christian, her faith started to grow and her strong determination to follow God's guidance was evident in her actions and way of life. Rebecca is very friendly, and we often spent time talking about her friends as well. She cared for them too.

Rebecca joined me in Manila to continue her studies in college. Every Saturday and Sunday she was exposed to church life. She was discipled by my friend Marybeth, who was teaching Sunday School for Young People. During that time I became her counselor, clarifying difficult situations and allowing her to choose and understand God's way—not her own ways. She also enjoyed being with the young people in the church, listening to God's word preached by pastors, and mingling with the church members. All of them contributed a lot to her growing faith and love to God. I'm so thankful for what the Lord is doing to my sister.

Our bond as sisters and friends is also growing. We talk about God, biblical matters, hopes, and dreams for the future. We also talk about funny experiences. I call her "Kieth" as an identification of our closeness as friends who keep each other's secrets. And I call her Beck when I give orders and teach as an older sister. She often helped me in my church work, and then she joined the choir and other activities of the church. It refreshes my heart seeing her growing in love with God with God's people in the church, and also growing in love for the unsaved.

After graduating from college Becky decided to work abroad. This time *I* needed to seek God's guidance. It was so hard to let her go, but we trusted God, and we knew that both of us needed to be strong. At the time, we did not yet know that we would soon need to face the hardest thing—letting go of our father who went to be with the Lord. This time we made a final decision. We went to the seashore of Cagayan Valley. There we talked heart–to–heart while sitting in a boat along the seashore, gazing at the sea waves.

We felt the sea breeze and quietness of the atmosphere. After talking about many things, with the sun slowly setting, Beck finally said, "*Ate*, I need to go so that I can help our family." I just kept silent; my faith told me that I could trust her in the hands of a loving God.

During the years of separation I became an intercessor to her. We keep on writing about our joys and victories, sorrows and pains, and our answered prayers and prayer requests. We often talked about our family, our love lives, and many other things.

The first money that she sent to the Philippines was during my ovarian cyst operation, and this was indeed proof of Beck's help to me. Why me? Did I need to give the money to the doctor? God answered no, because God provided all my hospital bills by using different people whom he had chosen to place into my life. Even my OB/GYN, Doctor Melba Santos, and my surgeon gave their services for free.

I thanked God for the money and for his sovereignty in my sister Becky. I decided to invite my friends and those who prayed to give a thanksgiving fellowship for us to celebrate God's goodness and healing. We enjoyed the fellowship, and I felt so blessed and thankful, smiling with God and with the people as I saw them eating our merienda. Then I whispered in prayer, "My Lord, there goes the money." It came during my time of crisis, but it was spent for thanksgiving fellowship, Glory to God. Looking back, I know what God had done. He told me that **first fruit belongs to the Lord**. Beck continued to send money and declared it was for the family. God is so great!

Life is a journey. There are always hurdles and struggles in our Christian lives, but God is always there with us. I praise God for upholding and guiding my sister in her victories and trials.

Becky and I have also experienced years of silence where there was no communication at all, but both of us kept on hoping and praying and waiting for God to move and make things happen. During her joys and sorrows, we share them with God in prayer. There are times that I do phone counseling, listening, and encouraging for my sister. Through her trials I became creative in my praying. In face-to-face counseling, you can touch and show your sympathy, but ours is distance counseling and praying. Thank God, for he is **never limited in working at a distan**ce.

And God creatively answered those prayers. It is God who transforms:

- Sorrows into joy
- Sickness into health
- Struggles into victory
- Brokenness into wholeness
- Blessings into more blessings

In God's special way, he imparted to my sister a shadow of his unconditional love and forgiveness. God implanted in her heart the true riches that come only from him and through him. The **faith, hope, and love** of my sister are tested and molded through the years. The simple Kieth that I entrusted to his hands before she left our place is still in love with our God and King, whom she wants to serve. This is the God who holds her during her ups and downs, teaching her deeper and meaningful things in life so that she has something to share.

After reading the book I came up with this idea: that faith, love, and hope are like an air conditioner, which truly refreshes the soul so that our whole beings will have fullness of joy in every circumstance of our lives.

May God be magnified!

Chapter One
My Story

Why I Wrote This Book

I was very active in the Church from 1993 to 2002, when I was in Hong Kong and also when I came to Canada. My faith grew like a mountain and my love for God went deeper than the ocean. I always wanted to serve God full-time, even before I could commit to the church. Things happened so dramatically, like a brief glimpse. I fell in love with a business man, whom I will call "Ezra" (not his real name)—my sister gave him the name with a biblical reference.

Ezra was not a born-again Christian and he was the reason I received dis-fellowship from the church. I had disobeyed God and committed sin. The fact that I could no longer attend the church that I had lived with all my life and gave all my love to—and gave my heart to—was difficult. But it was an opportunity for me to follow my will and my heart's desires. Ezra and I dated for eight months.

In November 2003, Ezra broke up with me. The pain and the misery can only be described as a dead end for me. There was no exit to the left or to the right, to the back or to the front. The only opening I found was Heavenward. The church and my dearly beloved boyfriend had turned their backs on me. I wanted to die; life was without meaning anymore. I asked God to take my life at that moment but he didn't. I knew that he could if he wanted to. But instead of death, he gave me life again. "A New Life"! And that is why this book is written, because it's so true what David said: "Though my father and my mother forsake me, but the Lord will take me up."

I've written this book not only to the broken heart, to the despairing, to the lost, to the fatherless, to the widow, to the married or single, to the young or old—this book is for you. It is to the wealthy people and the poor, to the lukewarm child of God, to the backsliding child of God, to the people who want to know God, to the child of the living God—this is for you. I want you to have this unconditional love that God has poured out from my heart, and I know he can give it to you just the same. He said, "Without me ye can do nothing." (John 15:5b) My prayer for you as you read this book is that it can apply to your own life. I want your faith to become increased. I want your love to become abundant and I want you to overcome all and be ready to meet the Lord Jesus when he returns. I want us to meet again in Heaven when the time comes. I love you, my friend, with the precious, unconditional love of our Lord and Savior Jesus Christ, our soon coming King, the Alpha and the Omega, the beginning and the end. To him be all the glory, and honor and power both now and forever. Amen

This is my love letter to God when I was on the path of no return—my dead end. I didn't want to live anymore.

There was no way to the left or right, the only thing I could do was look upward.

Love Letter to God

My comfort,

Did I ever want to say I would die for you? Never did I! ... Even though I know for sure that you died because of me.

2

You died for my sin, that I may be free from death to life.

You show me the meaning of Love Divine, without condition, and you love me unconditionally, and I share the same with EZRA. I love him unconditionally. Now he doesn't want that kind of love. He wants a friendship, and I don't understand why. I love him so much. He means everything to me; without him, my life will never be the same again. I am complete when I'm with him; it is happiness that I couldn't describe, like I don't ask for anything more than that.

And this is what happens to me. What is life without being with someone you love? What is the purpose of my living without joy and happiness in my heart? There's only one thing and one wish I could have ... and that is to be with him forever. To share the borrowed life I have from you. I only have a small time, an unknown time limit to live on this planet earth. And if you give me a thousand years to live, I would spend that time with him, to show him the love that you have taught, shown, and given to me. But why does he not want to be with me? Am I not good enough for him? Can I not make him happy and be content? I know I can't do that. I know that there is no way I could make him feel complete. I know he doesn't need me. Because I don't have all the qualifications of what is he looking for? I'm just a poor lady, fat and ugly in his sight, and nothing I can do will make him love me and want me.

I am what I am because you created me this way. I'm not perfect but I tried at least to be perfect in your sight. Only for one thing I've done something wrong in your sight. I've ruined my life ... And you know that. Forgive me Oh God, forgive me.

The only thing I know is that he needs you more than anything else in this world, because you died for him too. Your

3

love will abound to his deepest heart and I pray that one day he will come to know you and be saved.

This life that I'm living is not mine; it's yours. Now if I can have one last wish before you take me home, I would wish that EZRA would come to know you, so that we may dwell in your house forever. Now my life is lifeless, without form. Because I have found out that he only wants me to be a friend. It could have been good if we were just friends from the start. But why did you allow us to be together and then separate us? Am I faithless enough to know that you are the God of Impossible things? That you can make impossible things become possible, and that you own and have the power over our hearts and minds if you want it. Why do I want to end my life if I know that you will never forgive me if I do commit suicide? Yesterday I felt that way. I'd rather be dead than living on this planet earth lifeless, without joy and happiness in my heart, and without EZRA in my life. How am I going to face the world without being with someone I really love, cherish, and adore? I would treat him like a priceless gift. To me he means everything. But now he wants to go away. How can I make him stay? You are the only one who could make him do so.

Now this life that I'm living, I don't deserve it. Everything you've given, I don't deserve it. Take this life of mine or I will take it to you, whatever the cost. If I still had been given the chance to live, I would spend that life with him and you, that your name will be glorified. If you can make a way in the wilderness and rivers in the desert, my hope and my faith will be forever the same. If we are meant to be, you will make a way for us. It may not be today, but it could be the next day. Hold me for I am weak and weary. Strengthen my weak knees and let me stand on a solid

4

rock. I do not want to put your name into shame. Give me wisdom to know the difference and accept the things I cannot change. Help me to be thankful in everything that happens in my life, whether good or bad, and especially in the bad things.

I love you Lord Jesus and I really do. I love you both.
You are my shelter in times of need,
A strong tower from the storm,
A refuge in times of trouble,
A comfort in the time of grief,
A healer in the time of sickness,
A provider in the time of need,
A friend in the time of sorrows,
A love to lean on when someone you love rejects you.

You are there for me in all these years. I am now what I am because you love me, and I know that you will make a way. I love you Father.

The Lord Answers My Love Letters

Fear thou not for I am with you, be not dismayed for I am thy God, I will strengthen you, yea I will help you.
(Isaiah 41:10)

My Comfort, My Shelter

Dear Lord,

Thursday night, I wanted to commit suicide. If EZRA let me go that night, I'm sure I did want to end my life. I was more depressed than I have been in my whole life; that never happened to me before.

I've eaten nothing for two days and only drank water. I cried two days and two nights without life and without form. And I was so weak and almost couldn't even move; I had so much grief.

I called EZRA and was crying on the phone and poured out my feelings to him. He told me I'd be ok. I said I will never be ok because I feel worse, I feel I don't have life anymore, and I said I can't go on. I can't.

I could not go on; not until you took my attention and pulled out my love letter and urgent request July 31, 2003.

I read it all... Your words are so alive to me you said...

Comfort ye, comfort ye my people; saith your God.

Speak ye comfortably to Jerusalem and cry unto her, that her warfare is accomplished that her iniquity is pardon.

For she hath received of the Lord's hand double for all her sins.

To whom then will you liken me or shall I be equal? Saith the Holy One, lift up your eyes on high and behold who created this things, that bringeth out their number: he calleth them all by names by the greatness of his might, for that he is strong in power not one faileth.

Hast thou not known? Hast thou not heard that the everlasting God, the Lord, the creator of the ends of the earth faileth not, neither is weary? There is no searching of his understanding.

He giveth power to the faith; and to them that hath no might, he increaseth strength. Even the youth shall faint and be weary, and the young men shall utterly fall.

But they that wait upon the Lord shall renew their strength. They shall mount up with wings as eagles. They shall run and not be weary. They shall walk and not faint.

Keep silence before me Oh Island; and let the people renew their strength. Let them come near; let them speak, and let us come near together to judgment.

But thou, Israel my servant Jacob (Rebecca) in whom I have chosen the seed of Abraham my friend.

To whom I have taken from the ends of the earth and called thee from the chief men thereof, I said unto thee, thou art my servant; I have chosen thee' and not cast thee away.

Promised: Fear thou not for I am with thee: be not dismayed; for I am thy God. I will strengthen thee, yeah I will help thee, yea I will uphold thee with the right hand of my righteousness.

For I am the Lord will hold thy right hand saying unto thee fear not; I will help thee. Fear not thou worm Jacob (Rebecca) and ye men of Israel and I will help thee, saith the Lord and thy redeemer, the Holy one of Israel.

Promised: Behold I will make thee a new sharp threshing instrument having teeth. Thou shall thresh the mountain and beat them small, and thou shall make the hills as chaff.

Thou shall fan them, and the wind shall carry them away. And the whirlwind shall scatter them; and thou shall rejoice in the Lord, and shall glory in the Holy one of Israel. (Isaiah 40:1-2, 28; Isaiah 41:1, 8-10-16)

I'll be looking forward to seeing that these things will come to pass, because you had promised me and nothing can compare to your promises. I love you forever.

It was during my third day of not eating that the Lord had spoken to me through his words. These are his words from the Bible and I always write them in paper and add them to my prayer request. These words gave me life, since I was without life anymore and I didn't want to physically live. But God's words are true and faithful; it's a re'ma from Heaven. Now I live, because God gave me back my life. He pardons my iniquity, he lifts me up, and now I am alive because he lives in me. He never ever leaves me, in spite of what I have done. He loves me still and is always there to carry me when I can't carry on anymore. He is my faithful friend, and not only my friend, but my God, in whom I trust. My Saviour, my Lord, Redeemer, comforter, tower of strength, my life, and my everything. To God be all the glory and honor and power both now and forever.

Egypt

I am the LORD, your God, which brought you out of the land of Egypt, to be your God: I am the LORD your God.
(Numbers 15:41)

When, the children of God were in Egypt, they were held captive by the Egyptians; they were slaves. So God called Moses to lead God's people free from slavery. God had promised his children a land that is flowing with milk and honey (Canaan). And the LORD said unto Moses, Command the children of Israel, and say unto them, when ye come into the land of Canaan (this is the land that shall fall unto you for an inheritance, even the land of Canaan with the coast thereof) (Numbers 34:12) (Exodus 3:17; 6:8) God desired for his people to be free so that they can serve God.

*Then the LORD said unto Moses, Go in unto Pharaoh, and tell him, "thus saith the LORD God of Hebrews, **let my people go, that they may serve me.**"*
(Exodus 9:1)

As long as they were in Egypt they could not have the freedom to serve God. They were in the wilderness for forty years; some of them died in the wilderness and couldn't reach the Promised Land. Even Moses, who was sent to lead them, wasn't able to reached Canaan. And God hath fulfilled his promise to them. God had brought them out with a mighty hand and with miracles and wonders, as described in Psalm 105.

My life has always been at peace with God. I knew how to live a holy life until the time when I meet Ezra. I was figuratively held captive and became a slave by my sin, which is fornication. I have committed sin against God. So during those times, when I wrote that letter to God, I died spiritually. My life was empty, it had no meaning, and there was no more hope for me to live again. I didn't want to live anymore, because what's the point of living without Ezra? I felt as if it was the end of my world. That was the point where I felt useless; I felt that I was nothing and that I was of no use. It was because of my sins that I felt those kinds of things. Sin is awful, dreadful, miserable, and hopeless, and it leads to a life without meaning or purpose. It was on the third day that God spoke to me through his word.

To whom I have taken from the ends of the earth and called thee from the chief men thereof, I said unto thee, thou art my servant; I have chosen thee' and not cast thee away.

Fear thou not for I am with thee: be not dismayed; for I am thy God. I will strengthen thee, yea I will help thee, yea I will uphold thee with the right hand of my righteousness.

Life came to me again, in that moment when God spoke his word.

I was never the same person again. Here I was, having committed sin before God, and still he told me that He is with me, that He never left me, that he will help me and will strengthen me. I just believed what God says in his word. And now I look back after seven years to find that this promise was fulfilled.

The Promise was:

Fear thou not – Have faith in me (GOD)
For I AM WITH THEE – The Great I AM is with me. (Exodus 3:14)
Be not dismayed – I don't have to be discouraged or faint.
For I AM thy God – For God the great I AM is my God.
I will strengthen thee – He will give me incredible strength.
I will HELP thee – God will help me, comfort me, raise me.
I will uphold thee – God forgive me, build me, and equip me.
With the right hand of my righteousness.

The second Promise was:

Behold I will make thee a
new sharp threshing instrument having teeth.
Thou shall thresh the mountain
and beat them small,
and thou shall make the hills as chaff.

I know that, truly, God has helped me, strengthened me, molded me, walked with me, guided me, built me, taught me, and used me, so with my mouth I will praise him and declare the marvelous and mighty things God hath done in my life. This book is written not because of who I am, but because of who God is in my life. God had looked down on me through the eyes of Grace. I don't deserve it. Amazing grace that's so amazing, I once was lost, but now I'm found. I named my gold fish "Charis," which comes from the Greek word Grace, so that I will never forget what the Lord has done in my life. And it was also the grace of God that this book came into reality. Also I named the Charity Foundation I had started Charis Now Foundation. If God allows me to have a child one day and it's a baby girl, I will name her Charis also. It is grace that

God reaches toward me, toward us through Christ's expense, and grace from God to you as you continue to read this book.

We all have Egypt in our lives, in the forms financial bondage, spiritual strongholds, slavery, sin, sickness, etc. All I can tell you is **Fear Not**! God desires to give you freedom from that slavery, so that you can fully serve God with all your heart and mind and soul. My prayer for you, my friend, is that God will open your heart and your mind so you can understand his word, and that you will come to know God's will in your life. As you read this book, may the Holy Spirit be your teacher and highlight the things he wants you to see and understand, so that you can fully obey God's will in your life.

Why Do I Need to Know These Things?

My people are destroyed for lack of knowledge: because thou hast rejected knowledge, I will also reject thee...
(Hosea 4:6)

I heard someone say, "I didn't want to read the book; I just didn't want to listen to the foolishness in the author's head." Does this sound familiar to you? The Lord said that it is because of lack of knowledge that his people are being destroyed. This is a warning to us. Is knowledge important? Is truth important? The answer is Yes! If knowledge is not important, then there would be no schools. In Canada, people must learn English well; otherwise, people would laugh at them. Because I am a Filipino, the way I pronounce words is different from the way Canadians do because of my heavy accent. For example, when I say "Whitney Houston," I pronounce it as Host-ton, and others can't understand me, because they say Huse-ton. See the difference of knowing and not knowing.

In the word of God, he doesn't laugh at us, but he corrects us. Being ignorant is not a sin, but it will make a huge impact on our destinies.

So this is important for you to know. I won't talk much about unnecessary aspects of myself, but I will tell you about my experiences and what God had taught me all these years. This means that it is important to know what you believe to be truth or a lie, because it is going to be your destiny, and it is what matters most in the final days. My dad taught me the importance of knowledge. He said, "When you have knowledge, no one can take it away from you." And it's really true, they can take all your money and belongings, but they cannot take what you have learned. It is all in your head. My friend had finished taking her MBA and she gave me all her books. I asked her why she didn't want to keep them, and she said, "I don't need them anymore; it's all in here." (She said this while pointing to her head.)

Even if you lost all your money, you can get it back again— even a double portion—because you have the ability, skill, and knowledge that makes you different from other people. It's in your head; your brain can store more memories than even a computer can.

Knowledge

And to knowledge temperance; and to temperance; patience; and to patience. Godliness, and to godliness, brotherly kindness, and to brotherly kindness, charity. But he that lacketh these things is blind, and cannot see afar off, and hath forgotten that he was purged from his old sins.
(1 Peter 1:6-9)

Knowledge is essential. It is important and it is a must-have.

Lack of knowledge could affect our lives in many ways. It could destroy our relationships, cause us to mismanage our money, make us invest in the wrong things, and lose everything. We might marry the wrong person, or we might even take for granted our health if we know nothing about health and, worst of all, if we do not know that there is life after the physical death, we might die without salvation. Hosea said, "my people are destroyed for lack of knowledge."

What is the purpose of knowing it?

All scripture (The Holy Bible) is given by inspiration of God, and it is profitable for doctrine, for reproof, for correction, and for instruction in righteousness.

*That the **man of God may be perfect**, thoroughly furnished unto all good works.*
(2 Timothy 3:16-17)

The good news is that the Bible is the word of God. The Bible is "thropneustor" (God–breathed) (2 Timothy 3:16) or God-inspired. Inspiration is the strong conscious breathing of God into men qualifying them to give utterance to truth. It is God's speaking through men. God is the author and the Holy Spirit.

The **Bible** was written for:

a. **reproof**
b. **correction**
c. **instruction in righteousness.**

The Bible is now the best seller of all books. It is read by every group of people on the planet, and it is the mirror or the book of morals and the standard of people. It was written by the prophets, and the apostles, through the inspiration of the Holy Spirit. How did the Bible come to us? How did the apostles suffer for their faith? John the Baptist was beheaded. Paul and John, just to name a few, died because of their faith. And others had trials of cruel mocking and scourging. They suffered through more than bonds and imprisonment; they were stoned, they were sawn, they were tempted, they were slain with the sword. They wandered about in sheep-skins and goatskins; being destitute, afflicted, tormented. (Hebrews 11:36-37.) They lost their lives physically, because they knew that whoever loses his life for Jesus's sake will find it. (Matthew 16:25) They understood that there is life after death. Jesus didn't remain in the grave; he rose again. Jesus's body was glorified, and this life is eternal. And he alone has the power to give that life eternal to anyone who believes.

My sheep hear my voice, and I know them, and they follow
me: and I give them eternal life; and they shall never perish,
neither shall any man pluck them out of my hand.
(John 10:27-28)

God's Promises to You

God is looking for you.

*I will **seek** that which was lost, and **bring again** that which*
*was driven away, and will **bind up** that which was broken,*
*and **will strengthen** that which was sick.*
(Ezekiel 34:16)

God has a plan for you.

For I know the thoughts that I think toward you, saith
*the Lord, thought of peace, and not of evil, to **give** you an*
expected end.
(Jeremiah 29:11)

God wants to heal you.

*For I will **restore health** unto thee, and I will **heal** thee of thy*
wounds, saith the LORD.
(Jeremiah 30:17)

God wants you to Seek him.

Look unto me, and be ye saved, all the ends of the earth: for I am God, and there is none else.
(Isaiah 45:22)

God wants to save you.

I, even I, am the LORD; and beside me there is no savior.
(Isaiah 43:11)

God tells you do not fear!

Fear ye not, *neither be afraid: have not I told thee from the time, and have declared it? Ye are even my witnesses. Is there a God beside me? Yea, there is no God; I know not any.*
(Isaiah 44:8)

God wants to give you life more abundantly and eternally.

*The thief cometh not, but for to steal, and to kill, and to destroy: I am come that they might have **life**, and that they might have it more **abundantly**.*
(John 10:10)

Chapter Two

The Temporary Riches on Earth

The Richest Man in the World

- Vancouver Sun Dated February 27, 2004 -

Jim Pattison is Canada's third wealthiest individual. *Forbes* ranked Pattison 94th on its list of the billionaires WITH AN ESTIMATED NET WORTH OF $4.6 BILLION USD. Microsoft co-founder Bill Gates remains is perched atop the list for the 10th straight year. Bill Gate's net worth is now estimated at $46.6 billion. And Warren Buffet ranks number 2, with a net worth of $42.9 billion USD.

August 20, 2007, Carlos Slim was the richest man in the world with a $59 billion fortune from a telecom. (*Forbes* Magazine)

March 11, 2011 at <u>Forbes.com</u> Warren Buffet is now the richest man on planet earth; Carlos Slim is the world's second richest man, with an estimated net worth of $60 billion.

These people are so blessed materially and financially. They have everything they want in life. They don't have to worry about what they are going to eat or what they will wear tomorrow or the next day. In regard to wealth, they have security. There is nothing wrong with being rich materially or financially. In fact, it is God's will for his children to live in abundance. But abundance also depends on every person's contentment. Not everyone wants to be rich. I know some of my friends are content with what they have right now and they won't ask for anything more than that. I also know some who are already making lots of money and they want to make more. The question is, how much do you want in order for you to be content?

John describes it this way,

*Beloved, I wish above all things that thou mayest **prosper** and **be in health**, even as **thy soul prospereth**.*
(3 John 1:2)

There are three things God wants for us to prosper in:

1. **Financial or material blessings.** (God will provide everything you need) But my God shall supply all your needs according to his riches in glory by Christ Jesus. (Philippians 4:19)

2. **Physical health.** (Health, healing of sickness) And I will restore health unto thee, and I will heal thee of thy wounds, saith the LORD. (Jeremiah 31:17a)

3. **Spiritual blessings.** (Salvation of our soul) The thief cometh not, but for to steal, and to kill and to destroy: I am (Jesus) come that they might have life and that they might have it more abundantly. (John 10:10)

The word *prosper* is *euodoo* in Greek, which means "to have a good journey."

It's God's will that we earn enough to provide shelter for our family, food, clothing, and if we have more than enough for ourselves, then we can help others for the glory of God.

Is it possible to live without sickness? The answer is yes, and no. We are all vulnerable to sickness because we are not in

Heaven yet. In Heaven there is no more sickness, pain, or misery. We are still on this planet earth. From time to time we get headaches, colds, flu, viruses, fever, infections, food poisoning, etc. Other people might never get sick, so I do believe that for every sickness there is a cure. The medical community may not yet have found cures for all particular diseases. But it is God's will for us to be healthy, without sickness. If it is not possible, then the apostle John shouldn't have mentioned it. And Jesus already paid on the cross. He will heal our diseases, just as David said. You may have a billion dollars, and yet you are sick. I am sure that you desire to be healed. And God's healing is available for you.

God also wants your soul to be prosperous. This is the salvation of your soul, and the knowledge or wisdom from above. The Bible exists so that you are able to grow in spiritual maturity.

For what is a man profited, if he shall gain the whole world, and lose his own soul? Or what shall a man give in exchange for his soul?
(Matthew 16:26)

Story of a Rich Man

There was a certain rich man, who was clothed in purple and fine linen, and he fared sumptuously every day. And there was certain beggar named Lazarus, who was laid at his gate, full of sores, and desiring to be fed with the crumbs that fell from the rich man's table. Moreover, the dogs came and licked the sores or Lazarus. It came to pass that the beggar died and was carried by the angels into Abraham's bosom.

The rich man also died and was buried, and in hell he lifted up his eyes, being in torment, and saw Abraham far off, with Lazarus in his bosom. And he cried and said, "Father Abraham, have mercy on me and send Lazarus, that he may dip the tip of his finger in water and cool my tongue; for I am tormented in this flame." But Abraham said, "Son, remember thou in thy lifetime receivedst thy good things and likewise Lazarus evil things: but now he is comforted and thou art tormented. And beside all this, between us and you there is a great gulf fixed: so that they which would pass from hence to you cannot; neither can they pass to us that would come from thence."

Then He said, I pray thee therefore, father, that thou wouldest send him to my father's house:

For I have five brethren; that he may testify unto them, lest they also come into this place of torment.

Abraham saith unto him, They have Moses and the prophets; let them hear them. And he said, Nay, father Abraham: but if one went unto them, from the grave, they will repent.

And he said unto him, If they hear not Moses and the prophets, neither will they be persuaded, though one rose from the dead.
(Luke 16:19-31)

The Reality of Heaven and Earth

In this story, we learn the reality of Heaven and hell. (Luke 16:22-23.)

We learn that there is life after physical death and that there is accountability, and we learn the reality of physical death.

We have something in common, which tells us that whether you are rich or poor, you are still going to face death. We don't know when it will come to us. But the difference between Lazarus and the rich man is that Lazarus believed in God. He was so poor that he ate whatever crumbs fell from the rich man's table. The rich man knows God but doesn't believe there is judgment. When he was in torment, he then believed, but it was too late for him to repent of his sin.

He suddenly remembered that he still had five brothers that didn't believe, and that if Father Abraham would send Lazarus back to earth to his father's house then they would still have a chance to believe and become saved. We currently live in the generation of "to see is to believe." We (and the rich man) are often like Thomas, who, unless he could see and touch the hands of Jesus, would not believe. But Jesus told Thomas, **"Thomas, you have now seen and touched and you believe it, yet blessed are those who have not seen and yet believed."**

And the rich man again said, "Send Lazarus, that he may testify to them, because I have five more brothers, lest they will also come into this torment." Father Abraham told him, "They have Moses, they have the prophets."

We have the apostles and prophets who wrote the Bible. We have churches now left and right. We have global television preaching the word of God. We have missionaries to go around the world to preach the gospel to every creature. The 106.5FM radio station (local) is there preaching the word of God in the evening from 9 p.m. to 11 p.m. We have born-again Christians around our workplaces. We have family and friends—yes friends—and I am one of them to tell you now that that's why this book was written just for you. That you will not be destroyed because of lack of knowledge. Others have been destroyed, not because they didn't know, but because they didn't believe and they didn't obey the voice of the LORD.

I pray that God will now open your hearts and mind, as you continue reading this book.

And I saw a great white throne, and him that sat on it, from whose face the earth and the Heaven fled away; and there was found no place for them. And I saw the dead, small and great, stand before God; and the books were opened: and another book was opened, which is the book of life: and the dead were judge out of those things which were written in the books, according to their works.
(Revelation 20:11-12)

From the story of the rich man and Lazarus we can learn:

✝ The Reality of Judgments

✝ The Reality of Physical Death

✝ The Reality of Life after Physical Death

✝ The Reality of Accountability

✝ The Reality of Rewards

✝ The Reality of Eternal Separation

✝ The Reality of Heaven and Hell

✝ The Reality of Sowing and Reaping

But most of all, that there are two sets of books in Heaven: the book of work, and the book of life. The moment you came

22

into this planet earth or came out from your mother's womb, you were alive and you had a name. You now have a book of your life, which is the book of your works. For example:

Example: Book of works by Becky Farkoush
Born March 11, 1954

Place	Date/Time	Works of Flesh	Works of Spirit
Philippines	June 1983- 9 a.m.	Lie to Mom	
Philippines	June 16, 1986 – 3 p.m.		Accept Jesus Christ
Philippines	April 3, 1981- 3 p.m.	Steal money- Mom's	
Hong Kong	June 5, 1984- 9 a.m.		Join the Choir
Canada	November 2004- 2 p.m.	Committed Fornication	
Canada	December 2004- 5 p.m.		Re-dedicate life to God.

I assume that the book of works is black and white ink and paper, which is better than a notebook and pen here on earth. A book of works is recorded by the angels. From the day I was born until the day that I will die (God forbid), all my works, and my actions (good or bad) are recorded into that book. How am I going to escape from that book? Because God has assigned an angel to watch over all of us, we know in our hearts that everything written in our own personal book of works is true. And on top of that, God is all-knowing. He knows your beginning and your ending. I will be judged according to what is written in my book of works (Accountability). And then God opened another book, which is the book of life (also called the Lamb's Book of Life [Revelation 21:27b]). This is, of course, just an example below.

Example: Lamb's Book of Life

Name	Date of Birth	Date Born Again	Reason of Death	Date of Death
John Baptist	Unknown	BDC	Beheaded	BDC
Stephen	Unknown	BDC	Stone to death	BDC
Paul Apostle	Unknown	BDC		ADC
Abraham	Unknown	BCC	Old age	BCC
Moses	Unknown	BDC	Old age	BCC
Eunoch	Unknown	BCC	Didn't die	Was translated to Heaven
Elijah	Unknown	BCC	Didn't die	Was translated to Heaven

BDD – Before the death of Christ

BCC – Before the Coming of Christ

ADC – After the Death of Christ

And what if my name is not found written in the book of life?

24

Revelation 20:15 says, **And whosoever was not found written in the book of life was cast into the lake of fire** (the second death, or hell. [Revelation 20:14]). This is now called the eternal separation between the child of God and the child of Satan (Judgments).

That for every child of God, He prepared for us Heaven which is the New Jerusalem.

And I saw a new Heaven and a new earth, and the first earth were passed away; and there were no more sea. And I John saw the Holy City, New Jerusalem, coming down from God out of Heaven, prepared as a bride adorned for her husband. (Revelation 21:1-2) (Heaven)

The Reality of Hell

And I saw an angel came down from heaven, having the key to bottomless pit and a great chain in his hand. And lay hold on the dragon, that old serpent, which is the Devil, and Satan, and bound him a thousand years. And cast him into the bottomless pit, and shut him up and set a seal upon him; And the devil that deceived them was cast into the lake of fire and brimstone, where the beast and the false prophet are, and shall be tormented day and night forever and ever. (Revelation 20:1-2, 3a, 10)

My question now for you is: how can you escape hell? Is your name written in the Lamb's Book of Life? Do you have a place in Heaven? Will you receive a reward after the white throne judgment or will you receive damnation? If your answer to these questions is, "NO! I don't know! Maybe! I want to know!" then you need to keep reading this book. If your answer to these questions is "Yes!" then you still need to read this book. There are riches in Heaven cover to cover that you can learn from the LORD and, even more, he can reveal them all to you.

A Prayer for You

Father in Heaven, I come before you into the throne of grace.

I worship you for the beauty of your holiness. I stand in the gap of this sister or brother reading this book. Father, have mercy, have favor in their life.

I'm asking that you will open their eyes, hearts, and minds so that they can understand your word. Bless them now physically, emotionally, and, most of all, spiritually. Reveal to them the real riches of your kingdom, so that they too can have salvation.

Guide them in your truth and set them free indeed.

This I ask in the precious and mighty name of Jesus Christ our Lord and Savior Amen.

The Incurable Spiritual Disease

September 18, 2010

I went to the bathroom at 12:00 in the morning. I went back to bed and I felt as if my whole body was spinning. I felt like I was going to faint. My stomach was in so much pain that it felt as if I would be knocked unconscious. I prayed right away in the Spirit and asked God to help me, but my stomach pain still did not go away. So I called Choice but he was busy talking on the other line. Then I called Rock and asked him to come over, but he was downtown so it may have taken him an hour to come, so he suggested calling Madeth instead, who lived two doors beside me.

I asked her to call the ambulance and so she did.

The ambulance came after seven minutes and checked on me. They asked me if I wanted to go to the hospital with them; I said yes.

The medic asked me, "On a scale of one to ten, how much pain is your stomach in?" I answered and said, "I don't know, the pain is settling, but it makes me question my faith."

When we got into the hospital it was 12:30 a.m. I started vomiting. Every thirty minutes I had to go to the bathroom. At 3:00 a.m. they called me and checked my heartbeat. The nurse who attended to me told me that my heartbeat was normal.

I asked her why it took so long for them to call me. She said there was only one doctor that night and it was the busiest night they had had at the Burnaby hospital.

She told me to wait outside and they would call me again for another checkup.

I went back and had a seat. While I was waiting for my second time to be called, I asked the Lord, in my mind, why he sent me there, and the Lord said, "PRAY."

I asked the Lord, "Am I supposed to pray for myself first, for my own healing?"

So instead, I started praying for all the people inside the hospital. For the doctor, for the staff, and for all the people who were sick there. I noticed that the people around me had their eyes on me. This was because I had been going in and out of the bathroom for the previous three hours. So when I closed my eyes and prayed, I knew their eyes would still be on me.

At about 5:00 a.m., I started watching people coming into the hospital. I saw:

- A woman who was going to give birth, with her husband and grandmother.

- A woman, her mother, and her daughter (about five years old).

- A family of three—mother, father, and a young boy.

- An old man and wife together.

- A young lady who got involved in a car accident; her face was bloody near her eyes.

- A man on a stretcher, lying down and surrounded by police officers at the acceptance desk.

- A young man with a bloody mouth.

- An old man who was in a wheelchair, with his wife walking beside him.

And the Lord spoke again and said, "Did you see all these people?" I said, "Yes, Lord." The Lord continued, "They are all waiting for the doctor to heal them physically. If one person here doesn't know me, they will perish without salvation."

For what is a man profited, if he shall gain the whole world, and lose his own soul? Or what shall a man give in exchange for his soul?
(Matthew 16:26)

What does it profit a man if he gains the world and loses his own soul? The answer is NOTHING! You can gain nothing but the wrath of God if you do not believe and do not do his will.

So I started praying for the salvation of each of those people.

At 7:00 a.m., the hospital staff attended to me and gave me an IV drip because I was dehydrated.

They took a blood test and a urine test, and everything was normal—praise God. We went home by 9:30 a.m.

I went home and slept. The next morning I still went to church.

Monday morning, I was singing, "People need the LORD." I was crying and speaking in heavenly languages. And the people I saw at the hospital flashed back to my mind. God again was telling me that people need the LORD, that sin is deadly. **A person without salvation is a spiritual disease that's an incurable disease of eternity.** And the LORD reminded me of this book that I had been writing since 2004. That somehow I can reach out to some of you through my testimony. And God will speak to your heart through my testimony. The reality is… there is life after death.

And the sea gave up the dead which were on it; and death and hell delivered up the dead which were in them: and they were judged every man according to their works. And dead and hell were cast into the lake of fire.
(Revelation 20:13-14.)

This is the second death.

The Bible says it is appointed to man once to die and after that is the judgment. Any disease can be cured, but no one can cure the spiritual disease except God, who provided a way and a ransom for you and me. It's only through the death of his son Jesus Christ that I may be free from the spiritual death of eternity in hell. I will talk more about this in the middle of the chapter about the love of God, that he sent Jesus Christ to ransom us and be our Savior from our sins.

A Prayer for You

Father in Heaven, I come before your throne. I worship you for who you are, and glorify your name in all the earth.

I stand in the gap of the person reading this book. Father, open the eyes of their understanding, so they can comprehend your words.

I bind all the forces of Satan against them, and bring them into the marvelous light of Jesus. So that they can know and understand your word and they too can be saved for the glory of your name.

I ask you then Father to protect them from the enemy and give them your divine protection.

Draw them close to you as you had drawn me closer to you.

And give to them the Real Riches that you had given me. This I ask in Jesus's mighty name amen.

Chapter Three
Faith

*And now abideth **faith**, hope, charity, but the greatest of this is charity.*
(1 Corinthians 13:13)

*But without **Faith it is impossible** to please him. (God) For he that cometh to God **must believe**, that he is, and that he is a **rewarder** of them that diligently seek him.*
(Hebrews 11:6)

O Woman Great is Thy faith

Then Jesus went thence, and departed into the coast of Tyre and Sidon. And behold, a woman of Canaan came out of the same coast, and said unto him, saying; Have mercy on me, oh Lord, thou son of David; my daughter is grievously vexed with a devil. But he answered her not a word. And his disciples came and besought him saying send her away; for she crieth after us. But he answered and said, I am not sent but unto the lost sheep of the house of Israel. Then came she and worshipped him, saying, Lord, help me. But he answered and said, it is not meet to take the children's bread, and cast it to dogs. And he said, truth Lord: yet the dogs eat of the crumbs which fall from their master's table. Then Jesus answered and said unto her, O woman, great is thy faith: be it unto thee even as thou wilt. And her daughter was made whole from that very hour.
(Matthew 15:21-28)

The Meaning of Faith

*Faith is the substance of things hope for **the evidence of things not seen.***
(Hebrews 11:1)

So then faith cometh by hearing, and hearing by the word of God.
(Romans 10:17)

My Story

Faith was sown in my heart when I started hearing God's word through my sister Virgie. I was only in elementary school when she first told me about what Jesus did at Calvary. That he died on the cross to save me from my sins. So I made a prayer for forgiveness, and thanked God for giving me his son to die for my sins, and I accepted him into my heart as my Lord and Savior. That's all I did and knew, but I accepted the Lord Jesus Christ in my heart that day and Virgie was a witness to me. We often had a Vacation Bible School whenever she came home. This was the start of my faith. It was thirteen years ago, and at that time I didn't fully understand the whole meaning of faith and the wonders of God's amazing grace and love for me.

The first step of faith was so tiny, but I began to exercise it. I was on my second semester in college. It was the first day of school, and I needed to go early because I wanted a seat in the front row. It was a first-come-first-served chair. If you missed the first class you most likely would be seated at the back. But to my surprise, my sister didn't want me to go to school, because we had to do something that day. She told me it was only first day of school and most likely we wouldn't start important class work yet. But I reasoned out to her that I wanted to go because I didn't want to sit in the back. To my surprise she told me, "Beck, your faith is so tiny, you can't even trust God with your chair. God can take care of it." I said ok. I realized she was absolutely right. God is able to do that. If I wanted a seat in the front row, God would be able to do that for me. All I needed was to trust God with these little things (e.g., the chair).

The next day I went to school and asked my friend about the previous day's class. She told me that the instructor had not shown up for the first class, so I had missed nothing. I was so happy and thanked God for what he had done for me. I was able to sit in the first row. I was so impressed by what God did, and by what an amazing God we serve.

Nothing is Impossible With God

But Jesus beheld them, and said unto them, **"With men this is impossible; but with God all things are possible."** (Matthew 19:26)

I began to quote this verse and my motto has always been "Nothing is impossible with God."

My sister Virgie worked as a full-time employee in the church. The name of the church is Resort Village Christian Church. I went to school from Monday to Friday and stayed in my aunt's place in Manila. On Fridays after school, I would go to Las Pinas, where my sister attended church, and I slept at the worker's house. Sundays were the most exciting days for me because that is when our church services were held. I helped my sister in the church. I admired the workers so much because of their love for God. I especially admired Pastor Arlan, his wife, Ate Mercy, Sis Beth, Brother Al, and Bro Awe. I'm so blessed to have had them in my life and for what they have done in the church. My faith grew and I learned more about God with them through Bible study. We also did evangelism together. I finished my study as a Secretarial

and become one of the top ten in my class. After I had graduated as a Secretarial, I looked for a job right away in the
Philippines. My aunt told my sister that she knew an agency
that was hiring and that I should go to Singapore. So I tried to
apply; this was in April of 1989. My dream had always been
to just serve God. So going to another country? This was not
even in my wildest dreams. All of my friends wanted to go
abroad. But it was never my personal wish to go anywhere
else. I applied anyway. We didn't have much money when I
applied. I just had this little bit of faith in me that my God
would provide whatever I needed. In June 1989, my Dad was
diagnosed with a complicated heart disease, kidney failure,
and high blood pressure; he passed away that same month.
It was the following July that I received the job offer to go to
Singapore as a caregiver. I left the Philippines on August 1989
and I was able to go to Singapore with borrowed money. We
used all of our available money for my dad's hospitalization
and funerals, and we had nothing left afterward. But God
was so faithful to us in still providing me with funds to go. I
left in August 1989. Truly, God taught me to put my faith on
him alone, and I learned to trust him completely through his
word. He proved to me over and over again that he is a God
that is able to go exceedingly and abundantly above all that
we can ever ask or think or imagine. He is not an un-able God
that we are serving, He is all-able, and all things are possible
for him if you just believe. Maybe you have lots of money to
spend; you are so blessed and you should thank God for it.
He alone is the owner of your life. He created you as a human
being, and you never exist on this planet earth without him.
That alone can make you believe that he is the creator of the
universe, the Almighty God who created everything that you
see and touch, as well as things you do not see.

God created all the different kinds of trees that bear the
fruits we enjoy eating. He made the sun to give us light during the day and the moon by night. God created the rivers

and oceans so that we can have all the different kinds of fish to eat. God gave us our brains to be able to think and create. People invented airplanes; we can travel from one place to another just from the use of airplanes, jets, cars, and boats. Nothing exists without the Creator—the God of Abraham, Moses, and Jacob. He is the God of the whole earth. He is my God whom I want you to meet and have an intimate fellowship with. My prayer is that as you read this book your faith becomes like a mountain that cannot be moved, shaken, or destroyed by any circumstances that come into your life.

I hope that your love will abound and will flow like a river to everyone you touch and get close to. I hope that your hope will increase, and your faith will not be shaken, no matter what circumstances you face. I hope that one day you will be ready to meet the Lord Jesus Christ when he returns. And most of all, I hope that you may know the depth, the height, and the width of the love of God in you.

Faith – "pistis" (Hebrew word) means, primarily, firm persuasion, or a conviction based upon hearing.

Faith had begun in my heart when I heard about the word of God. Like the Caananite woman—she heard about the Lord Jesus Christ, that he was able to heal the sick, make the lame walk, and cast out devils. So when she came to see Jesus, her faith began upon hearing.

The Trial of Faith

The story of the Caananite woman is the best example I have in the Bible because it touches my heart so deeply. And it was then that God began teaching me to have great faith in him. This woman had three negative responses or answers to her plea.

1. Jesus didn't say a word to her and his disciples asked her to leave. (Verse 23)

2. Jesus told her that she was not part of the promise of Israel, because she was a Gentile woman. (Verse 24)

3. Jesus told her that it was not good to give blessings to the dogs (meaning Gentile or Caananite people); it has to be first to Israel, and they must be first-class blessings only.

Despite what was said to her, she persevered in her true faith and knew that Jesus would be able to heal her daughter. She reasoned it out with wisdom and perseverance, that even though she was a Gentile woman, she was not part of the blessings of the children of Israel. But she also believed in God's purpose for Gentiles to receive blessings indirectly when he blesses Israel.

The Trial of My Faith (Phase I)

Jesus became the Lord of my life.

*That the **trial of your faith**, being **much more precious than of gold** that perishes, **though it be tried with fire**, might be found unto **praise** and **honor** and **glory** at the appearing of our Lord Jesus Christ.*
(1 Peter 1:7)

In June 1989, my dad was diagnosed with a complicated heart disease, high blood pressure, and kidney failure. My mother, my sister, and I went to see him at the hospital in Tuguegarao Cagayan. As I looked at my father, I began to pray to God; I prayed that he would heal my father in that moment. I had learned by then that he is the God who can heal the sick and he has the power to do impossible things. I put my faith in God, knowing that healing my father was perhaps the most impossible thing that I could ask for, yet still believing that he would heal him. But my faith in that instance was so strong that I was completely surprised when God did not heal my father.

36

I felt that God had failed me and did not hear my plea. The doctors and nurses attempted to revive my father's heart, but it was all to no avail. They simply did not have the power to bring him back to life. When my father passed away, I truly felt that God had failed me. I felt that he had not been listening to my plea. I did not cry, although my heart was aching from the pain and silent grief. I felt so much hate at that moment, both in my mind and in my heart.

I had to talk to God and ask him the questions in my mind. I spoke with him only in my mind, because I believe God can hear our thoughts and knows what we think before we can even think it. I said to my God, "Why did you not heal my father? You know that I love him so much. You have all the power to heal him and give him life. Why?? You forgot me at this moment, so I am going to forget you, too, as my God."

I continued to wrestle with God. I continued to blame Him. I continued to wonder why he would do this to me. I was so bothered that I could not eat. I became completely detached from my friends and family. My mom and my sister and my cousin all tried to console me, but I pushed them away—figuratively and, at one time, literally. I acted like a crazy woman without any understanding. All the while, my brother and sisters just cried and said nothing. I loved my dad so much, and I never expected for him to leave us so early in life. I could not free myself from the thought that God had abandoned me, failed me, and disregarded my prayers.

I continued to struggle in my relationship with God for about a month. My sister, at around that month, came back from Manila with some big news for me. I was reluctant to listen to her, but she persisted and let me know that I had received employment in Singapore. I told her that I was no longer interested in going to Singapore—I was still so hurt and withdrawn. She then said, "Listen, it's not me, your choir director told me to tell you this." This made me begin to open my ears and listen. My sister continued and said, "When we accept

Jesus as our Lord and Savior, we don't accept him as Savior only but also as Lord. When you said 'Lord,' that means he is the Lord of everything." That's all she told me, and I was left to continue what I had been doing.

At that moment, the Lord spoke to me in a soft, small voice and said, "Have you accepted me as your Savior?" I answered, "Yes, Lord, I accept you as my Savior." The Lord continued, "Have you accepted me as your Lord?" I answered again and said, "Yes, Lord." Tears flowed from my eyes and I said, "Oh Lord I'm sorry, please forgive me! Please forgive me. If you always know what is best for us, then it must be best that my dad passed away now, rather than suffered for many months in pain." So I went to my room and, for the first time, I cried and poured out my grief.

I didn't tell my sister what happened to me, but I went to Manila with her and then agreed to go to Singapore. I gave my testimony in the church, telling of what the LORD had done for me, and I cried again. I didn't know that they had been praying for me ever since they learned about my situation through my sister Virgie.

I was very immature in my faith at that time when I was struggling with my God. I knew that he had all the power to heal my dad if it was his will. But I have since learned the most powerful wisdom and knowledge, that whatever happens in my family and in my life, God is still God and he knows what is best for us. He is the Lord of everything he created. He is the potter, I am the clay. God molded us and made us in his likeness.

I thank my God every day for the people that he brought into my life. Each of them has a very special part in my life, to make me grow and mature in my faith. I had failed my second trial of faith, but I gained great wisdom from it. Glory to God! I've learned that our God is an all-knowing God; he sees the future and is always present. So he knows what is best for us.

We only need to trust him fully. We also need to embrace our loved ones and show them that we love them before they are gone. Seize every moment that you are together and embrace life with them; give all your best to love and care for them. Do not wait until they are already gone and they can't hear you.

You may be in the same situation as me; perhaps one of your loved ones has passed away and you are still wondering why God allowed this to happen to them. Good man or evil man, young or old, we are all going to taste death. We just don't know when it will come upon us. Always remember that the life you have is not yours; it's given to you as a borrowed life from God. It's yours to enjoy, and God wants you to experience everything that he has created. It's up to you if you use your life for good or for bad. But if you live wisely here on earth, you will have a reward, and I will talk about that in the last chapter of this book.

The Reward of My Faith

O woman Great is thy Faith, Be it unto thee as thy will.

My story: The trial of my great faith

While I was working in Singapore, I had saved enough money for my expenses to come to Hong Kong. I was in Hong Kong for one year, and then I went home temporarily to the Philippines to get all the requirements to apply for a job in Canada. One Sunday at church, our pastor taught about the Canaanite woman who had a daughter that was possessed by a devil. I somehow knew then that God was going to test my great faith.

It was March 1997 when I got the employment letter from the Canadian Embassy. I was jumping up and down from overflowing joy that day; it was God's surprise present for me on my birthday. I took a medical examination the same week that I got the employment letter.

Two weeks later, my employer in Hong Kong gave me a release letter. They were going to move out to a smaller apartment.

I suddenly had a problem. I couldn't stay longer in Hong Kong if I did not have an employer. However, I wondered who would hire me if they knew I would soon be going to Canada. God gave me wisdom and knowledge on what to do. I talked to a friend of mine who owned an agency and explained to him my situation. I asked him if he would be able to support me; he agreed right away. Just like that, my problem was solved.

Yet another problem arose, however, when I needed to process my employment paperwork. My employer had left for a business trip and was not able to provide me with the documentation I needed to stay in the country. I was given a two-week visa and was told that I must find another employer or I would be sent back to the Philippines. Although I knew finding employment elsewhere would be difficult since I would soon be leaving for Canada, I had no choice but to seek another job.

Before I could even consider finding a different employer, I was required to have another medical examination. Typically, it takes a month to get an appointment for a second exam. The doctor was incredibly kind to speed up the process for me, because I only had two weeks left to be in the country. If I hadn't been able to have my exam, I would have been deported no matter what.

I prayed to God and asked him what I should do at that point. I asked him, "What's next Lord?" I was in the sky train station when, suddenly, the small voice of the Holy Spirit spoke to me. "Call your employer's friend." So before I took the sky train home, I made a phone call on the pay phone. I called my ex-employer's friend Mr. Yu and explained to him my situation. I asked him if he would be willing to sponsor me for the time being, until I got my visa to Canada. He told me to call back the next day, because he had to talk to his wife about it. In the night, I was praying that God would work in their hearts and that they would be willing to support me on this journey. So I called him the next day and he said, "Yes, we are willing to help you. Let me know what papers I need to give you so you can process them. And come over tomorrow and I will give them to you." I said, "Thank you very much," and told him what papers he needed to give me. I was so happy and overwhelmed with joy, for I knew that God was with me. God makes sure that every step I take is under his provision and control.

I went back to the immigration office the next day and processed my papers. I was officially able to stay and work in Hong Kong while waiting for my visa to go to Canada.

I was so excited to go to Canada that I decided to book my ticket to fly there. I called the airline and asked to book my flight. I told them that I did not yet have my visa, but I would call them if something changed. Booking my flight at that point was an exercise in my great faith. Here's what I wrote, by faith:

Book the ticket – REGINA SASKATCHEWAN
Date of Booking – Tuesday April 15, 1997
Date of Exodus – April 30, 1997- Canadian Pacific
Exodus – 1:30 p.m. Hong Kong
Joshua- 9:50 am Vancouver
Connected to Jordan River (CP 1344)
Departure Vancouver – 11:30
Arrival Regina – 14:45
Promised Land – Canaan – Canada

Chapter Four
The Power of Faith

Jesus answered and said unto them, verily I say unto you, ***if ye have faith,*** *and doubt not, ye shall not only do this which is done to the fig tree, but also if ye shall say* ***unto this mountain be thou removed, and be thou cast unto the sea; it shall be done.***

And all things, whatsoever ye shall ask in prayer, ***believing ye shall receive.***
(Matthew 21: 21-22)

My friend heard about my letter from immigration and told me, "I heard that you are going back to the Philippines." I replied to her and asked, "Who told you I'm going back to the Philippines?? I'm going to Canada."

And that is exactly what happened. Because I believed, with all my heart, what God has promised to me. I had a few setbacks, and my original intention of leaving in April 1997 changed. Instead, I left on June 19, 1997. Glory to God! God had promised me a land that is flowing with milk and honey, and this land is Canada for me. It was a very big challenge of faith for me, because when blessings come, many negatives tend to also come to try to kill my faith. The following circumstances I underwent seemed to allow no way out.

1. My employer terminated my contract.

2. The immigration office gave me two weeks of stay in Hong Kong.

3. My medical was not good; the doctor said I needed a re-medical (wait a month for a medical checkup).

4. I needed to find an employer to be able to stay in Hong Kong.

5. I needed money to be able to go to Hong Kong.

In spite of all these negative circumstances, God had taught me to trust in his word and promises.

May 5, 1997

Revelation: Canaan Arrival

To you I will give the land Canaan as the portion you will inherit.
(Psalm 105:11)

You are worthy to be praised, yes I will proclaim all the wonders that you have done in my life. My mouth will sing it, shout it, and proclaim it among the congregation, among the heathens, all the wonders of your love and faithfulness in my life. Thank you Father for the privilege to come out now. I am ready to go. I'm excited, extremely excited. My thanks will never end, a simple thanks is not enough but I have streams of joy and overwhelming happiness, joy and peace. I love you LORD.

May 16, 1997

Isaiah 55:12 (the mouth of the Lord had spoken)

You will go out with joy and be led forth in peace; the mountains and the hills will burst into song before you, and the tress of the field will clap their hands.

Father, thank you for the promises and the confirmation that I can go to Canaan in the coming week. I will go out

with joy and be led forth into singing, and the congregation will clap and clap their hands for praising you because of all your mighty hands hath done.

I am so happy Father, really happy. Thank you Father. I praise you and worship you for all the wonders of your love and faithfulness.

PRAISE YE THE LORD!

Amen.

May 21, 1997

Psalm 144:1-2

> *Praise be to the Lord my rock, who trains my hands to war, my fingers to fight, my fingers for battle.*
>
> *He is my loving God, and my fortress, my stronghold and my deliverer. My shield in whom I take refuge, who subdues people under me.*

My Father, praise and singing be to you, my rock and my stronghold. I thank you for all the things you have done in my life. I can't do anything without you. It's all because of your amazing GRACE; that's why I am still here. Be it unto me then according to your promises, according to your word, according to your revelation you've given, that I will be ready to testify this Sunday. Prepare me then in Jesus's name Amen.

May 21, 1997 (Becoming Impatient)

Isaiah 54:4-5

> *Do not be afraid, you will not suffer shame, do not feel disgrace, you will not be humiliated. You will forget the*

shame of your youth and remember no more the reproach of your widowhood. For your maker is your husband- the Lord almighty is his name- The Holy one of Israel your redeemer. He is called the God of the whole earth.

Today you promised that my visa would come, and tomorrow I'm going to pick it up, and this Sunday I will go and testify, and the 30th is my exodus arrival to Canada. Thank you Father. Thank you so much. In Jesus's name! Amen.

May 23, 1997 (Becoming More Impatient)

My Deliverer,

My Father, thank you so much for the answer to my prayer this afternoon. I don't want to stay here anymore. Now it's time to go. But I cannot go until my visa comes.

Does my visa come today? Will I be able to have a testimony this Sunday? Father please give, or bring to pass, all the promises that you have spoken to me. Do not delay it any longer. Bring it to pass. I want to see the reality of my faith. Be it unto me then according to your word, according to your promises.

Father please! Please Father!

I'll be very happy if you give me time to have a testimony this Sunday. Please Father.

In Jesus's name! Amen.

May 28, 1997

Psalms 30, Psalms 28

7:35 a.m.

My Rock and my Fortress,

To you I lift up my soul, my heart is fixed. Oh LORD, I will not be moved nor will I be shaken. Because of your promises, because of your word is truth, and you are able to do or fulfill all the promises that you had given long ago. Make or let them come to pass now Father.

Please do not delay it, lest I'll be weary in waiting. Remember Oh LORD the suffering I had endured when I passed through the fire. Remember all the things that I've done. Remember my FAITH that you strengthen and make great. I am looking for you to let it be according to my faith. What's lacking in my faith again? I have works and I have faith; couldn't that be enough to fulfill all the promises you have spoken to me?

Father I trust you and I trust your word. You are true, you are real, you are worthy to be praised. You are eternal, unchanging. That means you will forever be the same. So I will look for you as long as I live.

Father please. Be it unto me according to your words and promises. In Jesus's name Amen.

The Rewards of Faith

But without Faith it is impossible to please God, for who that cometh to God must believe that he is, and that he is a rewarder of them that diligently seek him.
(Hebrew 1:6)

June 11, 1997 5:15 p.m.

My Father and my Deliverer,

A simple thanks cannot say how I feel. Thank you Father for the answer to my prayers. Thank you for my visa via

Canada. I got it in Jesus's name. I feel it and I know I got it because of your promises.

Monday was really a wonderful day for me, for I felt your mighty presence. I was jumping up and down praising you, and there was what felt like a fire on my tongue that I couldn't control, praising you with loud praises, shouts of praise and triumph. Thank you Father. That's what I'm longing for, to be in your presence all the time, to overcome all the time, and to love you all the time. Give me then a time, so I can share all the wonders of your mighty love for me.

That they may know you from the rising of the sun till it sets that you are God and there is none like you. That people may praise your name and glorify your name.

I'll be hoping my visa will come this week so I can testify this Sunday.

June 15, 1997

I know that everything is fine now and thank you for the revelations again. Please do not allow the enemy to mix up my dreams. I just want a dream from you. If you give me a revelation through dreams please fulfill it, just like all the promises you are able to fulfill. You promised me that you will never put me to shame. I look for your promises because they are my life and my joy. Fulfill your promise to your servant, that my enemies may see it and be put to shame. Thank you for the strength, and for renewing me each day. Thank you once again.

Amen.

June 11, 1997 9:00 p.m.

My Jesus,

What a relief. What a joy. What wonderful good news. I got it at last.

It's what I'm longing for.

One song is not enough. I need more now that I received it.

Thank you Father for my visa via Canada. It's really, really, really great. You're so great, marvelous, mighty in honor and praise. It was really a matter of time and patience, but in the end I got it.

I can hardly express my thanks and my joy keeps over-whelming me for all these things that you have done. I'm ready to testify LORD, thanks a million Oh Lord!

Praises to your name!

God has fulfilled all the promises he has given me. Not one has failed.

God has also taught me how to fight the good fight of faith, how to trust him despite the negative circumstances, and how to keep proclaiming God's word and promises. I gave my testimony that Sunday and they were all amazed by what I had gone through, and they declared what the Lord hath done for me.

I left Hong Kong on June 19, 1997. Just as my faith was tried, so will your faith be tried.

August 6, 1997 - Canada

My Rock and Savior,

Glad to be here, thanks for all the fulfillment of your prom-ises to me. They are so real to me now. They came into reality. I can't express my thankfulness and my happiness for having those fulfilling promises. Thank you Lord Jesus.

Thanks for my good employer; it is excellent! Thanks for everything and for the blessings that I received. My salary is $1,000, no charge for the room, and free food. I am free to move around the house and use everything in it. Thanks for giving me such a beautiful house and room. But through it all, I was so thankful for a wonderful employer and three kids, whom I love most.

Thanks for bringing me here. I'm so happy and peaceful. But one day, when I dreamed about a certain man, I had fallen in love with him. Could it be a dream or just a map or what? One thing I know is that dreams come true. How can I ever run away from the dream? Help me Lord. Amen.

<u>I stand with faith and trust that God is going to do miracles in my life.</u> In the beginning, when my visa arrived, he said to me, "O woman great is thy faith, be it unto thee as thy will." Just as Paul also said, "Show me your faith without works and I will show you my faith with works, for faith without work is dead."

And now I'm already in Canada. I have been here thirteen years and I am writing this story of mine for God's glory. I can tell you with all of my heart that the greater the blows the greater the blessings. And if you persevere in your faith and prayer, you can get what you ask for from God. Whether it be a healing of your afflicted body, a miracle, a financial breakthrough, a salvation of your family, or whatever you ask, believe you can have it and you shall have it. It may be a matter of time, maybe months or years, but God always gives whatever we ask of him.

If ye then, being evil, know how to give good gifts unto your children, how much more shall your Father which is in

heaven give good things to them that ask him?
(Matthew 7:11)

After all these things happened to me, I gained wisdom from above and I can say, "Great faith accomplishes great and mighty things."

How to Have Faith

*So then **Faith cometh** by hearing, and hearing by the word*
of God.
(Romans 10:17)

In the story of the Canaanite woman, she just heard that Jesus can heal the sick and can cast out demons. From that moment on, she believed and went to see Jesus. She got what she asked for because of her great faith. I got what I wanted because of my persistent great faith.

***Fight the good fight of faith, lay hold on eternal life**,*
*whereunto thou art also called, and has professed **good***
***profession before many witnesses**.*
(1 Timothy 6:12)

Faith comes by hearing the word of God. When was the last time you heard God's word? When was the last time you heard about the love of God, that God sent Jesus, his only begotten son, to redeem us from the coming wrath? Were you convicted by the Holy Ghost? Did you respond and say, "Yes Lord I will obey and follow you"? Do you believe what the Bible says? It says that there is a creator, and that we are created beings. It says that one day we are going to face our creator and we will be judged according to our works.

Salvation is a free gift; you don't earn it or work for it. It is only received through **FAITH**. Faith is believing that God exists and trusting God's words are true and just. Salvation is a gift from God to anyone who believes in him. Grace is the grace of God, and it means unmerited favor. You don't have to earn it to be saved; all you need is to believe or to have faith in God.

Zacchaeus was a tax collector and he was a rich man. He heard that Jesus was coming to the Town of Jericho. He couldn't get closer to Jesus because there were too many people in the crowd and he was very short. So he ran and climbed up a sycamore tree to see Jesus.

Notice that Zacchaeus was very persistent. He wanted to be noticed by Jesus. Everybody else was following Jesus, but Zacchaeus had his own idea, "If I can climb up into the tree, then Jesus will notice me." His idea was brilliant; Jesus noticed him right away. On that day when Zacchaeus met Jesus, he was never to be the same person again. Zacchaeus stood and said unto the Lord, "Behold, Lord, half of my goods I give to the poor, and if I have taken anything from any man, by false accusation, I restore him fourfold." (Luke 19:8) And Jesus said unto him, "This day is salvation come to this house, forsomuch as he also is a son of Abraham." (Matthew 19:9) Notice Abraham is the father of faith. Read Hebrews Chapter 11; the whole chapter talks about faith.

Rich men do not climb trees; they make appointments. They think differently from the poor and the middle class. Rich people take risks and are not afraid of doing so. They have a strong determination and are persistent about winning no matter what the cost of it.

They are very well educated in almost all things, except for the word of God.

That's why the rich man rarely can enter into the kingdom of God—because he trusts in his abilities and skills rather than trusting in God.

How many trees have you climbed just to hear the preaching of the word of God? Are we so eager to hear about salvation? There are so many books out right now that you don't have to climb trees to hear it—just buy it. You can go to the Christian church and hear the word of God. When our favorite singers come to town, we buy tickets a month before the concert. But when it comes to the word of God, we can hardly even wake up and go to church on a Sunday morning.

Salvation is by grace. Even when we were dead in sins, hath quicken us together with Christ, (by grace ye are saved;) **For by grace ye are saved through faith**; and these not of yourselves: **it is the gift of God**. (Ephesians 2:5,8)

Just us Zacchaeus followed Jesus and had salvation because he believed, the Samaritan woman also believed and received healing for her daughter. You too can receive salvation, healing, miracles, and financial blessings. All you need to do is have faith in God.

But without faith it is impossible to please him (God). For he that cometh to God must believe that he is, and that he is a rewarder of them that diligently seek him. (Hebrews 11:6)

Now it's up to you to believe or not. You only need to believe that God is God and that nothing is impossible for him, for all things are possible with God. If you still don't believe, then pray a prayer like this: "LORD God help my unbelief." Or say, "Oh God increase my faith in Jesus's name. Amen."

*That the God of our Lord Jesus Christ, the Father of glory, may give unto you the **spirit of wisdom** and **revelation in the knowledge** of him: The eyes **of your understanding being enlightened**; that **ye may know what is the hope of his calling**, and **what the riches of the glory of his inheritance** in the saints.*
(Ephesians 1:17-18)

How BIG is Your FAITH?

And the Lord said, if ***ye had faith as a grain of mustard seed****, ye might say unto this sycamore tree, Be thou plucked up by the root, and be thou planted in the sea,* ***and it should obey you****.*
(Luke 17:5)

The mustard seed is the smallest seed of all, but if you have even this small amount of faith, you can command. Command those things you want in life to come to you and they will come. You can command those things that you do not like—such as sickness, debts, or anything else—to come out from your life, and it will be done. You can say, "You, headache (sickness), I command you to leave my body in Jesus's name Amen."

But you may be surprised. When you command the headache and it doesn't go away, then you may be very disappointed.

When I was in Hong Kong, one of my right-hand fingers became infected. It smelled very bad and became black. It bothered me so much. When I came to Canada, I took a serious look at it and began to command it to heal. I lit a candle and let the melted candle wax drip onto my finger to help kill the germs inside. It was the most painful thing I could ever have done to myself. But my goal was to kill the germs and cure the infection. So I did it a few times and then I completely stopped. It didn't heal right away. I just looked at my ugly finger and said, "Lord, my finger is so beautiful now. Thank you Lord for healing my finger." So every time I looked at my hand all I would see was a beautiful finger through the eyes of my faith. In reality, it was still stinking and black and ugly. However, I woke up one day and my finger was completely healed. It was beautiful, just as I had said it would be, and it contained no scars from its infection. All the Glory to God for the healing of my finger!

Fiery Financial Trials

In 2001, I became a landed immigrant, so I decided to step by faith and start a business. I joined Primerica Insurance and other businesses that can be done on the side. I had just gotten my car at that point and had found an apartment to live in. I lived with a few roommates, one of whom was a friend of mine and the others were sisters in the church I was attending at the time.

I applied for Employment Assistance (EI). I was on my first EI and was receiving more than $200 a month after two weeks. I applied for an office job and I got accepted as an "on call" from one of the offices in downtown Vancouver. The job unfortunately did not pay enough, so I applied at and was accepted by the Canadian Superstore at the bakery on Rupert Street. I started as part-time, so I still didn't have enough money to live on.

That was the toughest year of my life. I remember my roommate crying because we had no food. And I remember praying at the kitchen table and thanking God for whatever we did have. The food we ate came from my roommate's mom. We only had rice, eggs, and sausages. We were always late in paying our rent. And we had to borrow money because we never had enough.

During that time, I had gotten into a car accident; I accidentally bumped into a Mercedes Benz on a rainy day. I was driving at thirty kilometers per hour and I wasn't paying attention to the road. The car in front me was at a full stop and I was dialing a friend on my phone. It was too late for me to stop, so I bumped the car. I was charged about $3,000. Of course, I did not have the money to pay them, so they charged my car insurance a 40 percent surcharge—this increased my insurance premium to about double for the next four years. And I also lost my 10 percent discount because of that.

My car insurance was eventually canceled because there was no money in my bank account. We had to borrow some money to pay it so that I could keep the car.

I knew that this was a time of trials and temptation, so I stood by faith. I decided to go back into a live-in caregiver position in September 2002, until my financial life got back in order.

After two years I was ready again to live on my own. As I write this book, I have been here in this apartment for seven years. I still have my car and I am now on a 30 percent discount with my insurance. I now have a cleaning business. It's just a year old. I have a few clients and a few employees.

I had named my car Beulah, which means "the married one," and "the Lord delights in you." And sure enough, God was so faithful. When I see Beulah, I see God's faithfulness, mercy, and favor in my life.

Healing of My Wounds

In 2005, I got sick in my secret parts. I didn't know what it was, but it was so incredibly painful. I couldn't go to work for one week, so I even lost my part-time job because of it. I went to the doctor, and he said that I had herpes. He said that I might go to the hospital if it gets worse. I wasn't alarmed at all. I said to God, "Lord you are bigger than my illnesses, you are the only one who can heal me."

And you know what God had told me? He gave me this verse:

No weapon that is formed against thee shall prosper;
and every tongue that shall rise against thee in judgment
thou shalt condemn. This is the heritage of the servants of the
LORD, and their righteousness is of me, saith the LORD.
(Isaiah 54:17)

And I believe it. I took the medicine the doctor gave me, but I mostly put my trust in God that he would be the only one who could heal me. After ten days, the doctor was surprised; I was all better. He had even given me the wrong medication and wrong diagnosis. It was God who honored my faith. And all the glory and honor to him alone.

For verily I say unto you, That whosoever shall say unto this mountain, Be thou removed, and be thou cast into the sea; and shall not doubt in his heart, but shall believe that those things which he saith shall come to pass; He shall have whatever he saith.
(Mark 11:23)

I am not saying to you that you don't need to go to a doctor when you are sick. You need the doctors; they are the ones who will help and diagnose you if you have an illness. God can also use them to treat illness and disease. God can do some miracles through them—God works in so many different ways, not just by faith. One thing I can tell you is that the doctors can't do anything without God.

Jesus answered to, verily I say unto you, if ye have faith, and doubt not, ye shall not only do this which is done to the fig tree, but also if ye shall say unto this mountain be thou removed, and be thou cast unto the sea; it shall be done. And all things, whatsoever ye shall ask in prayer, believing ye shall receive them.
(Matthew 21: 21-22)

Your faith, in addition to prayer, is the most powerful force in the universe. You can command, and you can have what you ask for. Faith is the absence of doubt. If you doubt, you are like someone on the sea; you will be tossed to and fro. You will never get what you ask for when you doubt from your heart.

Prayer of Faith

Father God,

Thank you for, I am fearfully and wonderfully made, created in Your image and Your likeness. I come before Your throne, and ask you to open my heart and my mind, help my disbelief. Thank you for Your words, You said in Your words, that if I have a faith like the seed of the mustard seeds, I can move mountains. May this faith now in my heart, grow, so I can move all the mountains that come in my life (sickness, debts, emotions, financial problems, stress). Because You said that there is nothing impossible for You, for all things are possible in Your sight. I now commit to You my faith and I trust that You will honor my faith. Because You also said in Your words, that whatever You said, it doesn't come back to You void, but it will fulfill what You had said. (Isaiah 56:10-11) Thank you Father, this I ask in the mighty name of Jesus amen.

FAITH WITH ACTION

*Even so **faith**, if it hath **not works, is dead**, being alone. Yea, a man may say, Thou hast faith, and I have works: show me thy faith without works, and I will show you my faith by my works. **As the body without the spirit is dead, so faith without works is dead also.***
(James 2: 17, 18 26.)

When you start proclaiming God's word, it is a very powerful weapon you have every day—especially when you are undergoing spiritual warfare. Through the word of God, you can move whatever mountains or valleys that come into your life. Mountains represent trials, persecutions, sickness, spiritual strongholds, etc. Your patience will be tested, but if you doubt not, you will receive what you have asked for. Hold onto this belief, because the more you believe, the more the shadow of gloomy clouds will disappear. The circumstances around you will say, no way, there's no way out, or they will tell you that you can never get what you ask for. Be of good cheer my brothers and sisters, I've been there, and God has proven it to me over and over again that his word never fails.

When I was holding onto my faith, I called the agency to book my flight on April 30, 1997. I made this declaration every day.

I will go to Canada on April 30, 1997. (2x)

I will go to Canada on April 30, 1997. (2x)

I will go to Canada on April 30, 1997. (2x)

I will go to Canada on April 30, 1997. (2x)

I will go to Canada on April 30, 1997. (2x)

I will go to Canada on April 30, 1997. (2x)

I will go to Canada on April 30, 1997. (2x)

I wrote this in my notes, and I said it every day. It was only two months and three days that I had to wait. *I will go to Canada on April 30, 1997 (14x).*

Then I changed the date again to May and then to June.

In the Bible, Naaman was instructed to go to the Jordan River, to dip his body seven times; on the seventh submersion he was healed of leprosy. I have to say it seven times or double it, just my idea, and it works.

On June 19, 1997, I flew to Canada. My faith had been tested; so many negative things happened, but I didn't doubt what the Lord had promised to me. When the negatives happened, he confirmed it all to me through his words, the Bible, and dreams.

Great Faith Accomplishes Great and Mighty Things

This is what I've learned through all these years. My faith started at nothing and is currently mighty and great.

I have used my faith in every step I take, every move I make, every journey I go on, and every situation I am in. My faith is not only for the mighty things I want to achieve, but it is for my everyday life as well.

The righteous shall live by faith. For we walk by faith and not by sight.

When I wanted to buy a car, I went shopping for something brand new. The people who are faithless in the church were talking behind my back. But my friend who is close to me told me what they said about me. They said, "How is she going to buy a car? She doesn't have a job. Is she crazy?"

I was laughing inside. Because I knew in my heart that I was going to buy a car. When they said that, I had already been working for three months. I couldn't be approved for a brand new car because I didn't have a credit history (I was very new in Canada). But I got a car secondhand. It was a 1991 Toyota Corolla. The people who thought I was crazy were very surprised. They couldn't stand it. Some of them also went on to buy new cars shortly after I did. They decided that if I could do it, they could as well. To God be the glory for the things he has done. And lastly, believe it or not, my car is still working to this day! My friend Robert has had three cars since he has known me, yet my car is still alive and kicking. So he made a conclusion that my car is made from Heaven. Glory to God!

Faith Versus Worry/Fear

One of the ministries I am doing now is to pray for other believers along with non-believers. I felt the need to add this topic because I realized that many children of God still worry, despite their faith. The opposite of worry is faith, and worry is a shadow of things to come. When you worry, you worry a "shadow" of things that have not yet happened. We are more valuable than sparrows and we need not to worry.

Even the sparrow or the lilies of the field, they do not work, but our Heavenly Father supplies their needs.

Fear ye not therefore, ye are of more value than many sparrows.
(Matthew 10:31)

I remember, when God was teaching me about faith, all he was asking me to do was to trust him; that means having faith in God, because he can reserve that little chair for me. So right there, in 1988, I learned to trust God in the little things and, most of all, in the bigger things.

I never let negativity enter into my mind. If it does, I will quickly say the word of God and confess the promise of God, which is my sword in the spirit.

Here was the verse God taught me, "But Jesus beheld them, and said unto them, With men this is impossible; but with God all things are possible". (Matthew 19:26). So this was my motto "Nothing is Impossible with God."

I once read a book about worry and anxiety. The author claimed that one of the reasons people get sick is because of worry.

Worry and fear go hand in hand; when you start to worry, fear will enter into your heart. When you fear, you either run or hide. Hide from the reality of the problem, or run away instead of solving or facing the problem with your faith in God. Know that God is going to help you, because you are walking by faith and not by sight. So the choice is up to you. If you want to be healthy, choose faith. If you want to get sick, choose worry. I have chosen to live by faith, walking by faith and talking by faith. I can only tell you about my faith. And I brag about the grace of God in my life. I can see it through the eyes of my faith. I choose to live by faith every day of my life, through the grace of God and his favor in my life.

There are so many examples of great faith in the Bible. One is Hebrews, Chapter 11:

By faith, Able offered unto God more excellent sacrifice than Cain. V4a

By faith Enoch was translated that he should not see death; and was not found, because God had translated him before his translation he had this testimony, that he pleased God. V5

Through faith Sarah herself received strength to conceive seed, and was deliver of a child when she was past age, because she judged him faithful who had promised. V11

By faith Abraham, when he was tried, offered up Isaac' and he that had received the promises offered up his only begotten son. V17

By faith Joseph, when he died, made mention of the departing of the children of Israel; and gave commandments concerning his bones. V22

Fight the Good Fight of Faith

Fight the good fight of faith, lay hold on eternal life, whereunto thou art called, and hast professed a good profession before many witnesses.
(1 Timothy 6:12)

Looking unto Jesus the author and finisher of our faith;
who for the joy that was set before him endured the cross,
despising the shame, and is set down at the right hand of God.
(Hebrews 12:2)

Being a born-again Christian is not that easy. It is the most challenging, exciting, difficult, and yet very rewarding walk of life. When trials come, that's when you've been tried. You will discover if your faith will stand the test or not. It is easy to serve God when things are going well and you have no problems. But the most difficult time is when you face scary trials, testing, and temptation. Trials of not having a job, not having money, not having food to eat, not having shelter, having sickness, or having your wife or husband leave you.

How will you deal with those trials and how will you respond? That, my friend, will determine your level of maturity in the spirit. You can grow mature day by day by every trial that you have stood and conquered.

If everyone around you stops serving the Lord, will you also stop? If everyone stops loving his neighbor, will you? If you are left alone and no one is on your side about what you believe, will you stand? If everyone compromises, will you?

The Bible says that we are more than conquerors to him that loves us.

Who shall be able to separate us from the love of Christ? Shall tribulation, or distress, or persecution, or famine, or nakedness, or peril, or sword? Nay, in all these things we are more than conquerors through him that loves us. For I am persuaded, that neither death, nor life, nor angels, nor principalities, nor powers, nor things present, nor things to come, nor height nor depth, nor any other creature, shall be able to separate from the love of God, which is in Christ Jesus our Lord.
(Romans 9:35,37-39)

There is nothing that can separate us from the love of God. Trials? No! Tribulations? NO! Temptations? No! Boyfriend? No! Whether husband, wife, sickness, wealth, power—none can separate you from the love of God. Most of the time it is our own personal will that separates us from God. It is that *we* left God, not that God left us. God never leaves, nor does he forsake us.

So let's fight with all our might, with all our strength, for our faith, until Jesus comes. We can conquer all through Jesus, who loves us and gave himself for us. We can conquer all because he has given us his holy spirit, and even our faith. So let's hold on to the eternal life to which we are called. And let us fix our eyes upon Jesus because he is the author and finisher of our faith.

I wrote this poem when I was in Hong Kong, after all the trials I had gone through.

FAITH Makes ALL Things POSSIBLE

When you walked through a crooked way
When you passed through the wilderness
And when you faced a stormy weather,
Believe that there is always a way out, a highway of Faith
If you are in the mountain of trials
If you are in the oceans of hopeless
And if you are in the rivers of sorrow
Believe that there is always a break through refreshing living water
Trials, sorrows, and disappointment crush the bones
Joy and contentment make the bone grow fat
Trust and hope open up opportunities and produce more expectation
Love and devotion leadeth you to serve and obey his word

While love makes things easy, and Faith makes all things possible

When you have Faith

A crooked way becomes straight

A wilderness becomes green pastures

Stormy weather becomes fine sunny weather

Because Faith makes impossible become possible

Your trials like mountains become a level ground

Your hopelessness like the ocean becomes a universe of Hope

Your rivers of sorrow become rivers of Joy and Life

Because Faith makes all the difference of who you are

By Rebecca Daluddung Hong Kong 1997

God's Own Special Tool

God uses so many kinds of tools to mold us, so that we can serve him wholly. This reminds me of what a wonderful God we are serving. This reminds me of a time that I visited a hardware store. I was looking at all these thousands of tools, so many different kinds of nails, small and big, and you can also find something to pluck the nail out when you want it gone. While I was there pondering and amazed at all these kinds of tools, God was speaking to my heart. And I began to think that he has many tools to use for his children. We are not all the same; we are different from one another. Characters, attitude, color or skin, different tastes and likes ... We have different backgrounds and values; we are so unique. Everyone is special and unique. This tool may work for me, and it may not work for you. Let's say that I want to take the big nail that is stuck to the wall. Now I'm going to use the small hammer to pluck it out. Do you think I can take it out? The answer is no, but if I will use the right tool, then yes, I can take it out.

It is the same thing with our God. He uses so many ways to draw us closer to himself, because of his great love for us.

Other people find God in the midst of their sickness and when bad things happen to them. Other times, when they don't seek God, they find God through their Christian friends. It goes on and on.

Oftentimes when people hurt us, and when we feel rejected, God knows when we really need him and he uses that special tool to draw us to himself. Because God loves us so much, He cares even with the little things we need. How much more must he care for the eternal things we need, such as salvation of our souls?

God Uses Tools to Mold Us

And the vessel that he made of clay was marred in the hand of the potter: so he made it again another vessel, as seemed good to the potter to make it.

O house of Israel, (your name_____) cannot I do with you as this potter? Saith the LORD. Behold, as the clay in the potter's hand, so are ye in mine hand, O house of Israel. (Jeremiah 18:4, 6)

When God called you and me, he didn't call us alone to serve him and be with him in Heaven. He also has a special plan for us. He also molds us and makes us to become more effective in our service.

When I was in the process of molding, this was God's message for me.

"Have patience with me, God is not finished with me yet."

This message was actually a picture frame hanging in my best friend's apartment. God was telling me this over and over again whenever I visited her. It reminded me that God is not finished with me yet—that he is in the process of molding me and shaping my life to be in accordance with his will.

*Wherein ye greatly rejoice, though now for a season, if need
be, ye are in heaviness through manifold temptations:
That the trial of your faith, being much more precious than
gold that perisheth, though it be tried by fire, might be found
unto praise and honour and glory at the appearing of Jesus
Christ.
(1 Peter 1:6, 7)*

*But the God of all grace, who hath called us unto his eternal
glory by Jesus Christ, after that ye have suffered a while, make
you perfect, establish, strengthen, settle you.
(1 Peter 5:10)*

God uses hurt or pain to draw me closer to him. The more
pain and disappointment I feel, the closer I get to him and
call upon him. I know I am not perfect yet, and during this
time God taught me the real meaning of love. God uses trials
and hardship to strengthen my faith and love for him. When
my love and faith had been tested by fire, if I didn't fail or turn
away from God, then I could be found worthy of his calling,
and my life would be a living sacrifice that gives glory and
honor to God. And I was not only full of faith, but also full of
love, and patience, and forgiveness, and, best of all, I learned
to be content and grateful for everything that has happened
to me, whether good or bad. I can boldly say, God giveth and
God taketh away, Blessed be the Lord God almighty.

*For our light affliction, which is but for a moment, worketh
for us a far more exceeding and eternal weight of glory;
While we look not at the things which are seen, but at the
things which are not seen: for the things which are seen are
temporal; but the things which are not seen are eternal.
(2 Corinthians 4:17-18)*

Chapter Five
LOVE - Charity

And now abideth faith, hope, charity, **but the greatest of this is charity.**
(1 Corinthians 13:1-13)

Love is Eternal

Love...suffereth long, (Patient)

Love...is kind,

Love...envieth not,

Love...vaunteth not itself

Love...is not puffed up,

Love...does not behave itself unseemly,

Love...seeketh not her own, (unselfishness)

Love...is not easily provoked,

Love...thinketh no evil, (purity)

Love...rejoiceth not in iniquity, but rejoiceth in truth.

Love...beareth all things,

Love...beleiveth all things,

Love...hopes all things,

Love...endureth all things.

Love never fails

Three Kinds of LOVE

1. Phileo – means tender affection. Love of family, relatives, and friends.

2. Aeros – means fleshly love between a husband and wife or a sweetheart.

3. Agape - means Love of God (Love that values and esteems).

Agape - It is unselfish love, ready to serve.

The love of a husband and wife, phileo love will fade away. But the agape love doesn't fade away. It's eternal and it endures through hardships, trials, and temptations. You may be surprised to see a newlywed couple end up divorcing after only six months. Even couples who have been married for a long time with multiple grown children have divorced. Divorce is increasing rapidly. There are fathers who kill their own sons and brothers who kill their brothers. You probably love your friends when they are good to you, but what happens if they cheat on you, stab you in the back, or do something you don't like? And even a mother killing the small fetus in her womb: that's abortion. She might not realize she is killing an innocent life; she doesn't even give her baby a chance to be born. Our world is in so much chaos and misery. The two towers falling on 9/11 in the United States was a disaster. So many people had suffered and died. The news always talks about the bad things that happen—the bad economy, murders, etc.

The phileo and aeros loves both pass away. It's because those two kinds of love actually don't last at all. Maybe we're friends today and become enemies tomorrow. It's gone like the wind.

Phileo and aeros loves actually fade away. It is so common in North America for marriages to last for only months, or perhaps a few years. Why? Because we are only human beings. We are not perfect. Even born-again Christians who are devoted in their faith are not exempted from temptation. We all commit mistakes. But there is hope for you, my dear sister or brother. This is the reason why this book is written, because of the Love of God. God loves you, and that's why this book is in your hands right now. To let you know about God's love and his redemption, and that he is coming again to take you and me. Every problem has a solution. I once heard a preacher named Majed say that you can have two options: you can be a solution to the problem, or you can be a part of the problem. Which one will you choose now?

Here's why the phileo and aeros loves disappear or why they are not permanent. We are only human beings, and nobody is perfect except God. Let's look at the case of Maria (not her real name). Maria is a born-again Christian. She works for a living and earns more than her husband does. She complains to me that her husband doesn't help around the house. They went for counseling, but nothing worked. The problem has continued on and on for the past four years. Even though Maria loves her husband and her kids, she thought this was too much for her to bear. She couldn't carry it any longer. So she wanted a divorce. The problem with this couple is that they don't have the love of God in their hearts. We may ask, "But Maria is a born-again Christian, wouldn't she of course have the love of God?" If she really has the love of God, she should have the agape love, which means that it is the willingness to serve and to love without any condition. You might wonder, "How can I love those people who don't love me?" Very simple—when you really have the love of God in your heart, this is the unselfish desire to love them unconditionally. When this happens to you, you can understand me more.

As I have mentioned previously, years ago I fell in love with a man whom I will call Ezra. In the Bible, Ezra is a priest. God used Ezra to revive his people Israel to worship him again. This priest was devoted to God—but the Ezra that I fell in love with was just the opposite. Ezra is a very sweet, caring, and loving man, and he cared about me a lot. After eight months he broke up with me. But my love for him never stopped. One day I was complaining about Ezra to God, and God told me, "Love him as I love you." I asked, "How Lord?" And God said, "How many times have you failed me and yet I still love and forgive you?" Then I thought about how God loves me and how faithful he is in my life, how he always forgives me when I commit sin, and how great is his mercy and grace toward me in spite of my brokenness and unworthiness and imperfection. God always welcomes me and never turns his back on me. So God had taught me to love him unconditionally. And also God taught me to be content with whatever time he can give me. Many times Ezra failed me, yet my love for him is still the same. After four years with Ezra, one day I told him, "If it is only my love that I am holding onto, I was already gone. But because God told me to love you the way he loves me, that's why I'm still loving you." He told me that's impossible, "How can you love me like God? You are not God." I answered and said, "Yes, I am not God, but I can love the way he loves." Years after this event, one day Ezra told me, "You had taught me how to love and showed me the real meaning of love." No matter where he goes or what Ezra does, he will never forget me. It is because Ezra has seen and tasted the love of God that flows through me. All I did was to love him just as God had loves me. I had demonstrated my love for him not only through words but though actions, and I had taught him the real meaning of love. I had showed him how to love, or the real meaning of unconditional love. That was God's love flowing through me.

True, my dear friend, we can love the way God loves us. If God so loves us, why can't we love others, the way God loves us? We can love because God is love. (1 John 4:7,8) Beloved let us love one another, for love is of God, and everyone that loveth is born of God and knoweth God, he that loveth not knoweth not God for God is love.

If your husband or wife has failed you, or your friends have failed you, you can't love them if you are still in the phileo or aeros love. It will only stay there and go no further. That's why divorce is increasing rapidly. You can be part of them or you can make a big difference. I know that God's love is available to you if you ask him, because he has given me that love. Just remember no one is perfect. If Jesus Christ is able to raise Lazarus from the dead, he is also able to resurrect your dying marriage and dying love for your husband or wife, or even to your parents or friends.

Love Covers a Multitude of Sins

*Above all things have fervent **Charity [Love]** among yourselves: for charity shall **cover the multitude of sins**.*
(1 Peter 3:8)

Agape loves does that, when Jesus died on the cross to save us from our sin. That love says, "Greater love hath no man than this, that a man lay down his life for his friends." There is no greater love I ever found that is so pure and so holy and that will be able to die for me. Jesus Christ is the only one that can do that for you and me and the only reason he did it is because of love.

Christ died for us even though we are sinners. He loves us so much that he made a way for us to be saved from eternal destruction (Hell).

When your love abounds and increases, hate is going to melt away. I choose to love and forgive no matter how much I have been hurt or rejected, and how much I hated what others did to me. Love covers a multitude of sins, not just one mistake or two but a multitude that's uncountable. Choose love today, tomorrow, and always.

FORGIVENESS

*Let all bitterness, and wrath, and anger, and clamour, and evil speaking, be put away from you, with all malice: And be ye kind one to another tenderhearted, **forgiving one another even as God for Christ's sake hath forgiven you**. (Ephesians 4:31-32.)*

***C**onfess your faults one to another*, and **pray** *one for another, that ye may **be healed**, the effectual fervent prayer of a righteous man availeth much.*
(1 Peter 5: 16)

"If you want to be happy, then learn how to forgive and forget."

I heard someone say, "I may forgive her, but I will not forget what she has done." That's not forgiveness at all. When God forgives us, he forgets it all. Just as he said in Isaiah 44:22, "I have blotted out as a thick cloud, thy transgressions, and, as a cloud, thy sins." As far as the east is from the west so far hath He removed our transgression from us.

If God, who created us, can forgive our sins and remember them no more, who are we not to forgive our fellow man? We are only creatures who are supposed to submit to our Creator. If we keep on looking for the small speck on our brother's eyes, yet we cannot even see the big speck in our own eyes, then something is wrong.

A woman was taken by the scribes and the Pharisees and they brought her to Jesus. They told Jesus that she was caught in an act of adultery and she deserved to be stoned to death according to the law of Moses. They wanted to know what Jesus's opinion about her was. But I love what the Lord Jesus said in verse 7: "He that is without sin among you, let him first cast a stone at her."

Notice that he says he who is without sin will be the first one to cast a stone to her. So all of them left, because they were convicted by their own consciences. Only Jesus had the right to accuse her or cast a stone on her because Jesus is without sin. So the Lord asked the woman, "Woman, where are those thine accusers? Hath no man condemned thee?" She said, "No man, Lord." And Jesus said unto her, "**Neither do I condemn thee: go and sin no more.**" (John 8:11)

This was the beginning of a transformation in the life of this woman. She was forgiven and Jesus gave her a second chance. "**Go and sin no more.**" A second chance and a favor. I call it **GRACE**. Her life would never be the same again since she saw the light of Jesus and became a follower of Christ.

Wouldn't it be wonderful when our accuser declares **NOT GUILTY! YOU ARE FORGIVEN! YOU ARE FREE!** We don't have the right to judge other people or condemn them. Our part is to tell them the will of God and they can choose to obey or disobey. We are all going to stand in the judgment seat of Christ, so who are we to judge our fellow men?

Jesus said, "He that rejected me, and receiveth not my words, hath one that judgeth him: the word that I had spoken, the same shall judge him in the last day." (John 12:48) The very words of Jesus will judge us in the last days. So it will be how much that we have heard and what we do about the word of God that we will be judged on. It's not how much we didn't hear and didn't do. My part is just to tell you what I have learned, and share how I obey the truth and live with it before I can preach to you.

Our part is to pray for the lost and reach out to them and pray for our brothers and sisters who have fallen from faith.

This woman received forgiveness, and became free from her accusers. She was no longer condemned. She had FREEDOM.

Jesus set her free. "If the son therefore shall make you free, ye shall be free indeed." (John 8:36)

Jesus Christ not only freed this woman, but he frees all of us. Jesus hath suffered enough to pay the penalty for our sins.

We are free indeed, because Jesus has set us free. We can now love just as God loves us and we can do his commandments

Any sins we have committed can be forgiven. All we need to do is to repent and ask God for forgiveness. For the child of God, I say, God hath freed us from the power of sin, therefore we should no longer be a servant of sin. But a servant of God. God hath given us the power to obey though his spirit. So we should no longer serve sin. Paul said:

Flee fornication. Every sin that a man doeth is without the body. What? Know ye not that your body is the temple of the Holy Ghost which is in you, which ye have of God, and ye are not your own? ***For ye are bought with a price: therefore glorify God in your body, and in your spirit, which are God's.***
(1 Corinthians 6:18-20)

"Go and sin no more." It is an expression of **GRACE**. Jesus is more interested in her soul and gave her a second chance to undo her life.

We are supposed to pray for our brothers and sisters who have committed sin, and help them to stand up again and find forgiveness and grace from God. We are not to condemn them and let them continue to wallow in sin and unrighteousness. Our part only is to tell them the truth about God, and about the consequences of every action they make. Their part is to make choices. And we also cannot judge them, because Jesus said to not judge, so you won't be judged. Because there is only one who can judge us, and that is the one who created us. Jesus is both the judge of the dead and the living.

Learning to forgive is the hardest thing a person can do. But when you understand the law of forgiveness it becomes easy. When God taught me how to forgive others of what they had done to me, I did forgive them. It is because in order for you to be forgiven from your sins, you must first forgive others of what they had done unto you.

Forgive, and You Will Be Forgiven

If you forgive not other to what they have done to you, neither will your Heavenly father will forgive your sins. (Matthew 6:14-15)

That is so simple, but too difficult to obey for many others, especially if they commit an offense that really needs justice. But just as I have said, that God is love, if you love God, then you must obey his commandments. He said "If you love me, keep my commandments." Forgiveness is something that someone else doesn't deserve. It's canceling their faults and trespasses, like canceling debts, and they don't owe you anymore. Love for God bids you to forgive others, because God has forgiven you, and you ought to forgive others too. You can choose to forgive or not, that's a choice of obedience, to God's will or your own will.

Jesus utters before his death, "**Father forgive them for they know not what they do.**"

Do you have any idea that the people inflicting pain on you don't know what they are doing? Others think that when they kill someone, they are offering it to their god. You may know or not that you still have to forgive them. Jesus forgave those who persecuted him, mocked him, ridiculed him, spit on him, and tortured him. He is still able to forgive them. Jesus is without sin, yet he can forgive others, like you and me. If others can forgive, if your husband and wife can forgive, if your parents can forgive, if your neighbor can forgive, if the whole community and nations can forgive, if this whole earth can forgive, there would be no war at all. What a world it would be. It would be peace first in our hearts and then in our surroundings.

When God taught me to forgive, it was hard for me in the beginning. I cried out to God and said, "What he did is unacceptable, or so unreasonable. He doesn't deserve my love and my forgiveness." But God had given me this verse: Matthew 6:14-15. And I was convicted by the Holy Ghost.

I felt like God was talking to me through this verse and said, "How many times have you committed sins against me, yet I still forgive you. And remember, if you can't forgive others from what they have done to you, neither can I forgive you if you ask forgiveness, if you don't forgive others." Since then, I always forgave other people for whatever things they had done to upset me or mistreat me. Oftentimes they don't know what they are doing. If God's love is in your heart, you can forgive unconditionally. Other people forgive, but they never forget what the other party has done to them. And in return they will never do business with them or go near them. When God forgave us from our sins, he wiped them away by the blood of Jesus Christ. And he forgets it. As far as the east is from the west, so far hath he removed our transgression from us.

Nobody's perfect, because the person next to you might not even know the Lord Jesus Christ. By forgiving her, you open the window for her to look on a new way. She might even learn to forgive others the next time she has the same experience that you do.

If you don't know Jesus Christ yet, maybe it's time for you to forgive. Learn from the parable of the wicked servant.

The Parable of the Unforgiving Servant

Therefore is the kingdom of Heaven likened unto a certain king, which would take account of his servants.

And when he has begun to reckon, one was brought unto him which owed him ten thousand talents.

But forasmuch as he had not to pay, his lord commanded him to be sold, and his wife, and children, and all that he had, and payment to be made.

The servant therefore fell down, and worshipped him, saying, Lord, have patience with me, and I will pay thee all.

Then the lord of that servant was moved with compassion, and loosed him the debt.

But the same servant, went out, and found one of his fellow servants, which owed him an hundred pence: and he laid hands on him, and took him by the throat, saying, Pay me thou owest.

And his fellow servant fell down at his feet, and besought him, saying, Have patience on me and I will pay thee all.

And he would not: but went and cast him into prison, till he should pay the debt.

So when his fellow servants saw what was done, they were sorry, and came and told unto their lord all that was done.

Then his lord, after that he had called him, said unto him, oh thou wicked servant, and I forgave thee all that debt, because thou desirest me:

Shouldest not thou also have had compassion on thy fellow servant, even as I have pity on thee?

79

And his lord was wroth, and delivered him to be tormentors, till he should pay all that was due unto him.

*So likewise shall my Heavenly Father **do also unto you, if ye from your hearts forgive not every one** his brother their trespasses.*
(Matthew 18:23-35)

This parable is what is going to happen to anyone who doesn't forgive. Verse 35 says that you will be accountable first to God because you didn't forgive your brother or sister who wronged you. For we know him that hath said, "**Vengeance belongeth unto me, saith the LORD**." Again, The LORD shall judge his people. It is a fearful thing to fall into the hands of the living God. (Hebrews 10:30)

How Many Times Will I FORGIVE?

One of my friends told me that I shouldn't forgive Ezra. I had been forgiving him for four years and she thought I should stop forgiving. I asked her, "Do you know how many times you have to forgive?" When she told me it was seventy times seven, I told her she was right. (Matthew 18:21-22) You have to forgive many times. Here's my example: The life span of a man is about 70 years.

70 x 7 = 490 offence

1 year old = 1 offence

7 years old = 7 offence

70 years old = 70 offense

You have to live 490 years here on earth to forgive. Who is going to live on this age? None!

That means we have to forgive 490 times. Seventy years is the approximate life span of a man. Let's just say that your brother wronged you once when you were one year old, then once a year he committed one offence. So when you are seven years old, he has committed seven mistakes against you. When you are 70 years old, he has committed 70 offences. Still you didn't get to 490 offences. Which means as long as you are alive, keep on forgiving others. I have also applied this verse into my life so many times. If you love someone, the closer and deeper your relationship together, the deeper the wounds can be. If I have to dwell on the hurts, there is no way I can forgive them. But thank God, he always reminds me to forgive. Many times I have committed sins against God and he always forgives me. God has been so patient with me and is always forgiving. So in return, I always forgave Ezra, not because I loved him so much but because the Lord told me to love him as God loves me. So, I have to obey.

If you have a hard time forgiving, just pray to God to take away that hate or grief in your heart and pray also that God will put more love into your heart, whether that person had hurt you intentionally or unintentionally. They may or may not deserve our forgiveness, but we have to forgive them.

And be ye kind one to another, tenderhearted, forgiving one another, even as God for Christ's sake hath forgiven you.
(Ephesians 4:32)

How Did God Create Human Beings?

And the LORD God formed man of the dust of the ground, and breathed into his nostrils the breath of life; and man became a living soul.
(Genesis 2:7)

So God created man in his own image, in the image of God created he him; male and female created he them.
(Genesis 1:27)

God created Adam and Eve, in his own image and likeness. He created the earth through his word. He said, "Let there be light," and there was light. "Let there be firmament," and there was firmament. But when he created us, he made us according to his own image. God formed us from a dust from the earth, and breathed on Adam, and so Adam became a living soul. Adam and Eve were the first creations, God's own masterpiece. The difference between us and the animal kingdom is they are created through God's word. But we are his masterpiece, made by his own hands. God formed us according to his likeness.

You and I are special in God's eye, because he is our Creator. Therefore we are obligated to the one who created us. We are accountable to God. So if someone thinks that there is no God, that person is a fool. The Bible says, "The fool thinketh in his heart that there is no God."

Everything that God hath created, it was very good, there's nothing on earth that God created that is not good. (Genesis 1:31a)

God had put them in the Garden of Eden. Adam and Eve never worried about what they were going to eat, because God had told them to eat from every tree in the garden except for the tree that was in the center—the tree of the knowledge of good and evil. (Genesis 1:9) "And the moment they eat this fruit, they shalt surely die." Pay attention to this verse: Verse 17—And the LORD God commanded the man, saying, of every tree, of the garden thou mayest freely eat. But the tree of the knowledge of good and evil, thou shalt not eat of it: for in the day that thou eatest there of thou shalt surely die.

Our God gave commandments to Adam and Eve, because he wanted to see or test their obedience and faith in him. When he said, "When you eat it, you shall surely die," God was giving them the freedom of choice. They had a choice to obey or to disobey God's word.

The Fall of Man

God had told Adam and Eve to eat from everything in the garden except for the one tree that was in the center, which was the tree of knowledge of good and evil, but they disobeyed God and ate from it. This was because Satan came down to earth and deceived Eve by telling her that she can become like God herself. (Ezekiel 28:17) So Eve ate the fruit and gave it to her husband Adam. That's why God drew them away from the Garden of Eden and they then had to toil for their food. And the punishment for women is pain and difficulty during childbirth. And he told the serpent that he will be trampled down underground. In the Philippines, whenever we saw a snake, we called the neighbor and he would kill that snake. If the snake got away it was very lucky not to be tortured on the head or killed. Satan was the serpent and he will receive punishment in hell.

And the punishment for Adam was: cursed is the ground for thy sake: thorns and thistles shall it bring forth to thee: in the sweat of thy face thou salt eat bread; till thou return into the ground; for out of it, wast thou: for dust thou art, and unto dust shalt thou return. (Genesis 3:16-17a,18-20)

After Adam and Eve had eaten the tree of life, their eyes were open and they hid themselves from the presence of God. They knew that they had disobeyed God. They didn't only lose the abundant blessing of God from the Garden of Eden, but they also lost God's presence the moment they disobeyed. It was a separation from God.

That's why nakedness and shame are the first fruits of sin.

Man Was Separated from God

Disobedience is a free will called sin. And sin separates us from God.

Although God loves us, he hates sin because he is holy and just.

The Bible tells us that we all have sinned and we come short of the glory of God. (Romans 3:23) There's no exception here; we are all sinners and we have died spiritually. That sin separates us from God because God is holy. The soul that sinneth it shall die. (Ezekiel 18:20) You may be living and have breath of life physically, but you are dead spiritually. Isaiah says that we all, like sheep, have gone astray, each of us went to our own way. (Isaiah 53:6) By the disobedience of one man, all had to die. Adam disobeys God in the Garden of Eden. And through that onward, paradise is lost. Adam and Eve used to hear God's voice, sense his presence, and enjoy all the bountiful blessings in the garden before they disobeyed God. And so we inherited this sin from them. The penalty of our sin is death. Sin doesn't evaporate; it is like a debt. So long as you are indebted you are not free from it until you pay it all. For the wages of sin is death. But the gift of God is eternal life through Jesus Christ.

Chapter Six
The Love of God

Agape Love means: The unselfish love ready to serve.

God
Reaches
At
Christ's
Expense

For God so loved the world, that he gave his only begotten son, that whosoever believe on him. [Jesus Christ] should not Christ but have everlasting life.
(John 3:16)

In the Old Testament, every year the Israelites would have to choose a lamb without blemish. The lamb had to be healthy, to be offered as a sin offering. They would bring the lamb to the high priest and the high priest would sprinkle the blood of the lamb on the altar. Then their sins would be forgiven that year. So every year they did it, to cover their sins.

Jesus has done it for all of us, once and for all.

He did it neither by the blood of goats and calves, but by his own blood. He entered into the holy place, having obtained eternal redemption for us. For if the blood of bulls and of goats, and the ashes of heifer sprinkling the unclean, sanctifieth to the purifying of the flesh:

How much more shall the blood of Christ, who trough the eternal Spirit offered himself without spot to God, purge your conscience from dead works to serve the living God.
(Hebrews 9:12-14)

He is the only perfect sacrifice for our sins, because Jesus is without blemish or sin. He did it once and for all.

Because of God's love for mankind, he sent his only son as a sin offering of your sins, my sins, and the sins of the whole earth.

And he will give birth to a son, and his name will be called Emmanuel, which means God is with us. For he will save his people from their sins.

Isaiah also says:

He is despised and rejected of men; a man of sorrow, and appointed with grief… surely He hath bore our grief's and carried our sorrows, yet we did esteem him stricken, smitten of God and afflicted. But he was wounded for our transgressions, he was bruised for our iniquities, the **chastisement of our peace was upon him; and with his stripes we are healed.**
(Isaiah 53:4-5)

We are supposed to die for our own sins.

But God made him an offering for our sins. He took the penalty on the cross. Christ died on your behalf and my behalf. It is only through Jesus's death that we can be free and receive grace. That's the love of God. Grace is something that we don't deserve, because we are sinners and we deserve to die for our own sins. But with God's own love and mercy and grace, we found favor in his sight, through the suffering of his son Jesus Christ. This grace is unmerited favor.

The suffering Savior JESUS CHRIST (Redeem us from our sins)

1. **Scourge our Savior Jesus Christ** (Matthew 27:26)

The Roman scourge consisted of the victim being stripped and stretched against a pillar or bent over a low post, with his hands being tied. The instrument of torture was a short, wooden handle to which several leather thongs were attached, with bits of iron or bore tied to the thongs. The blows were laid on the victim's back by two men, one lashing the victim from one side, one lashing from the other side. This resulted in the flesh being cut to such an extent that veins, arteries, and sometimes even inner organs were exposed. Often the victim died during the flogging.

2. **Scourging was hideous torture**: the inability of Jesus to bear his own cross was with no doubt due to this severe infliction. (Verse 32 Luke 23:26)

3. **A scarlet robe and the crown of thorns** (Matthew 27:28-29)

    Jesus is untied and placed in the middle of the Roman Battalion. (V27) The soldiers put a robe across his shoulders, placed a stick in his hand, and pressed a circle of branches covered with long thorns onto his head. The soldiers mocked him and struck him across the face and head, driving the thorns deeper into his scalp. (V30-31)

4. Crucify him (JESUS) (The heavy beam)

The heavy beam of the cross is tied to Christ's shoulder. He begins the slow journey to Golgotha. The weight of the wooden beam, together with sheer physical exhaustion, causes him to fall. Simon then is pressed into service to bear his cross.

At Golgotha the cross beam is placed on the ground and Jesus is laid upon it. His arms are stretched along the beams and a heavy square, wrought iron nail is driven through his hand (or wrist), first into the right, then into the left hand, and deep into the wood. Next Jesus is lifted up by means of ropes or ladders. The cross beam is bound or nailed to the upright beam, and the support for the body is fastened on it. Lastly, his feet are extended and a larger piece of iron is driven through the two. (V35)

5. Revile him

Jesus is now a pathetic spectacle. He is blood streaked, covered with wounds, and exposed to the view of the people. He experiences hours of pain in his entire body, fatigue in his arms, great waves of cramps in the muscles, and skin torn from his back. Then another agony begins—a crushing pain deep in the chest as fluid begins to compress the heart. He feels an intense thirst (John 19:28) and is aware of the ridicule of those who pass by the cross. (V. 39-44)

6. Why hast thou forsaken me??

These words mark the climax of sufferings of Christ for a lost world. His cry in Aramaic is, "My God, my God, why hast thou forsaken me?" He has experienced separation from God as the sinner's substitute. Here, the sorrow, grief, and pain are at their worst. He is wounded for our transgression. (Isaiah 53:3)

The LIFE is In the BLOOD

What is the human blood that flows through veins? It is a river that begins in the mountains and comes down to wash away all the mess, muck, and filth of humanity. The rivers take it out to the sea where God purifies it again with salt and by many other elements. He purifies it again by vaporizing it, taking it up into the clouds, and dropping it again on the mountaintops, then it runs down again. Rivers are God's cleansing system of the body. The blood that flows through you is a cleansing power. The blood is the life that flows of the soul and the body of man. Leviticus 17:17 says, "For the life of the flesh is in the blood. Your life is not in your bones or muscles; your life is in your blood. It is your blood stream that purifies your brain. Your brain must have a flow of blood or it will die. The blood flows throughout your body, purifying, rejuvenating, bringing strength, and producing power."

The heart is the center of emotions; it is the pump that sends life throughout your whole being. That could mean that if you are wrong in your emotions, you are wrong everywhere. If you do not have your emotions under control, your whole person will be affected.

Jesus didn't die because of a broken heart. He suffered an irregular heartbeat because of the loss of blood. The heart pumps irregularly if there is not enough blood. His blood was poured out the moment they scourged him. It was poured out for the redemption of our sins. When the soldiers pierced Jesus on the side, there was no more blood, but water came out of his body. The blood of the lamb only covered their sins for a year. But Jesus Christ did it once and for all. He said, **"It is finished!"** (John 19:30) His cry signified the end of his suffering and the completion of the work of redemption. (1 Peter 1:19) The debt for our sins had been paid in full, through Jesus's suffering. You and I are supposed to die for our sins, but Jesus came and died on our behalf, instead of you or me. And he is the perfect sacrifice for our sins, a lamb without blemish. (1 Timothy 2:6) He who knew no sin, God makes him to be sin for us. The first Adam died to sin, the second Adam lives.

7. The veil of the temple was rent (Matthew 27:51)

The meaning of the temple signified that a way was open into the presence of God. The curtain separated the holy place from the most holy place, and it barred the way into the presence of the living God.

In the Old Testament, the temple of God is divided through curtains. There is a holy place, where the people can come and worship God. But the holy of holiest is where only the High Priest can enter, because the presence of God there is so intense, you can feel the mighty presence of God.

Moses put a veil on his face when descending from Mount Sinai, thus preventing the Israelites from beholding the glory of God.

The Veil is removed or broken down, because Jesus already paid our sins in full by dying on the cross. He was crucified and died to redeem us from our sins. We can now enter boldly into his presence. For the wages of sin is death, but the gift of God is eternal life through Jesus Christ. No religion or denomination can save you; God's design is that we can only be redeemed through Jesus's death. Whether you are Greek or Jewish, American, Japanese, Filipino, Persian, European, or Chinese, whether your color is black or white or brown, God is calling you. He already made a way. Jesus died for your sins and the sins of the whole world. He is the perfect sacrifice, a lamb without blemish because Jesus is without sin. You can probably imagine someone wanting to die for a good man. But no one will ever want to die for a bad man. Jesus also took the place of Barrabas, and Barrabas was a murderer. You can't grasp the depth of God's love for you, not until you understand the suffering of Jesus in order to redeem you from your sin. I pray that through his suffering you will be able to know and understand the depths of his love for you and me. If you have watched *The Passion of the Christ* by Mel Gibson, that is the passion of God's love for you and me. Jesus came to save us from our sins and from the coming wrath of God.

JESUS IS THE WAY

Jesus saith unto him, I am the way, the truth, and the life: no man cometh unto the Father, but by me.
(John 14:6)

If you want to go to Heaven, there's no other way but with Jesus Christ; no religion or denomination can bring you there. The veil of the temple was rent into two. The death of Jesus and his suffering opened an invitation for us to come to him, because he conquered death and rose again. There's no other way. Some people think that to go to Heaven, they have to help the poor. Others believe that they will have to carry the literal cross in order to be forgiven and go to Heaven. Some even believe they need to sacrifice and do good to others in order for them to inherit eternal life. None of this is God's way to go there. Jesus is the only way. No man cometh unto the Father but by Jesus alone. Jesus is the only perfect sacrifice for our sins, because he is without sin. Religion is not the way to the Heavenly Father. Jesus is the only way because he died for our sins. He died once and for all. There is only one way and no other way to go to God—it is only through Jesus Christ our Lord.

There is No Salvation Other Than Jesus's Name

Neither is there salvation in any other: for there is none other name under Heaven given among men, whereby we must be saved.
(Acts 4:12)

Wherefore God also hath highly exalted him, and given him a name which is above every name: That at the name of Jesus every knee shall bow, of things in Heaven, and things in earth, and things under the earth;
And that every tongue should confess that Jesus Christ is Lord, to the glory of God the Father.
(Philippians 2:9-11)

Isaiah prophesied about Jesus. For unto us a child is born unto us a son is given: and the government shall be upon his shoulder: and his name shall be called Wonderful, Counselor, The mighty God, The everlasting Father, The prince of Peace. Of the increase of his government and peace there shall be no end.
(Isaiah 9:6-7a)

And behold, thou shalt conceive in thy womb, and bring forth a son, and shall call his name Jesus. He shall be great, and shall be called the Son of the Highest: and the Lord God shall give unto him the throne of his father David. And he shall reign over the house of Jacob forever; and of his kingdom there shall be no end.
(Luke 1:31-33)

He is the way you are looking for. Go back and look again at what the Lord Jesus went through, just to save us from our sins. He already paid for our sins through his death. You can name all the religions in the whole wide world, but only through Jesus's name will we be saved. And only to him will we bow down and confess and worship for the glory of God the Father.

JESUS IS THE TRUTH

IN THE beginning was the Word, and the Word was with God, and the Word was God. The same was in the beginning with God.

All things were made by him; and without him was not anything made that was made. In him was life; and the life was the light of men.
(John 1:1-4)

And the Word was made flesh, and dwelt among us, (and we beheld his glory, the glory as of the only begotten of the Father,) full of grace and truth.
(John 1:14)

JESUS IS THE BEGINNING

[Jesus] Who is the image of the invisible God, the first born of every creature.

For by him [Jesus], were all things created, that are in Heaven, and that are in earth, visible and invisible, whether they be throne, or dominions, or principalities, or powers: all things were created by him and for him: And he is before all things, and by him all things consist.
(Colossians 1:15-17)

Sanctify them through thy truth: thy word is truth.
(John 17:17)

In the beginning, the Word was God.

Adam, Eve, Abraham, and Moses only heard the Word. God had spoken to them through his word. And none had ever seen God at any time.

But the Word became flesh and dwelt among us. When Jesus Christ came to earth, and was conceived by the Virgin Mary. He came to save us from our sins. And he shall be called wonderful, counselor, the mighty God, the everlasting Father the prince of Peace.
(Isaiah 9:6)

This is that came by water and blood, even Jesus Christ; not by water only, but by water and blood. And it is the Spirit that beareth witness, because the Spirit is truth.
(1 John 5:6)

JESUS IS LIFE

I am the door: by me if any man enter in, he shall be saved, and shall go in and out, and find pasture. The thief cometh not, but for to steal, and to kill and to destroy: **I am come that they might have life**, *and that they might have it more abundantly. I am the good shepherd:* **the good shepherd giveth his life** *for the sheep.*
(John 10:9-11)

My sheep hear my voice, and I know them and they follow me:

And I give unto them eternal life; and they shall never perish, neither shall any man pluck them out of my hand.

My Father, which gave them me, is greater than all; and no man is able to pluck them out of my Father's hand. I and my Father are one.
(John 10:27-30)

And this is **eternal life, that they may know thee the only true God, and Jesus Christ, whom thou hast sent***.*
(John 17:3)

JESUS IS THE EXPRESSION OF GOD'S LOVE

Herein is love, not that we love God, but that he loved us, and
sent his Son *to be the* **propitiation for our sins.**
(1 John 4:10)

We love him because he first loved us.

It is possible to give without love, but it is not possible to love without giving. Since the fall of man through Adam and Eve, there was no hope for mankind. The penalty for our sins is death. It is because of the disobedience of one man, Adam, that we are all destined to die and will receive punishment for our sins. God looked down on us with love, and sent his only son Jesus Christ to die for our sins. This is the real, unconditional love of God. Because God is holy and he hates sin, we were separated from God because of sin. But God made a way for us to come back to him through the death of his son Jesus Christ. That is because of the obedience of a new Adam, who is Jesus Christ; now we receive mercy and grace in the sight of God.

Jesus is without sin. He came as a human born of the flesh so that the body he had would become a sacrifice of sin offering to God. It is for my sins, your sins, and the sins of the whole world that Jesus came and died for us.

The Bible says, "No man hath seen God at any time. If we love one another, God dwelleth in us, and his love is perfected in us. And we have seen and do testify that the Father sent the Son to be the Savior of the world." (1 John 4:12&14)

This is where the unconditional love began, through Jesus Christ. He is the unconditional love of God in spite of our sinful nature. He loves us and sent his only Son to die on our behalf. That's why Jesus said, "Greater love hath no man than this, that a man lay down his life for his friends. I am the good shepherd: the good shepherd giveth his life for the sheep." (John 10:11)

JESUS IS RANSOM FOR ALL

*For there is one God, and one mediator between God and men, the man Christ Jesus; Who **gave himself a ransom for all**, to be testified in due time.*
(1 Timothy 2:5-6)

Even as the Son of man came not to be ministered unto, but to minister, and to give his life a ransom for many.
(Matthew 20:28)

This is the good news for everyone, whether you are Greek, Jew, Gentile, Canadian, Japanese, Pilipino, American, Korean, Pakistani, or whatever nationality you have. You are part of God's salvation, first to the Jews and then to us. Jesus already redeemed us through his blood. So the invitation is for everyone and this is the gift of God, the eternal life through Jesus Christ.

JESUS IS THE BREAD OF LIFE

But he answered and said, It is written, Man shall not live by bread alone, but by every word that proceedeth out of the mouth of God.
(Matthew 4:4)

Verily, verily, I say unto you, He that believeth on me hath everlasting life.
I am the bread of life.
(John 6:47-48)

I am the living bread which came down from Heaven: if any man eat this bread, he shall live for ever: and the bread that I will give is my flesh, which I will give for the life of the world.
(John 6:51)

JESUS WAS GOD'S ONLY BEGOTTEN SON

Then answered Jesus and said unto them, verily, verily I say unto you, The Son can do nothing of himself, but what he seeth the Father do: for what things soever he doeth, these also doeth the Son likewise.
(John 4:19)

Verily, verily, I say unto you He that heareth my word, and believeth on him (GOD) that sent me, hath everlasting life, and shall not come into condemnation; but is passed from death unto life.
(John 4:24)

I can of mine own self do nothing: as I hear, I judge: and my judgment is just; because I seek not my own will, but the will of the Father which sent me.
(John 4:30)

I am come in my Father's name and ye receive me not: if another shall come in his own name, him will ye receive.
(John 4:43)

Chapter Seven
What Will I Do to Inherit Eternal Life?

And that from a child thou hast known the holy scriptures,
which are able to make thee wise unto salvation through
faith which is in Christ Jesus.
(2 Timothy 3:15)

1. **Have Faith in God.** But without faith it is impossible to please him: for he that cometh to God must believe that he is, and that he is a rewarder of them that diligently seek him. (Hebrews 11:6)

The only thing you can do is to first believe in God. Believe that God sent his only begotten son, Jesus.

Do you believe that Jesus died for your sins, and not only for your sins but the sins of the whole world? Your salvation now is up to you to believe it or not. Jesus already made a way, you only need to believe. Have faith in God.

2. **Repentance/Repent from all your sins.**

Then Peter said unto them, Repent, and be baptized every one
of you in the name of Jesus Christ, for the remission of your
sins, and ye shall receive the gift of the Holy Ghost.
(Acts 2:38)

Again when the wicked man turneth away from his
wickedness that he hath committed, and doeth that which is
lawful and right, he shall save his soul alive.
(Ezekiel 18:27)

*From that time Jesus begun to preach, and to say, **Repent** for*
the kingdom of Heaven is at hand.
(Matthew 4:17)

After the apostles received the baptism of the Holy Spirit, they became bold in proclaiming the gospel of Jesus Christ. The people asked Peter what they were supposed to do. Peter told them to repent of their sins. Repentance means turning away 100 percent from your sins. We all have sinned, but God's invitation to repent is when we acknowledge our sins before him and ask forgiveness. If you want to know what the sins you have committed are and do not know already, read the Ten Commandments. If you can remember all that you have done, then ask God for forgiveness, and ask him to cleanse you from all your sins.

3. **Confession - Confess that you believe in God, that he sent his Son.**

If we confess our sins, he is faithful and just to forgive us our sins, and to clean us from all unrighteousness.
(1 John 1:9)

We have to confess our sins before God and we have to confess with our mouth that Jesus died for our sins.

But what saith it? The word is nigh thee, even in thy mouth, and in thy heart; that is the word of faith which we preach;

That if thou shalt confess with thy mouth, the Lord Jesus, and shall believe in thine heart that God hath raised him from the dead, thou shalt be saved.

For with the heart man beleiveth unto righteousness; and with the mouth confession is made unto salvation.
(Romans 10:8-10)

Heart

Keep thy heart with all diligence; for out of it are the issues of life.
(Proverbs 4:23)

1. The heart is the center of intellect (Deut. 8:5)

   a. We meditate in our hearts

   b. We commune in our hearts

   c. Keep things in our hearts

   d. We imagine things in our hearts

   e. We reason things in our hearts

   f. We believe or don't believe in our hearts

   g. We sing in our hearts

2. The heart is the center of our emotions (Ex. 4:14; Jer. 15:16)

   a. We love or hate from our hearts

   b. We fear or don't fear from our heart

   c. We repent or do not repent from our hearts

   d. We grieve or feel trouble from our hearts

   e. We are humble or not humble from our hearts

   f. We are sad or happy from our hearts

3. The heart is the center of our human will (Joshua 24:23)

   a. We obey or disobey from our hearts

   b. We seek God or don't seek God from our hearts

   c. We ask God from our hearts

   d. We do all things from our hearts

That is why it is important that we guard our hearts. It is in your heart or from your heart that you really believe in God's word, and it is also from your heart that you accept his word.

But those things which proceed out of the mouth come forth from the heart; and they defile the man.

For out of the heart proceed evil thoughts, murders, adulteries, fornications, thefts, false witness, blasphemies. (Matthew 15:18-19)

4. Acceptance – Accept Jesus into your heart

For as many are receive him, to them gave he power to become the sons of God.
(John 1:12)

And it will come to pass, that whosoever, shall call on the name of the Lord shall be saved.
(Acts 2:21)

Salvation is a free gift; yet in order for you to receive this gift, you have to receive it with all your heart. You must receive and invite Jesus into your heart to be your Lord and Savior. Only then will you become a child of God.

Adoption takes place when parents sign the documents required in order for them to take full possession of the child they want to adopt. So in the same way Jesus paid your sins on the cross, and by just believing you can accept him. Only then will you have eternal life. (You only need to say, "Yes, Lord, I accept you, come into my heart to be my Lord and Savior.")

It is as easy as *A-B-C*. But people are confused, and do not know which way they will turn to. What matters most is that you believe it from your heart. David said in his psalms, "Search me Oh God and know my heart today, try me my

Savior, know my hearts I pray, see if there be, some wicked ways in me. Cleanse me from every sin, and set me free." Let it be our prayer not only today but every day in our lives.

PRAYER OF ACCEPTANCE

Our Father, in Heaven, I adore you, I worship you Oh God. I come before your throne today, please forgive me for all my sins, wash me and cleanse me from every sin I've committed unto you. Forgive me, as I forgive others who trespass against me. Thank you for sending Jesus Christ to die for my sins. I now accept you Jesus to be my Lord and Savior, please come into my heart, and let your will be done in my life from now on. Thank you for your love and grace, I don't deserve it Oh God. I thank you. This I ask in Jesus's mighty name, Amen.

If you say this prayer, then I will be the first one to welcome you into the kingdom of God. You are now a child of God and millions of angels are celebrating right now in Heaven for one person turning to God and repenting of their sins ... Welcome my brother/sister in Christ. You are now born, not of corruptible seed but by incorruptible seed of the word of God. (1 Peter 1:23) You are now born again in the spirit. (John 3:3, 5) Jesus answered, "Verily, verily, I say unto thee, except a man be born of water and of the Spirit, he cannot enter into the kingdom of God." (John 3:5)

A New Covenant in Your "Declaration of Liberty"

Behold, the days come, saith the LORD, that I will make a new covenant with the house of Israel, and with the house of Judah.

But this shall be the covenant that I will make with the house of Israel; after those days, saith the LORD, I will put my law in their inward parts, and write it in their hearts; and I will be their God, and they shall be my people.
(Jeremiah 31:31a-33)

And I will give them an heart to know me, that I am the LORD: and they shall be my people, and I will be their God: for they shall return unto me with their whole heart.
(Jeremiah 24:7)

And I will give them one heart, and I will put a new spirit within you; and I will take the stony heart out of their flesh: and will give them an heart of flesh:

That they may walk in my statutes, and keep mine ordinances, and do them, and they shall be my people, and I will be their God.
(Ezekiel 11:19-20)

And It shall come to pass afterward, that I will pour out my spirit upon all flesh: and your sons and your daughters shall prophesy, your old man shall dream dreams, your young men shall see visions: And also upon the servants and upon the handmaids in those days will I pour out my spirit. And I will show wonders in the Heavens and in the earth, blood and fire, and pillars of smoke.
(Joel 2:28-30)

Covenant of Peace

Moreover I will make a covenant of peace with them; it shall be an everlasting covenant with them: and I will place them, and multiply them, and will set my sanctuary in the midst of them forever.
(Ezekiel 37:26)

Peace I leave with you, my peace I give unto you: not as the world giveth, give I unto you. Let not your heart be troubled, neither let it be afraid.
(John 14:27)

Jesus Christ - the Mediator of the New Covenant

But now hath he obtained a more excellent ministry, by how much also he is the mediator of a better covenant, which was established upon better promises.
(Hebrews 8:6)

And for this cause he is the mediator of the New Testament, that by means of death, for the redemption of the transgressions that were under the first testament, they which are called might receive the promise of eternal inheritance.
(Hebrews 9:7-15)

Jesus Christ is the Great High Priest

But into the second went the high priest alone once every year, not without blood, which he [JESUS] offered for himself, and for the errors of the people: The Holy Ghost this signifying, that the way into the holiest of all was not yet made manifest, while as first tabernacle was yet standing: Which was figure for the time then present, in which were offered both gifts and sacrifices, that couldn't make him that did the service perfect, as pertaining to the conscience; which stood only in meats and drink, and divers washing, and carnal ordinances, imposed on them until the time of reformation.

But Christ come on high priest of good things to come, by a greater and more perfect tabernacle, not made with hands, that is to say, not of this building; neither by the blood of goats and calves, but by his own blood He entered in once into the holy place having obtained eternal redemption for us. For if the blood of bulls and of goats, and the ashes of an heifer sprinkling the unclean, sanctifying to the purifying of the flesh: How much more shall the blood of Christ, who through the eternal Spirit offered himself without spot to God, purge your conscience from dead works to serve the living God.
(Hebrews 9:7–14)

Jesus Christ Hath Entered Into the Holy of Holiest

For Christ is not entered into the holy places made with hands, which are the figures of the true; but into the Heaven itself, now to appear in the presence of God for us.

For then must he often have suffered since the foundation of the world: but now once in the end of the world hath he appeared to put away sin by the sacrifice of himself.
(Hebrews 9:24,26)

This was the covenant that I will make with them after those days, saith the LORD, I will put my laws into their hearts, and in their minds, will I write them: And their sins and iniquities will I remember no more.
(Hebrews 10:16-17)

The new covenant is the blood of Jesus. Only through the death of Jesus Christ have we obtained mercy, forgiveness of our sins, and freedom from sin and slavery. The old covenant was not effective, because even though they had the law, they had seen God's wonders and miracles in the desert. This was when they crossed the Red Sea, ate the manna from Heaven, drank water from the rock, etc. (Psalm 78:14-29)

For all this they sinned still, and believed not for his wondrous works. (Psalm 78:32) That's why a lot of them died in the desert for those forty years. Only a few of them ever reached the Promised Land (Canaan).

Once you have repented from your sins and accepted Jesus as your Lord and Savior, you will enter into a new covenant with God. Whether you like it or not, your life will change, because a truly born-again Christian will have the new spirit of 100 percent obedience to the will of God. I am crucified with Christ; nevertheless, I live. Yet not I but Christ liveth in me: and the life which I now live in the flesh I live by faith of the Son of God, who loves me, and gave himself for me. I do not frustrate the grace of God: for if righteousness come by the law, then Christ is dead in vain. (Galatians 2:20-21) Just as Paul testified about it, I can also tell you, only then is it possible to live in 100 percent obedience to the will of God. I can tell you this because it's my experience, as well as the experience of all of God's children who have repented and received the Holy Spirit. Life will never be the same again. Because we will be changed from glory to glory; strength from strength; holiness and righteousness and peace and joy in the Holy Ghost—that's the kingdom of God. And the kingdom of God is within you. You are now set apart for God as holy people and royal priesthood, so that you will show forth his marvelous works, his great love, and his faithfulness in your life.

You Now Have the Assurance of Salvation

That if thou shalt confess with thy mouth the Lord Jesus, and shalt believe in thine heart that God hath raised him from the dead, thou shalt be saved. For with the heart man believe unto righteousness, and with the mouth confession is made unto salvation.
(Romans 10:9-10)

1. Your sins are forgiven

If we say that we have no sin, we deceive ourselves, and the truth is not in us. If we confess our sins, he is faithful and just to forgive us our sins, and to cleanse us from all unrighteousness.
(1 John 1:8-9)

When we ask forgiveness of God, he always forgives us and is always faithful to us. He doesn't only cleanse us from our sins, but he also forgets our sins.

For this is my blood of the new testament, which is shed for
many for the remission of sins.
(Matthew 26:28)

2. Your sins become white as snow

Come now, let us reason together, saith the Lord: though your
sins be as scarlet, they shall be as white as snow; though they
be red as crimson, they shall be white as wool.
(Isaiah 1:18)

In winter, we seldom have snow in Vancouver. But when it
does snow, it usually rains the next day. It washes away the
snow. In 2006, the snow stuck for six days. I always love to
see the snow; it's so beautiful, so white, and so pure. This
reminds me of how pure and white my sins become after
God forgave them and forgot about them. So it is the same
thing with you: Jesus already paid the penalty of your sins.
That's why we can come boldly to God's presence and ask
forgiveness. Your sins may be red as crimson but they will
be white as wool because God can make them white as snow.

3. Your sins become erased and forgotten

As far as the east is from the west, so far hath he removed our
transgression from us.
(Psalm 103:12)

And their sins and iniquities will I remember no more.
(Hebrews 10:17)

Can you see the east from the west? No, you can't see that far
at all. That's how far our sins are forgotten.

I shall remember them no more.
(Isaiah 43:25)

When God forgives us our sins, he forgets them forever. The only thing he sees now is the blood of his Son Jesus, as a payment of our sins.

4. You inherit godliness (divine nature)

According as his divine power hath given us all things that pertain unto life and godliness, through the knowledge of Him hath called us to glory and virtue. Whereby are given unto us exceeding great and precious promises: that by these we might be partakers of the divine nature, having escaped the corruption that is in the world through lust.

And beside this, giving all diligence, add to your faith virtue; and to virtue knowledge; and to knowledge temperance; and to temperance patience; and to patience godliness; and to godliness brotherly kindness; and to brotherly kindness charity.
(2 Peter 1:3-7)

5. You are called to FREEDOM

Christ hath redeemed us from the curse of the law, being made a curse for us: for it is written, Cursed is every one that hangeth on a tree:

That the blessing of Abraham might come on the Gentiles through Jesus Christ, that we might receive the promise of the Spirit through faith.(Galatians 3:13-14)

6. You are buried with Jesus through baptism

Know ye not that so many of us as were baptized into Jesus Christ were baptized into his death? Therefore we are buried with him by baptism into death: that like as Christ was raised up from the dead by the glory of the Father, even so we also should walk in newness of life.
(Romans 6:3-4).

7. You become a child of God by faith in Christ Jesus

For as many of you have been baptize into Christ have put on Christ. There is neither Jew nor Greek, there is neither bond nor free, there is neither male nor female; for ye are all one in Christ.
(Galatians 3:26-29)

When you receive and confess in your mouth the Lord Jesus Christ, this is the second confession that you need to do. It is the public confession of your faith. It is also a symbol of the burial of Jesus Christ, that he died for our sins.

In 1994, when I first attended the Lighthouse Baptist Church in Hong Kong, I was baptized in the bathtub with a few other people.

The second time I got baptized was in 1995 at the Horshe Bay in Hong Kong.

I remember how fully fresh I felt and the power of God swept over me. I felt an overwhelming joy, free from guilt and shame. Whenever I see anybody become baptized, I see a new life, a new beginning, and a fresh start. I rejoice with unspeakable joy. It is a new beginning of your walk with the Lord and this is only the start of the Christian warfare.

8. God gives you the Holy Spirit as a seal

In whom ye also trusted, after that ye have heard the word of truth, the gospel of your salvation: in whom also after that ye believed, ye were sealed with the holy spirit of promise.
(Ephesians 1:13)

But the anointing which ye have received of him abideth in you, and ye need not that nay man teach you: but as the same anointing teacheth you of all the things, and is truth, and is

no lie, and even as he hath taught you, ye shall abide in him.
(1 John 2:27)

9. God gives you eternal life

And this is the record that God hath given to us eternal life,
and this life is in his Son.

He that hath the Son [Jesus Christ] hath life; and he that hath
not the Son of God hath not life.
(1 John 5:11-12)

10. You receive reconciliation from God

And having made peace through the blood of his cross, by him
to reconcile all things unto himself; by him, I say whether they
be things in earth, or things in Heaven. And you, that were
alienated and enemies in your mind by wicked works, yet now
hath he reconciled. In the body of his flesh through death, to
present you holy and unblameable and unreproveable in his
sight.
(Colossians 1: 20-22)

11. You become a son of God

For as many as are led by the Spirit of God, they are the sons
of God. For ye have not received the spirit of bondage again to
fear, but ye have received the Spirit of Adoption, whereby we
cry , Abba, Father. The Spirit itself beareth witness with our
spirit, that we are the children of God.
(Romans 8:14-16)

And because ye are sons, God hath sent forth the Spirit of his
Son into our hearts, crying, Abba, Father. Wherefore thou are
no more a servant, but a son; and if a son, then an heir of God
through Christ.
(Galatians 4:6-7)

12. You become an heir of the promise

And if children, then heirs; heirs of God, and joint-heirs with Christ; if so be that we suffer with him, that we may be also glorified together.
(Romans 8:17)

13. You are no longer condemned

There is therefore now no condemnation to them which are in Christ, Jesus, who walk not after the flesh, but after the Spirit.
(Romans 8:1)

14. You overcome

For whatsoever is born of God overcometh the world: and this is the victory that overcometh the world, even our faith.
(1 John 5:4)

He that rejected me, and receiveth not my words, hath one that judgeth him: the word that I have spoken, the same shall judge him in the last day.

For I have not spoken of myself; but the Father which sent me, he gave me a commandment, what I should speak. And I know that his commandments is life everlasting: whatsoever I speak therefore, even as the Father said unto me, so I speak.
(John 12:48-50)

15. We are the Children of Abraham

Even as Abraham believed God, and it was accounted to him for righteousness. Know ye therefore that they which are of faith, the same are the children of Abraham.
(Galatians 3:6-7)

16. You live by faith

But that no man is justified by the law in the sight of God, it is evident: for the just shall live by faith. And the law is not of faith: but the man that doeth them shall live in them.
(Galatians 3:11-12)

Chapter Eight

Agape Love Makes You Complete

Love is the fulfillment of the law.
(Romans 13:10)

For all the law is fulfilled in one word, even this; thou
shalt love thy neighbor as thyself.
(Galatians 5:14)

It is the divine love of God that makes you complete—not the aeros love or the phileo love that I mentioned earlier. When you become a born-again Christian, God's love is the first love you will receive. I remember when I first become born again in Spirit, I began to love other people and I wanted them to receive, or to know, what I just have received, which is the life eternal that Jesus offers to them that believe in his name. I did not want them to go to eternal damnation. That is God's love for us. He doesn't want us to go to hell; He created hell only for Lucifer and his angels and those people who follow him. This love still stirs up in my heart to this day—and that is why I wrote this book, because of that love. This love is still in my heart and I want all my friends and all the people that God will bring into my life to receive the eternal life that God has promised. I want the whole world to know about this love and accept it. My part is only to share it with you, but it's your choice to believe and accept or not to believe and reject it.

When you become born again in the spirit, the old spirit from you, which is the spirit of disobedience, will pass away. The new Spirit, which is the spirit of obedience, will come. That's why you are able to obey... And I will give them a new spirit, and I will give them one heart, and one way that they may fear me for ever, for the good of them, and of their children after them.
(Jeremiah 32:39)

Without the Holy Spirit in your life, you can never obey. It was only through the Holy Spirit that the disciples began to have power. Beforehand, Peter denied Jesus three times. After they received the Holy Ghost baptism, they all become fearless. They healed the sick, and did lots of miraculous signs and wonders.

It is only through the Holy Spirit that you can have power to obey. And you will be able to say, "Not my will Lord, but let thy will be done."

This love (agape love) of the Father will continue to grow in your heart, and you will completely obey him. This love is the fulfillment of the law. For Christ is the end of the law for righteousness to every one that believeth. (Romans 10:4) You won't have any more struggles when you follow his will. He said, "Love the LORD your God with all your heart and with all your mind and strength. This is the first and greatest commandment." If we take a look at the ten commandments, half of them are about loving the Lord and the other half of them are for your neighbor.

The Ten Commandments

I am the Lord thy God, which brought thee out of the land of Egypt, from *the house of bondage.*

1. *Thou shalt have none other gods before me.*

2.   *Thou shalt not make thee any graven image, or any likeness of anything that is in Heaven above, or that is in the
earth beneath, or that is in the waters beneath the earth:*

3.   *Thou shalt not take the name of the Lord thy God in vain:
for the Lord will not hold him guiltless that taketh his
name in vain.*

4.   *Keep the Sabbath day to sanctify it, as the Lord thy God
hath commanded thee.*

5.   *Honor thy father and thy mother, as the LORD thy God
hath commanded thee; that thy days may be prolonged,
and that it may go well with thee, in the land which the
LORD thy God giveth thee.*

6.   *Thou shalt not kill.*

7.   *Neither shalt thou commit adultery.*

8.   *Neither shalt thou steal.*

9.   *Neither shalt thou bear false witness against thy
neighbor.*

10.   *Neither shalt thou desire thy neighbor's wife, neither
shalt thou covet thy neighbor's house, his field. Or his
manserva*nt, or his maidservant, his ox, or his ass, or
anything that is thy neighbor's.

(Deuteronomy 5: 6-21)

When you love someone, obeying is just the fruit of it. Jesus
said, "If you love me keep my commandments." And that is
the greatest commandment. The second thing is to love your
neighbor as yourself, which is the other half of the ten commandments. When you love your neighbor as yourself, then
you want the best for him, and you will do him good, not

evil, all the days of your life. You wouldn't kill your neighbor, covet their wife or husband, or take their belongings. But you would indeed protect them from harm—or anything that you know will ruin their life. If you have this love in your heart, if my neighbor has this love in their heart, and if your community has this love in their hearts, our nations would be full of love. There would be no place for hate or war. The only thing that unites this world is this agape love. The love of God through Jesus Christ's death on Calvary made it possible for us to live with the law. (Galatians 3:12)

Then and only then can we fulfill the law, through love, because love is the fulfillment of the law. This is available for you; if you have not yet received God's love, receive him today.

What Makes You Content?

Is it relationships, wealth, good health, or power? None of these will make you content.

Man shall not live by bread alone, but by every word that proceedeth out of the mouth of God.

The reason why we need God's love so badly in our hearts is because, without it, we are lost. We can never be satisfied with our career, with our marriage, and with our life. Contentment is only found through God.

The relationship between the husband and the wife is called intimacy. They share everything and they have one body. This connection that bonds them is so intense that one cannot be happy or complete without the other. This intimacy is what God wants for us. Because he is the only one who can fill the emptiness in our hearts. The things that your husband or wife can't give you, don't look for them, only God can fill them. This is what my sister told me, and it is absolutely true.

That's why divorce is increasing so rapidly. This is the reason why people look for another wife or husband, because they couldn't feel the completeness that only God is able to give. And if you have this divine love, your marriage will be blessed, and your children and your offspring will be blessed as well.

When I met Ezra, I felt this contentment with him, I never felt this feeling with any man before, but only with him. I was so happy being with him that even when my friends or my family were not around me, I felt this incredible contentment of happiness and fulfillment. But sometimes we had disagreements, or something he said things that would make me angry. One thing that he cannot fill or ease in my heart is emotion. If I don't go to God on my knees, I can never be ok. But then I went with my brokenness and complained to God and asked him to heal my emotions and help me learn to forgive Ezra. Miraculous things then happened. I could face Ezra again as if nothing happened. It was a brand new start all the time. It is only God that makes you complete; without God in your marriage or relationship, it will surely fail.

This Agape Love Brings Joy and Peace

> But the fruit of the spirit is Love, joy peace, patient,
> longsuffering, gentleness, faith, meekness; temperance
> against such there is no law.
> (Galatians 5:22-23)

When I became a born-again Christian—when I accepted the Lord Jesus as my Lord and Savior—it was 1980 and I was in high school.

The first fruit I felt in my heart was the love of the people. I had the desire to share the love of God and what he has done for me. My heart was in evangelism right away. We always invited other people to come to our church or we went out giving tracts. When I was in Manila, we would go house to house, spreading the word of the Lord.

Then, when I was in Hong Kong, I did the same. I invited my friends and the people I met to come to church and they were converted. Namely: Emely, Josie, Jonah, Rose, Vangie, Evelyn, Agnes, Imelda. I invited all the people that I met to come to church with me in Canada, and every Sunday, I had a few visitors. But only few came to know the Lord Jesus Christ and become born again. And one of the reasons why this book is written is because I want to reach out to the unsaved people.

This love for the people is the agape love; it is the heart of God.

"The Lord is not slack concerning his promise, as some men count slackness; but is long suffering to us-ward, not willing that any should perish, but that all should come to repentance."
(2 Peter 3:9)

The second thing God taught me is to love the unlovable people. As a caregiver for many years, I had learned how to adjust to culture in Singapore, Hong Kong, and Canada. God taught me to love people for who they are, not for who I want them to be. But being a nanny, I was my employers' servant and had to do what they asked me to do. I had met all kinds of people with different attitudes and cultures and I had learned to adjust and love them for who they were. I remember one of the ladies I worked for saying that she expected that I would only last a month in my job, because the man of the house had such a fierce attitude. But I stayed for four years with them. I only left because I wanted to go to another country.

I have learned to love difficult people.

God also taught me how to love my enemies, although I never had any enemies in my life. But I consider those people who treat me badly and never welcome me to perhaps be enemies. I have learned to forgive and love them.

The most difficult part of loving is loving your enemy. The deeper the hurt and pain they cause in your life, the deeper the anger from your heart. Only God can melt this anger and turn it to a forgiving and loving heart. Without God in your heart, you will hate them till the end, and until they go down to the grave. God taught me how to love my neighbor as myself. It is easy to give something that you don't like. For example, you bought new clothes and you want to give away the old ones. You bought a new TV, new cell phone, or something else, and you want to give away the things you already used and that are out of style. This is actually called recycling. Instead of throwing them away, we give them to someone who is just starting their life and doesn't have anything. But I am talking about giving gifts. When I buy a gifts, it has to be of worth and of value and something that you can afford. That's what God had taught me: to love my neighbor as I love myself and care for myself.

Fruits of the HOLY SPIRIT

When you say you are a born-again Christian, yet these fruits are not in your life, you've got to look back, check your life, and ask yourself, "Do the fruits of the Holy Spirit live in me?"

Love - Toward your fellow men, especially to your brothers and sisters in Christ and to those who do not love in return (or to the unlovable).

Joy - Joy for the salvation of your soul, joy in the Holy Ghost, joy of answered prayer, but most of all joy in the midst of painful circumstances or trials.

Peace - Peace from God that passeth all understanding, and peace in the midst of war, in the midst of trials and temptations. Peace toward God and your fellow men. And when something you are counting on doesn't come through.

Patience - Toward others/yourself and when people keep failing you, and when things are not going quickly enough for you.

Kindness - Toward your fellow men and also to those who treat you unkindly, persecute you, or mistreat you.

Goodness - Toward your fellow men, especially to those who mistreat you or who have been intentionally insensitive to you.

Faithfulness - Toward God, your wife/husband, and your fellow men, but most of all, when someone proves unfaithful to you.

Gentleness - Toward your fellow men and those who have handled you roughly.

Temperance or Self-control - In the midst of intense temptations, trials, and sufferings.

LOVE your ENEMIES

But I say unto you, Love your enemies, bless them that curse you, do good to them that hate you, and pray for them which despitefully use you, and persecute you; That ye may be the children of your Father which is in Heaven: for he maketh his sun to rise on the evil and on the good, and sanded rain on the just and on the unjust.
(Matthew 5:44-45)

Overcome evil by doing good.

You may say, "That's impossible, I can't love my enemies, He killed my father/mother/children, so I am going to kill him too. He deserves to be condemned of his sin. I hope someone will kill him too. I will never want to forgive him/her."

Your enemies are the ones who hath done harm or offense in your life. Enemies are not only results of, for example, wars between nations, and kingdoms against kingdoms.

This is the hardest commandment from Jesus Christ, because it is easier to love someone who does good to you and those friends who help you and who are always by your side, in good times and bad. But to love the person who killed your father or mother is the hardest thing to do.

The opposite of love is hate, so you can choose to love or hate them. You can choose to forgive and forget or you can continue to harbor grief and resentment. The choice is yours. As for me, I will choose LOVE.

Chapter Nine
Love is the Greatest

*And now abideth faith, hope, **charity, but the greatest of this is charity**.*
(1 Corinthians 13:13)

Apostle Paul mentions the manifestation of the Spirit or the Gift of the Spirit.

But the manifestation of the Spirit is given to every man to profit withal

For to one given by the Spirit the word of wisdom; to another the word of knowledge by the same Spirit;

To another faith by the same Spirit; to another the gift of healing by the same Spirit.

To another the working of miracles; to another prophecy; to another discerning of spirits, to another divers kinds of tongues:

But all these worketh that one and selfsame Spirit, dividing to everyman severally as he will.
(1 Corinthians 12:7-11)

And he told them to covet the best gifts: Verse 31.

He goes on to say in 1 Corinthians 13:1-3:

THOUGH I speak with the tongue of men and of angels, and have not charity, I am become as sounding brass, or a tinkling cymbal. And though I have the gift of the prophecy, and understand all mysteries, and knowledge; and though I have all faith, so that I can move mountains, and have not charity, I am nothing.

And though I bestow all my goods to feed the poor, and though I give my body to be burned, and have not charity, it profiteth me nothing.

I read the book *Welcome Holy Spirit* by Benny Hin. I marvel at how anyone can speak in tongues. The book of Acts, chapter two, talks about the filling of the Holy Ghost. Since then I have longed to speak in tongues. I had been a born-again Christian for twenty-one years but I had never spoken in tongues.

It was 2008 when God gave me this gift. I learned over the years that love is the fulfillment of the law; that love is the most excellent gift you can have. In my mind, I spoke to God and said, "Lord I already have this gift, the agape love, which is the most important of all. If you give me the gift of tongues, it's just a bonus to me." And he did give me that gift—I did speak in tongues. Nobody can argue with me that the gift of tongues ceases to exist, because I experienced it myself. And not just once; every time I come to the presence of my Heavenly Father, I can use that gift to approach him.

I have learned over the years that when you keep using the gifts God gave you, he will give you even more. It's the parable of the talents, and he who is faithful with much will be rewarded even more.

Then I longed for other gifts, such as the gift of healing. I wanted so badly to heal the sick, like Peter. In the Bible, Peter said to the beggar, "Silver and gold I do not have, but in the name of Jesus, you will be healed." But I came to realize, that this love that God has poured in my heart was the best and most excellent gift a child of God can have. I thought, I only have faith to move mountains, but now I also have the

126

greatest gift, which is agape love. It is a divine love of God that has poured out of my heart. And that is the heart of the matter and the very reason this book is written—that love. I want to pass on to you this love that God has put in my heart. It won't be an easy road, but you will grow in love, when you die to yourself and obey God in every area of your life. This love of God is not seeking your own happiness. What matter are the questions: What is the will of God for me? Am I in the center of God's will? What can make my God happy? Jesus said, "**My meat is to do the will of him (God) who sent me.**" (John 4:34)

We are not going to do our own will but the will of God. When his will is done in our hearts, then this prayer will be manifested in our lives. When he said, "Thy will be done on earth, as it is in Heaven," it means that all areas of our lives will be surrendered to him. These areas are financial, dreams, your family, your marriage, and your career. As it was in Heaven, God's angelic beings only do the will of God. And if his will is done in our lives, his kingdom has come in our midst. That's why he said in his word, "The kingdom of God is within you," (Luke 17:21) And his kingdom is not in meat or drink, but in righteousness, peace, joy, in the holy ghost, and in faith and love. For the kingdom of God is not meat and drink; but righteousness, and peace and joy in the Holy Ghost. (Romans 14:17)

Is it possible to prophesy without love, to have faith without love, to speak in tongues without love, or to heal the sick without love? Paul stated that even if you have faith, you can move mountains; if you do not have love, you are nothing. There be no more prophecy in the last days, but only receiving of rewards. Knowledge will also cease, as will the other gifts that Paul hath mentioned. The only gift that lasts forever is love. This is the love of God, that he hath given us his only begotten son for our redemption and forgiveness of our sins, and he hath promised us eternal life. It is the love that is the fulfillment of the law. It is the agape love, and it is available for you if you have accepted the Lord Jesus Christ as your Lord and Savior.

The First and the Greatest Commandment

Love God

Hear, O Israel: the LORD our God is one LORD: ***Thou shalt love the LORD*** *thy God with all thine heart, with all thy soul, and with all thy might.*
(Deuteronomy 6:4-5)

How can we love someone whom we can't see? God is a spirit: and they that worship him must worship him in spirit and in truth. (John 4:24) When we come to God we must believe that he exists, and that he is the rewarder of those who diligently seek him. Do you believe that there is a God? Even the devil believes and trembles. We come to God through the eyes of faith; we can't see him, but we know that he exists— that God sent his son Jesus Christ to save us from our sins. We believe that the Bible is the word of God. His promises never fail; it is the truth that sets us free.

We love him (God) because he first loved us. (1 John 4:19) We must love God with all out heart (emotions), mind (intellect), with our soul (soul-salvation), and with all our might (fruits of our labor, strength).

That means God wants to be first in our life, in our family, and in our career. It is the first commandment.

This is the love of God, that we keep his commandments: and his commandments are not grievous.
(1 John 5:3)

Second Commandment

Love thy neighbor as thyself.

Love worketh no ill to his neighbor: therefore love is the
fulfilling of the law.
(Romans 13:10)

How are we going to love our neighbor as we love ourselves? The better question to ask is, how do we love ourselves? We give the best gifts to ourselves.

If you love yourself, you make sure you have everything you need. You give yourself the best of everything you can get.

When you love yourself enough, you don't harm your body, nor do you do stupid things to make yourself feel worse.

So if you love your neighbor, you don't commit adultery toward you neighbor's wife/husband, and you won't kill, steal, or bear false witness against your neighbor. But rather you would protect them somehow because you love them.

And if you see that your neighbor doesn't have any food, give them food.

That's how you ought to love your neighbor as yourself.

Love one another.

Beloved, let us love one another: for love is of God; and
everyone that loveth is born of God, and knoweth God.

He that loveth not, knoweth not God for God is Love.
(1 John 4:7-8)

This is my commandment, that ye love one another, as I have
loved you.
(John 15:12)

This commandment of the Lord Jesus Christ is to love. Love God first, then your neighbors, and then your fellow man. Love is the fulfillment of the law. So let us love one another.

A Faithful and True Friend

We can learn from the story of David and Jonathan. I am so blessed with knowing how they both loved each other.

Saul was the father of Jonathan. When King Saul was rejected as a king, David was the Lord's chosen one to replace him. David met Jonathan after triumphantly killing Goliath. Let's look at the characteristic of a true friend.

1. **He has one spirit and love.** Jonathan becomes one spirit with David and he loved him as himself. (1 Samuel 18:1)

2. **He makes a covenant.** And Jonathan made a covenant with David because he loved him as himself. (1 Samuel 18:2)

3. **He has an open hand.** Jonathan took of the robe he was wearing and gave it to David, along with his tunic and even his sword, his bow and his belt. (1 Samuel 18:4)

4. **He can be a shield in times of trouble.** Jonathan said to David, "Whatever you want me to do, I'll do it for you." (1 Samuel 20:4) This was when David was in danger through the hands of Jonathan's father.

5. **He made a promise.** Then Jonathan said to David, By the LORD, the God of Israel, I will surely sound out my father by this time the day after tomorrow! If he is favorably disposed toward you, will I not send you a words and let you know? (1 Samuel 20:12)

6. **He affirms his love.** And Jonathan caused David to swear again, because he loved him as he love his own soul. (1 Samuel 20:17)

7. **He is willing to take the cost.** Then Saul's anger against Jonathan, and he said unto him, "Thou son of perverse rebellious woman, do not I know that thou has chosen the son of Jesse to thine own confusion, and unto thy confusion of thy mother's nakedness? (1 Samuel 20:42)

8. **He gave a farewell kiss.** David arose out of a place toward the south, and fell on his face to the ground, and bowed himself three times; and they kissed one another and wept with one with another, until David exited.

9. **The Lord's witness.** And Jonathan said to David, "Go in peace, for us much as we have sworn both of us in the name of the Lord, saying, the Lord be between me and thee, between my seed and thy seed forever. And he arose and departed, and Jonathan went into the city. (1 Samuel 20:42)

10. **He is loyal.** I am distress for thee, my brother Jonathan: very pleasant hast thou unto me: thy love to me is wonderful, passing the love of women. (2 Samuel 1:26)

My dearly beloved, let us love one another, not just in flatterring words but in our deeds. Hereby perceive we the love of God, because he laid down his life for us: and we ought to lay down our lives for the brethren.

But whoso hath this world's good, and seeth his brother have need, and shutteth up his bowels of compassion from him, how dwelleth the love of God in him?
(1 John 3:16-17)

One of the riches we have is our family and friends. God has given us a family, our own flesh and blood, so that we can love them unconditionally—to watch over them and make sure their needs are meet. That love always forgives and forgets; there is no hate or non-forgiveness remaining in our home. Our walls should have written on them, "Love is here, hate is prohibited." A lot of families have been broken because of hate; they harbor resentment and non-forgiveness in their hearts. They don't talk for ages because they can't forgive someone else.

The friends we have are one of the riches God gave us. We should love and care for each other. Let's love one another, and pray for one another.

Chapter Ten
Love Not the World

Love not the world, neither the things that are in the world. If any man loves the world, the love of the Father is not in him.

*For all that is in the world, the **lust of the flesh**, and the **lust of the eyes**, and the **pride of life**, is not of the Father, but is of the world.*

And the world passeth away, and the lust thereof: but he that doeth the will of God abideth forever.
(1 John 2:15-17)

What is in our world today?

Three Things in the World

1. Lust of the flesh

2. Lust of the eyes

3. Pride of life

Let's go to America and take a little look at a city that is very different from all the countries and cities around the world.

When America was first colonized by the pilgrims, they offered prayers on that first Thanksgiving day. Even to this day, Americans offer prayers as a continuation of that heritage. And when you pick up a dollar bill or any piece of change, you will see four words that say "In God We Trust".

It is a symbol that God is the strength of America. Perhaps the man who summed it up best was Carlos P. Romulo, a soldier, a statesmen, and a Philippine patriot. He was a former President of the UN General Assembly. When he left America he said this:

I am going home, America-farewell. For seventeen years, I have enjoyed your hospitality, visited every one of your fifty states. I can say I know you well. I admire and love America. It is my second home. What I have to say now in parting is both a tribute and a warning: Never forget, Americans, that yours is a spiritual country. Yes, I know that you are a practical people. Like others, I have marveled at your factories, your skyscrapers and your arsenals. But underlying everything else is the fact that America began as a God loving, God-fearing, God worshipping people, knowing that there is a spark of Divine in each of us. It is this respect for dignity of human spirit which makes America invincible. May it always endure.

And so I say again in parting, thank you, America, and farewell. May God keep you always- and may you always keep God.

American people have this original American dream: "We hold these truths to be self evident; that all men are created equal; that they are endowed by their creator with certain unalienable rights; that among this are life, liberty, and the pursuit of happiness." That's why America was blessed by God even unto this day. It is because it was founded on the faith in God.

The essence of the American spirit is expressed in the inscription on the Statue of Liberty.

STATUE OF LIBERTY

Give me your tired, your poor, your huddled masses yearning to breathe free...

Yearning to breathe free...

134

...yearning to taste the fullness of life;

...yearning to stretch dormant muscles and operate in full capacity;

...yearning to tear down old barns and build new ones;

...yearning to have security and enjoy life in old age.

This is also the reason why Americans are very successful. And there is no doubt that this essence or spirit is what most everyone has as a burning desire to accomplish in their life. This is not wrong at all, because if you have the ability to do something and make it happen, it is for the glory of God.

I would think that money is the pride of life, because if you have a lot of money, you have more power, and you can do a lot of things that others can't do. And the love of money is the root of all evil. It is important to remember, though, that it is not the money that it is evil, but it is the love of money that is the issue. If your heart is evil, you would likely do anything to get money no matter what the cost. That means it may cost evil to your neighbor or love ones. It is the love of money that makes you do evil for the sake of getting rich. If you love God more than you love money, then you become the master of the money, and money becomes your servant. Therefore, you command where the money goes, for the glory of God. On the contrary, if you love money more than God, then you became the servant of the money. Therefore, money will command you to do evil things in order to get it.

But every man is tempted, when he is drawn away of his own lust, and enticed. Then when lust hath conceived, it bringeth forth sin: and sin, when it is finished, bringeth forth death.
(James 1:14.15)

Good heart, good money; evil heart, evil money. The thing that is most wrong is the accumulation of wealth for your

135

own self at the cost of others people's lives. It is the accumulation of wealth without God. That's why success without God is nothing.

Everything in our world today is beautiful. God created it for us to enjoy. And this world is a better place to live, because we have this so-called freedom.

- Freedom to speak and to practice one's religion

- Freedom of assembly

- Freedom to petition the government.

Imagine living in a world that has no freedom. It would be chaos. I have been in Canada for thirteen years and I love this place. It is my home sweet home. It's the most beautiful place I've ever been. It's a place where you can see all the Rocky Mountains. Canada Place downtown is my favorite place to go when I need quiet time with the Lord. I often go to Amble Side after work and take a long walk beside the water. I go to Whistler if I want to see the snow; I don't know how to snowboard so I just watch. Stanley Park is where I go when I want to go sightseeing. And if I want to see the sunset I will go to Burnaby Mountain or Amble Side in West Vancouver. If I want to see the beauty of Downtown, then I will drive to the upper British property, where most of the million-dollar houses are; from there you can see Downtown. There are so many beautiful places here in Canada—not only Vancouver but also Banff National Park, Vieux Quebec, Prince Edward Island, Waterton Lakes National Park, Saint Anthony, Newfoundland, Labrador, Alberta, and Saskatchewan.

Although my family is in the Philippines—where there's no place like home—God brought me here and now this is my "Home Sweet Home." And I love it here.

This world that we are living in right now will one day be ruined. Whatever you have built or treasured will be cast away. Not one stone will be left; it all will be destroyed.

When ye therefore shall see the abomination of desolation, spoken of by Daniel the prophet, stand in the holy place (whoso readeth, let him understand;)

Let them which be in Judaea flee into the mountains: Let him which is on the housetop not come down to take anything out of his house: Neither let him which is in the field return back to take his clothes.

For then shall be great tribulation, such as was not since the beginning of the world to this time, nor ever shall be. (Matthew 24:15-18&21)

Jesus had said that nothing like this would have ever happened before. It would be a great tribulation, spoken by Daniel. Read the whole book of Daniel, especially chapter 11. The bad news is that there will be a great tribulation; the wicked will be more wicked. But the good news is that the people of God will be stronger.

And arms shall stand on his part, and they shall pollute the sanctuary of strength, and shall take away the daily sacrifice, and they shall place the abomination that maketh desolate. And such do wickedly against the covenant shall he corrupt by flatteries: but the people that do know their God shall be strong, and do exploits. (Daniel 11:32-32)

We are so consumed with making more money, buying houses, and earning more on investments. We need to understand that in the last days, we can't even bring it with us or inherit it forever.

We rebuild our houses to make them look new. We spend so much time trying to perfect our bodies as well. Both of these things are not permanent; all physical things will eventually be ruined. We make ourselves beautiful—for what? If you don't have salvation, the body and soul you have now will only end up being burned into eternal hell.

And many of them that sleep in the dust of the earth shall awake, some to everlasting life, and some to shame and everlasting contempt.
(Daniel 12:2)

We are not made for this world alone, we are made for eternity. Just as Jesus said in his word,

I have given them thy word; and the world hath hated them, because they are not of the world, even as I am not of the world.

I pray that thou shouldest take them out of the world, but that thou shouldest keep them from the evil.

They are not of the world, even as I am not of the world.
(John 17:14-16)

We had a real destiny, an eternal destiny for ever and ever in Heaven or in Hell. After this world will pass away, there will be a new Heaven and a new earth.
(Revelation 20:1-4)

And we have a citizenship in Heaven that will never be renewed or erased.

*Now therefore ye are **no more strangers and foreigners, but fellow citizens with the saints**, and of the household of God.*
(Ephesians 2:19)

That's why Jesus said love not the world or anything in the world, the lust of the flesh, the lust of the eyes, and the pride of life. But he that doeth the will of God will live forever.

What you SOW is what you REAP

*Be not deceived; God is not mocked: for **whatever a man soweth, that shall he also rea**p. For he that **soweth to his flesh** shall of the flesh **reap corruption**; but he that **soweth to the Spirit** shall of the Spirit **reap life everlasting.**
(Galatians 6:7-8)*

This has been my philosophy or my way of life: "What you sow is what you reap." You can't go wrong with this.

What are you sowing right now? Good or bad? Hate or love? Justice or injustice? Righteousness or unrighteousness? If you plant an apple seed right now, then later on you are going to reap an apple tree that will bear fruit. So don't expect to harvest pear fruit, because in the first place you have planted an apple tree. It is the same thing with our body; if we keep eating junk food, and we eat all the fatty substances and don't exercise at all, then we will reap what we have sown. We cannot eat all we want to only satisfy cravings. We will become unhealthy people with no strength left for the day, and we can even get all kinds of sicknesses by eating unhealthy foods.

I also personally believe that AIDS is one of those things that people reap by just having multiple sex partners over time. I am not sure that some people in those circumstances really understand the principles of sowing and reaping.

The choices you make today will play a very important role in your life. They are going to be your destiny. What you sow is what you are going to reap. If you sow righteousness and holiness, you will reap eternal life. If you sow wickedness and unholiness, you will also reap destruction in hell.

Being a born-again Christian is not a guarantee that you are going to Heaven. Neither is accepting the Lord Jesus Christ into your heart. Do you think it is by grace you have been saved?

The answer is a BIG NO!

Lest there be any fornicator, or profane person, as Esau, who for one morsel of meat sold his birthright.
(Hebrews 12:16)

Once someone has become born-again Christian and has repented from their sins and become a child of God, they sometimes go back to their old sinful habits. This makes them like Esau, who sold his birthright for just a bowl of food to satisfy his physical hunger, not thinking about the eternal reward of that action.

Wherein in time past ye walked according to the course of this world, according to the prince of the power of the air, the spirit that now worketh in the children of disobedience.
(Ephesians 2:2)

If you really accept Jesus in your heart and have committed your life to following him, the seal of the Holy Spirit is on you and will guide you into all truth. Your life will never be the same again.

But if you turn away from God, and you *think* you believe in Jesus Christ and that, because by faith, you have been saved, you will still continue to sin. God forbid there should be more sinners in Heaven that never experience the complete regeneration of the Holy Ghost. It would not only be unfair to others who died for their faith, but it would also create confusion in Heaven. Our God is a God of order. Jesus said, "The words that I speak unto you will judge you in the last day." So if you are a born-again Christian and you are still participating in sins of fornication, adultery, or uncleanness, you know that it is wrong and you still do it. Don't wait for his second coming to repent. Now is the time. God is calling you to come out of it and be separate. God, in his bountiful mercy, is asking you to be set apart from them. Come out from there and be separate. Depart ye, depart ye, go ye out from thence, touch no unclean thing; go ye out of the midst of her; be ye clean, that bear the vessels of the LORD. (Isaiah 52:11)

I love you, my brothers and sisters. You know the Lord and perhaps you said you love him. Obedience is better than sacrifice. There is no other way than to trust God's word regarding what he said he will do. Our part is to obey. And once you have experienced the love of God, obedience is no longer the issue; our love is the motivation to obey God. The Lord Jesus said, "If you love me keep my commandments." He also said, "He that hath my commandments, and keepeth them, he it is that loveth me: and he that loveth me shall be loved of my Father, and I will love him, and will manifest myself to him." (John 14:21)

It is of our own will and desire to follow God—and the same applies when we reject him. It is our own will and way that we do what we want because we love ourselves more than God. But it is written that what you sow is what you reap. The choice is yours. But I also warn you that no matter what choices you make, there are consequences of those choices. I've been there; it was only because of God's mercy and grace for me that I was able to come out. I was disobedient. I followed my own will. I told God, "I can follow you but please, not in the area of my love life. I love Ezra and I can't live without him." But God said that he loves me with an everlasting love. (Jeremiah 31.3) He was so patient with me. I did not always obey him. But through it all, God delivered me out of it. I did obey him with gladness because God wanted me to love Ezra as he loved him. God loved Ezra's soul and he wanted him to have salvation. So I had to love Ezra, including his soul, with a pure heart. I have prayed for Ezra all these years, hoping that if he would become a born-again Christian, then I would be free from the sin of fornication if he would marry me. But it didn't happen, because I was the one blocking his salvation. I didn't love his soul in the way that God loved his soul, so that he would not go to hell. Once God helped me to understand that, my spirit was able to willingly obey him and I became committed to following him. I obtained victory over it. So I can tell you the same thing: God loves you and he doesn't want you to perish. If you love your soul, then flee from fornication and adultery or uncleanness. If you love your partner as God loves them, don't be a stumbling block to you partner, or even to those people around you. Help them to come to know Jesus Christ. They will see God's love in your life. And if you truly love God, then you will obey him. I pray that God's mercy and grace may be upon you and that God will open your heart and mind to understand the fullness of his salvation in you and his perfect will in your life.

Sow to yourself in righteousness, reap in mercy; break up your fallow ground: for it is time to seek the LORD, till he come and rain righteousness upon you.
(Hosea 10:12)

Lust of the Flesh Versus Fruits of the Spirit

*This I say then, Walk in the spirit that **ye shall not fulfill the lust of the flesh**.*
(Galatians 5:16)

Lust of the Flesh means sinful acts or sinful nature.

Now the works of the flesh are manifest, and they are: (Definitions from *Webster's New World Dictionary*)

1. Adultery - sexual intercourse with a married person

2. Fornication - sexual intercourse with an unmarried

142

person

3. Uncleanness - not clean

4. Lasciviousness - exciting lust means excessive sexual desire

5. Idolatry - worship of idols or excessive reverence for, or devotion to, a person or thing

6. Witchcraft - the power or practice of witches

7. Hatred - strong dislike, ill will, or hate

8. Variance - varying or being variant; discrepancy - degree of change or differences; official permission to bypass regulations; not in agreement or accord

9. Emulation - trying to equal or excel; surpass; to imitate a person or thing; admire

10. Wrath - intense anger; rage or fury; any action of vengeance

11. Strife - contention; fight or quarrel; struggle

12. Seditions - a stirring up of rebellion against the government

13. Heresies - a religious belief opposed to the orthodox doctrine of a church; any opinion opposed to an official or established view

14. Envying - discontent and ill will over another's advantages, possessions, etc.

15. Murders - the unlawful and malicious or premeditated killing of a person; to kill a person unlawfully or with malice

16. Drunkenness - intoxicated – to make drunk; caused by or occurring during intoxication

17. Reveling - to revel; to make merry; to make much pleasure in.

Of the which I tell you before, as I have also told you in the past, that they which do such things shall not inherit the kingdom of God.
(Galatians 5:19-21)

But the fearful, and unbelieving, and the abominable, and murderers, and whoremongers, and sorcerers, and idolaters, and all liars, shall have their part in the lake which burneth with fire and brimstone, which is the second death.
(Revelation 21:8)

Be not deceived; God is not mocked: for whatever a man soweth, that shall he also reap. For he that soweth to his flesh shall of the flesh reap corruption; but he that soweth to the Spirit shall of the Spirit reap life everlasting.
(Galatians 6:7-8)

It is so clear that whatever we sow we are going to reap. The reason I gave the meanings of these lusts of the flesh is because the Lord wants me to include them.

This reminds me of one man who attends the same church that I attend. When I showed a certain verse, he asked me the meaning of lasciviousness, and I told him I didn't know. I thought he knew because he speaks English much better than I do. The most important thing is that we know the meaning of each word so that we know how to avoid each sin when Satan strikes with them in our lives.

I always avoided men who are married and still try to date me, because God said, "What God joined together let no man separate." Believe me, I have had countless married men ask me on dates, and they were all very successful. But because I know that adultery is a sin, I fled from them. Nevertheless, Satan was not yet through with me. He knows I will not commit adultery, so he set his arrows of fornication toward me. Little did I know at the time, but Satan got me with that sin.

But I thank God that he loves me so much that he didn't allow me to stay in that sin. I was chastised and rebuked through the word of God. I learned from this that, truly, I am a legitimate child of God.

Ye had not resisted unto blood, striving against sin. And ye have forgotten the exhortation which speaketh unto you as unto children, My son, despise not thou the chastening of the Lord. Nor faint when thou art rebuked of him: For whom the LORD loveth he chasteneth, and scourgeth every son whom he receiveth.
(Hebrews 12:4-6)

God is so faithful to me that he was able to deliver me from the hands of Satan, and now I am free from it. All the glory and honor and power belong to God. You too, my dear brother or sister—God said we will more than conquer all through him who loves us, because greater is each person when Jesus is in him. But before we can overcome or conquer anything, we must be willing to obey God. God can do anything, but if we are not willing to obey, we choose our own will. Then we have no one to blame but our own selves.

If you are a child of God and your partner is not, but he or she is a born-again Christian, you are responsible for, or at least play a part in, his or her salvation. We live by example and should share God's love and God's word with them. If God is not seen in our lives, then we have to question ourselves. Is God really the author or maker of my life? Is God glorified in my life? In my relationship? In my career? Is this the will of God, or my own will?

You and you alone can answer these questions.

In North America today, countless young people are not taught the values of purity. In my own country, in the Philippines, this is a very big thing for us. It is something that you can give as a gift for your future husband and him alone. When I gave away this gift, I almost couldn't go on with my life anymore. I felt so impure and miserable and lost, and I felt that I was being used. I had sold myself for nothing. And I let Satan use me as a doormat. But God was not finished with me yet. He set me free.

That's why this book is written, because I want to let you know you can be set free, too, if you allow God to work in your life. If the Son makes you free, you will be free indeed. If God sets you free, then make a decision to follow him no matter what happens. We are not yet perfect. We are all changed from glory to glory. And if you are able to conquer, then help others to come out of that pit of hell.

I am bold to tell you this, because I love you as God loves you. I don't want you to live like that. I warn you also like Paul did to the Corinthians, "Know ye not that the unrighteous shall not inherit the kingdom of God? Be not deceived: neither fornicators, nor idolatress, nor effeminate, nor abusers of themselves with mankind. Nor thieves, nor covetous, nor drunkard, nor revilers, nor extortioners, shall inherit the kingdom of God. And such were some of you: but ye are washed, but ye are sanctified, but ye are justified, in the name of the Lord Jesus, and by the Spirit of our God." (1 Corinthians 6:9-11)

I pray that God may open your heart and mind, that you may be able to see and understand his will. I pray that he will allow more grace to be upon you.

A PRAYER FOR YOU

Heavenly Father I come before you right now into the throne of grace to obtain mercy and favor for all your sons and daughters who are reading this book, and those who are still struggling in the flesh, the sting of death and hell.

Father, I am standing in the gap for them right here right now.

Father, forgive, have mercy, have favor. Father, forgive their sins, their shortcomings. Cover them through the blood of Jesus. Father, restore them, rebuild them, draw them closer to you for the glory of your name.

You are able to deliver them from every sin ... because your hands are mighty to save. Set your people free ... so that they will come to know, love, and serve you all the days of their lives.

Father, thank you for your forgiveness, thank you for your mercy. I ask you then to open their hearts and minds as they continue to read this book. Reveal to them the real riches in Heaven. This I ask in Jesus's mighty name. Amen.

The fruit of the Holy Spirit is: (Galatians 5:22-23)

Love - a strong affection or liking for someone or something.

Christian love has God for its primarily object, and expresses itself of all implicit obedience to his commandments. Christian love, whether exercised toward the brethren, or toward men generally, is not an impulse from the feelings. It does not always run with natural inclinations, nor does it spend itself only upon those for whom some affinity is discovered. Love seeks the welfare of all, Rom. 15:2, and works no ill to any, 13:8-10; love seeks opportunity to do good to all men, and especially toward them that are of the household of the faith, Gal. 6:10.

Joy - a very glad feeling ; happiness, delight

Peace - freedom from war; an agreement to end war; law and order; harmony; concord; serenity, calm, or quiet; hold (or keep) one's peace to be silent

Longsuffering - bearing trouble, patiently, for a long time

Gentleness - gentle; of the upper classes; refined, courteous; generous; kind; kindly patient; not harsh or rough

Goodness - the state or quality of being good; virtue; kindness

Faith - to trust; unquestioning belief, specifically in God, religion etc.; complete trust or confidence; loyalty

Meekness/Meek - patient and mild; too submissive; spiritless

Temperance - self restraint in conduct, indulgence of the appetites, etc.; moderation; moderation in drinking alcoholic liquors or total abstinence from them. There is therefore now no condemnation to them which are in Christ Jesus, who walk not after the flesh, but after the Spirit. (Romans 8:1)

WALK IN THE HOLY SPIRIT	WALK IN THE LUST OF THE FLESH
Love God and love your neighbor as yourself	Adultery, Fornication, Hatred, Murder, Strife
Joy in the Holy Ghost	Reveling
Peace with God and your fellow men	Wrath, Seditions
Longsuffering	Envying
Gentleness	Strife
Faith in God	Idolatry, Heresies, Witchcraft
Meekness	Emulations
Temperance	Drunkenness, Lasciviousness, Murder

Against such there is no law. And they that are Christ's have crucified the flesh with the affections and lust.
(Galatians 5:22-24)

The Role of the Holy Spirit

Book of Colossians

The Role of the Holy Spirit in our lives:

1. The mark or seal of God's ownership. Verse 1:13
2. The first installment of our inheritance. Verse 13
3. The Spirit of wisdom and revelation. Verse 17
4. The spirit helps us draw near to God. 2:18
5. The Spirit helps us to be a holy temple of God. 2:21-22
6. The Holy Spirit helps strengthen our inner being. 3:16
7. Motivates unity in the Christian Faith 4:3,13
8. Holy Spirit grieves when there is sin in our life 4:30
9. Convict the world with sin.
10. Holy Spirit desire to fill us and empower us. 5:18
11. Holy Spirit helps in our prayer and spiritual warfare. 6:18

Let Us Live in the Spirit

If we live in the Spirit, let us also walk in the Spirit.
(Galatians 5:25)

My last phrase for this chapter is **Stand Fast**.

Stand fast therefore in the liberty wherewith Christ hath made us free, and be not entangled again with the yoke of bondage [sin].
(Galatians 5:1)

When you gain the ground of holiness and righteousness, do not go back again. Christ hath set you free, so let us not use our freedom to indulge the sinful nature but rather glorify God through yielding to the Holy Ghost.

A PRAYER FOR YOU

Father, thank you for revealing your words to us. You have called us friends, because you didn't hide these things from us. You desire us to be holy and blameless in your sight. Father, I come into the throne of grace, right here, right now, for this sister or brother who is reading this book. Father, I am asking for your mercy. Please forgive her/him for whatever sins they have committed unto you. Father, have mercy, have your favor upon them. Have your eyes look unto their needs, look beyond their weaknesses. Father, forgive, for the sake of your elect, forgive. Break every yoke of sin right here, right now. Break everything that is not acceptable in your sight.

Send forth your anointing upon them, so they can have power to obey your word and to do your will. So that they will declare your mighty works in their life, as well as your goodness, mercy, and favor in their life.

I break every yoke, every bondage of sin, every burden right now upon you, in the name of the Lord Jesus Christ of Nazareth who was raised from the dead.

BE SET FREE In Jesus's mighty name. Your life will never be the same again. You will walk in victory by the Spirit of God. You are more than a conqueror through him who loves you. I decree, that you will walk in faith, love, and victory. You will never be the same again. This I ask in Jesus's name. Amen.

Chapter Eleven
Real Eternal Riches

If therefore ye have not been faithful in the unrighteous mammon, [Money] who will commit to your trust the true riches?
(Luke 16:11)

For what is a man profited, if he shall gain the whole world, and lose his own soul? Or what shall a man give in exchange for his soul?
(Matthew 16:28)

Labor not for the meat which perished, but for the meat which endureth unto everlasting life, which the Son of man shall give unto you: for him hath God the Father sealed.
(John 6:27)

The Richest Man in the Bible

King Solomon is the richest man in the Old Testament. He has six hundred threescore and six talents of gold. All his drinking vessels were of pure gold. He had four thousand stalls for horses and chariots, and twelve thousand horsemen. He had seven hundred wives, princesses, and three hundred concubines. So King Solomon exceeded all the kings of the earth for riches and for wisdom. (1 Kings 10: 14, 21, and 23) (1 Kings 11:3) (2 Chronicles 9:13-28)

Covenant Between God and Solomon

*And the Lord said unto him, I have heard thy prayer
and supplication, that thou hast made before me: I have
hallowed this house, which thou hast build, to put my name
there forever; and mine eyes and mine heart shall be there
perpetually.*

*And if thou will walk before me, as David thy father hath
walked, in integrity of heart, and in uprightness, to do
according to all that I have commanded thee, and will keep
my statues and judgments:*

*Then will I establish the throne of thy kingdom upon Israel
forever, as I promised to David thy father, saying there shall
not fail thee a man upon the throne of Israel.*

*But if ye shall turn from following me, ye or your children,
and will not keep my commandments and my statutes which I
have set before you, but go and serve other gods, and worship
them:*

*Then will I cut off Israel out of the land which I have given
them; and this house, which I have hallowed for my name,
will I cast out of my sight; and Israel will be a proverb and a
byword among all people,
(1 King 9:3-7)*

David was the father of Solomon. David loved God, for he was
a man after God's own heart. David taught Solomon about the
God of Abraham, Isaac, and Jacob, and he is the God of David.
He had given them the Ten Commandments, covenants, and
God's promises. Solomon's love for God was great, because
he was the one who built the temple of God. He asked God for
wisdom, so God gave him not only wisdom, but also wealth
and power. But through all his blessings, Solomon turned
away and served other gods. 1 Kings 11:3; 5-7: He went after
Astoreth, the goddess of Zidonians and after Milcom. He

tolerated the false god of his wives, and turned his heart to them; and worshiped the god of Sidonian goddess Astoreth involving immoral rituals and the worship of the stars, the Moabite god of Milcom or Molech (involving child sacrifice Leviticus 18:21; 20:1-2) and the Ammonite god Chemosh (a sun god).

Because Solomon didn't fully obey the voice of the Lord, as a result of his sins, the kingdom was divided into two. He reigned forty years as king in Israel.

And this is what King Solomon said, "**In everything there is a season, and a time to every purpose in life a time to be born and a time to die [verse 9]. What profit hath he that worketh in that wherein he laboureth?"**

Verse 12:

I know that there is no good in them, but for a man to do good in his life.

And also that every man should eat and drink, and enjoy the good of his labor, it is the gift of God.
(Ecclesiastes 9: 11-12)

I returned and saw under the sun, that the race is not to the swift, nor the battle to the strong, neither yet bread to the wise, nor yet riches to men of understanding, nor yet favor to men of skill; but time and chance happeneth to them all.

For man also knoweth not his time: as the fishes that are taken in an evil net, and as the birds that are caught in the snare; so are the sons of men snared in an evil time, when it fallen suddenly open them.
(Ecclesiastes 12:13-14)

Let us hear the conclusion of the whole matter:

Fear God and keep his commandments, for this is the whole duty of a man. For God shall bring every work into judgment, with every secret thing, whether it be good, or whether it be evil.

The moment you were born onto this planet earth, God already had a plan in your life. Some were born poor and some rich, but no matter how poor or how rich you are, you and I have something in common.

*Then shall the **dust return to the earth** as it was; and **the spirit shall return unto God who gave it.***
(Ecclesiastes 11:7)

And it is appointed unto men once to die, but after this the judgment.
(Hebrews 9:27)

It is a fact that we all are going to die, like the rich man and Lazarus. We just don't know when. What we do know is that after a person dies, there is judgment. We know that this life and body that we have are not ours, and they will return to the one who created them.

Since this body is created by God, how do we live our life while we are still on this earth? King Solomon said that, "Chance happens to us all." How do we steward our life here on planet earth while we still have the chance to live here? Do you ever consider how long God will give you the chance to live? Do you know that your life is a borrowed life? God has created you. The chances you have, and the choices you make, will one day be accounted for before God. That's why I keep saying that the choices or actions you make will have a very important impact in your eternal life. Choices you make will determine your destiny. Yes, it is going to be your destiny. In the story of Lazarus and the rich man, notice that even though the rich man already died physically, he could still see and feel. This is because we are a spirit being, and we have a soul.

Our body is like a shell. Once we die, our spirit leaves the body. No matter how you might torture a dead body, it cannot complain of pain. The spirit inside your body is what can feel and see and touch. For what is a man profited, if he shall gain the whole world, and lose his own soul? Or what shall a man give in exchange for his soul? (Matthew 16:28)

The wealth of this whole earth is not even comparable to the worth of one man's soul, because all the temporal riches on this earth will pass away. Only your soul is eternal; it will either be eternally condemned in hell or eternally rewarded in Heaven. You could be rich with material things but still have no riches in Heaven. Jesus said that it is difficult for the rich man to enter into the kingdom of God. It is difficult because he loves his wealth more than God and the things of God. And so he forgets that he also has his soul. God has made us, soul, body, and spirit. It is your spirit that will come back to God—or not come back. Look at the parables of the kingdom. What they don't know is that the riches that they have right now are only temporal; they can't bring them to Heaven or even hell.

If you are rich and are reading this book, I want to tell you that God loves you and that Jesus Christ died for you. The riches that you have here on earth are only temporary riches. You can't take it with you. What matters to God is your soul. He doesn't want you to perish.

You can be a millionaire here on earth and still go to Heaven, if you repent of your sins and ask Jesus to come into your life. God gave you wealth, more than enough, for yourself and to bless others. You can use your wealth to glorify God by helping the poor and those people who are fatherless. Maybe you can adopt twelve kids into your home; that would be a great way to use your wealth.

Lazarus, on the other hand, was really poor, and yet he loved God. Lazarus means "my God is my helper."

Blessed are the poor where theirs is the kingdom of God. This doesn't mean that if you are poor you automatically go to Heaven, but the poor can be rich in faith. Through their poverty they cling to the Lord. It's not so hard to believe in God when you are poor. If you are a poor child of God, don't worry; you are rich in faith. Keep investing for the kingdom of God.

The Parable of the Rich, Foolish Man

As the partridge sitteth on eggs, and hatcheth them not; so he that getteth riches, and not by right, shall leave them in the midst of his days, and at his end shall be a fool.
(Jeremiah 17:11)

And he spake a parable unto them, saying,

The ground of a certain rich man brought forth plentifully:

And he thought within himself, saying, what shall I do, because I have no room where to bestow my fruits?

And he said, This will I do: I will pull down my barns, and build greater; and there will I bestow all my fruits and my goods.

*And I will say to my soul, Soul, thou hast much goods laid up for many years; take thine ease, **eat, drink**, and **be merry**.*

*But **God said unto him, thou fool, this night thy soul shall be required of thee**: then whose shall those things be, which thou hast provided?*

So is he that layeth up treasure for himself, and is not rich toward God.
(Luke 12:16-21)

This parable is still evident in our world today. In Canada, when I drive around the city, I always see where old houses have been torn down and new houses are being built up in their place. And I believe that is not only happening in Canada but throughout the whole world. And not only with houses, but with new TVs, cell phones, etc. Our world keeps on changing. We can't even keep up with the new style of dress, houses, cars, and phones.

There is nothing wrong with having a brand new cell phone, computer, house, or dress, or accumulating wealth. I even attended a millionaires mind in training. There was such a huge attendance at the training, which means a lot of people want to become millionaires.

It is the accumulation of wealth without God in our life that is the wrong thing.

If you go back to an earlier chapter, I mentioned the heart.

*For the **love of money** is the **root of all evil**: which while some coveted after.*
(1 Timothy 6:10a)

It is loving money more than God that makes you covet. Therefore, the heart is the problem, not the money. If I have a good heart, and I know the will of God, then I will give to the poor, donate to charity, adopt some children, sponsor a child, or give my tithes. There are so many good things you can do when your heart is right with God. But if you love money more than you love God, then you will do the opposite. You will do anything to get more money. There are millionaires and billionaires who are prospering because they know how to accumulate wealth. There is no problem with becoming a millionaire, but here is my message for you: If you have spent all your life accumulating wealth for yourself, without God in your heart, then you are a fool, just as the Bible tells us. And you are not only a fool, but you are also wretched, miserable, poor, blind, and naked.

Because thou sayest, I am rich, and increased with goods, and have no need of nothing; and knowest not that thou art wretched, and miserable, and poor, and blind, and naked. (Revelation 3:17)

What Revelation 3:17 means is that without God in your heart, you are wretched, your soul has no salvation, and you will be miserable without God. You are poor because you have no inheritance or rewards in Heaven; you are blind, meaning you do not see the truth or the plan of God in your life (salvation); and you are naked, meaning you are not clothed with righteousness or holiness, which is the Holy Spirit. The Holy Spirit will dwell in every believer's heart.

If you are a millionaire reading this book, you are still the poorest of the poor in God's eye if you don't have God in your heart or salvation of your soul. So God, in order for you to become rich, said, "I counsel thee to buy of me gold tried in the fire, that thou mayest be rich; and white raiment, that thou mayest be clothed, and that the shame of thy nakedness do not appear; and anoint thine eyes with eye salve, that thou mayest see." (Revelation 3:17-18)

This means that you have to receive the gift of salvation, the word of God, and know and understand the plan of God to be saved. You also need to receive the Holy Spirit (white raiment), which will guide you into all truth, that thou mayest see the good and perfect will of God.

You were not born into this world just to become millionaires or billionaires. If you think that way, then you missed what is the most important plan of God in your life. Ecclesiastes 9:3 says that there is one event that will happen to us all, and that is death. The time you spend here on earth will be over.

But, my friend, do you know when that time will come? No one knows when their time will be up. I always told other people that the moment you were born here on earth, you already had a due date on your forehead. But only God can see and know it because he knows all things and knows the future.

But if your time is over, where will your soul be?

What will happen to all the wealth that you had accumulated?

Ecclesiastes 5:14 says, "But those riches perish by evil travail: and he begetteth a son and there is nothing in his hand. As he came forth of his mother's womb, naked shall he return to go as he came, and shall take nothings of his labour, which he may carry away in his hand."

Just imagine for one second when you stand in the judgment seat of Christ.

Will God tell you, "Well done, thou good and faithful servant, enter now into my kingdom"? Or you will hear him say, "I never knew you, depart from me, ye that doeth iniquity"? What if your name is not written in the Lamb's Book of Life?

*And death and hell were cast into the lake of fire. This is the second death. And **whosoever was not found written in the book of life was cast into the lake of fire**.*
(Revelation 20:14-15)

The worst thing that can happen to a man or a woman, whether he or she is rich or poor, is for him or her to be forever cast into the lake of fire, which is the second death. This is the eternal separation of the child of God to the non-children of God. It is an eternal separation also from God.

We are all accountable to God; your wife or husband or children can't give their salvation to you. You and you alone can work out your salvation. Whether you are rich or poor, we are all going to receive a reward, a reward of good works or reward of bad works. And God will judge us according to what we have done—not according to what we have not done. My prayer for you, my dear friend, as a millionaire, is that you will repent and accept Jesus as your Lord and Savior. The choice is still up to you.

As many as I love, I rebuke and chasten: be zealous therefore and repent.
(Revelation 3:17-19)

Message to the Rich Person Who Doesn't Have Salvation

God said, "I counsel thee to buy of me gold tried in the fire, that thou mayest be rich; and white raiment, that thou mayest be clothed, and that the shame of thy nakedness do not appear; and anoint thine eyes with eye salve, that thou mayest see." (Revelation 3:17-18)

What is My Glory?

Thus saith the LORD, Let not the wise man glory in his wisdom, neither let the mighty man glory in his riches:

But let him glorieth glory in this, that he understandeth and knoweth me, that I am the Lord which exercise loving kindness, judgment, and righteousness, in the earth: for in these things I delight, saith the Lord.
(Jeremiah 9:23-24)

When we speak about glory, oftentimes, we can know a person's glory by the way they speak.

The glory of the moon is the sun. One morning, I was driving to go to work in West Vancouver. It was this morning that the moon was still up in the sky where the sun sets in the west, and obviously the moon could no longer glow in the dark because it was 7:45 in the morning and the sun was about to rise. As I drove, I was gazing at the moon. When the sun rose, it reflected on the moon, and the moon brightened for a few minutes. It was obvious that when the sun greeted her, she responded with great delight and decided to shine.

Likewise, the glory of the husband is his wife, and the glory of the children is their parents. When a husband talks, he talks a lot about his kids or his wife. And if a woman is in love, she talks all about her love with her friends. Usually, when people have talents, riches, or power, they glorify themselves and boast about it all. Little do they know that all these things are temporary.

The Lord told us not to boast about the wisdom or talents that we have, or the riches that we accumulate, but to instead understand and know God. We are to know that he is a God:

1. **Who exercises loving kindness**

2. **Passes judgment (Deuteronomy 1:17)**

3. **Is full of righteousness**

Because he said: "Behold, the days come, saith the LORD, that I will punish all them which are circumcised with the uncircumcised; uncircumcised in their heart." (Jeremiah 9:25-26b)

I want to highlight the word *Judgment:*

1. Judgment - krisis - primarily denote "a separating" "then a decision, judgments"

2. Krima - denotes the result of the action signified by the verb *krino,* to judge

3. Hemera - "A day" is translated judgments, 1 Corinthians 4:3, Revelation 1:10, "The Lord's day", a period of a divine judgment

4. Gnome - "a means of knowing" to know - came to denote "a mind understanding" a) a purpose b) a royal purpose, a decree, c) judgment opinion. *Vine's Complete Expository Dictionary* pp337

Judgment, then, is the decision upon which the defendent is accused and had evidence that the things he committed are true, thereby he will be called guilty.

And there will be a day of Judgment. If you want to know more you can read the book of Revelation.

We have to know that God is not only a God of love, but of righteousness. He is just and of judgments. As I mentioned earlier, God has created you and me, and the soul of men came from God.

Behold, all souls are mine; as the soul of the father, so also the soul of the son is mine: the soul that sinneth, it shall die.
(Ezekiel 18:4)

That's why God has the right to judge us, whether we like it or not.

I thank God that I have had the privilege to talk to Ruel, the number-one money earner at my previous company called Excel Telecommunications. He earned millions of dollars with Excel and currently makes the most money every year in our new company called Fortune High-tech. I was curious when I first listened to him while we are in Dallas, Texas to attend the "Excel Excellebration" of our company. He was talking about faith then, and now he is talking about sowing and reaping. I told him that he was speaking my language.

And just in the nick of time, while this book was being written, I had the opportunity to meet him personally, and was able to ask him three questions:

1. What makes you successful? What is the source?

2. Are you content?

3. What makes you content?

He answered and said, "Visions make you successful. God is the source. No, I am not content. People who are content don't grow."

Ruel is a born-again Christian; that's why he knows and understands the source of his success—that without God he can do nothing. He had visions that make him successful, and I give all the glory and honor to God, because he is the source of Ruel's success.

Without visions, people perish. So if your visions are to make more money without God, you gain nothing. We must then have visions first to God who created us; that is what gives us life. Then make visions to do his will while we are still here on earth. In whatever we do, whether business or personal, we do all to the glory of God, because there will be a day of judgment.

Whom are You Serving?

God is the creator, He created Heaven and earth.

IN THE beginning God created the Heaven and earth.
(Genesis 1:1)

He created everything that you see and everything that you can't see.

He created the moon and the stars, the seas and the dry land, the grass and the trees that bear all kinds of fruit, the beasts of the forest, the fishes, etc. (Genesis 1:1-25)

And God created man _____(your name) in his own image. We are the masterpiece of God. So God created man in his own image, in the image of God created he him; male and female created he them. (Genesis 1:27)

God created the things humans need, before he created man on earth.

Without all this, we would have starved to death. If you go to the market and look for vegetables, you can see all kinds of vegetables and fruits. God has created them for us to enjoy. The trees are older than human beings. Have you ever thought of that? The things that you see were already here before us. God in his own wisdom designed to give us all we need before he created us. What a wonderful God we are serving!

He is the True God

But the LORD is the true God; He is the living God, and an everlasting king: at his wrath the earth shall tremble, and the earth shall not be able to abide his indignation.

He is the God of the whole earth. There is only one God, whether you call him, "Allah" as the Koran or Muslim friends call him, or you call him "Dios" in Spanish and Tagalog. There is only one true God.

Thus saith the LORD the king of Israel, and his redeemer the LORD of host; I am the first, and I am the last; and beside me there is no God.
(Isaiah 44:6)

There is No Other God Besides God

Thus shall ye say unto them, the gods that have not made the Heavens and the earth, even they shall perish from the earth, and from under this Heaven.

He hath made the earth by his power, He hath established the world by his wisdom, and hath stretched out the Heavens by his discretion.

When he uttereth his voice, there is a multitude of waters in the Heavens, and he causeth the vapours to ascend from the ends of the earth; he maketh lightning's with rain, and bringeth forth wind out of his treasures.
(Jeremiah 10:10-12)

Are you serving the God of Abraham, Isaac, and Jacob? The God of the apostles who wrote the Bible? The God who did wonders in Egypt and had done so many mighty miracles? God sent Moses to be a leader of the Israelites, so that they would go to the land that was promised to them, the land that is flowing with milk and honey, the land of Canaan, so that they may serve God. The Promised Land that God had promised his people is actually to have a good journey here on earth. And the second Promised Land would be the new Heaven and the new earth, which is to come. And he is still the God that I am serving today, the God who made Heaven and earth, the God who gave his only son to the world to redeem us from the coming wrath. The God of love, and mercy, and loving-kindness. But he is also a God that is just and righteous and will execute judgment to the unjust. He is the only true living God and the only one God. There is no god before him or after him. He is the God of the living and the dead. Joshua said to the Israelites, "Choose now whom you will serve, whether the God of the heathen. But as for me and my house we will serve the Lord." And I will say the same thing, that as for me and my household, we will serve the Lord. I thank God that in my family, we are all now born-again Christians and everyone is serving God. When I started writing this book one of my younger brothers, Meliton, was not saved yet. But I am holding onto God's promise, "Believe in the Lord Jesus Christ and you will be saved, you and your family." And my desire is not only for the salvation of my family, but for my cousins, neighbors, friends, and for all the people that I meet and will meet. That they too will come out of their bondage and serve the living God. What about you my friend, whom are you serving?

God Knows Our Heart

The hearts deceitful above all things, and desperately wicked: who can know it? I the LORD search the heart, I try the reins, even to give every man according to his ways, and according to the fruits of his doings.
(Jeremiah 17:9-10)

God knows our heart and mind; he knows what we are thinking. He knows when we are sad and happy. He knows when we undergo trials and problems. He knows our deepest hurt, our deepest longing, and our deepest dreams. And God doesn't look upon our outside appearance; he looks into our heart. God sent Nathan to the house of Jesse, to anoint the King of Israel. Jesse had twelve sons, and they were all strong and good-looking. But God was looking into David's heart. He was a man after God's own heart. So when people look at your appearance and criticize you, just remember God is looking in your heart.

God Knows Where We Are (God is Omnipresent)

Am I a God at hand, saith the LORD, and not a God afar off?

Can any hide himself in secret places that I shall not see him? Saith the LORD. Do I not fill Heaven and earth? saith the LORD.
(Jeremiah 23:23-24)

166

David asked, "Where can I hide from your presence? If I go to the deepest part of the sea, you are there, if I go the outermost part of the earth you are there." My dear friend, we cannot hide from God because He is present everywhere at the same time, and nothing is hidden in his sight.

God Knows the Future (God is All-knowing)

He knows the future and sees the future. He knows his children and he knows when he is coming. He knows what is going to happen in your life.

He is all-knowing.

God is Love

Beloved, let us love one another: for love is of God; and everyone that loveth is born of God, and knoweth God.

He that loveth not knoweth not God; for God is love.
(1 John 4:7-8)

God is Holy

For thus saith the high and lofty One that inhabiteth eternity, whose name is Holy; I dwell in the high and holy place, with him also that is of a contrite and humble spirit, to revive the spirit of the humble, and to revive the heart of the contrite ones.
(Isaiah 57:15)

God is Just (Justice)

He is the Rock, his work is perfect: for all his ways are judgment: a God of truth and without iniquity, just and right is he.
(Deuteronomy 32:4)

Tell ye, and bring them near; ye let them take counsel together: who hath declared this from the ancient time? Who hath told it from that time? Have not I the LORD? And there is no God else beside me; a just God and Savior; there is none beside me.
(Isaiah 46:21)

God's Word Never Fails

For as the rain cometh down, and the snow from Heaven, and returneth not thither, but watereth the earth, and maketh it bring forth and bud, that it may give seed to the sower, and bread to the eater: So shall my word be that goeth forth out of my mouth: It shall not return unto me void, but it shall accomplish that which I please, and it shall prosper in the thing whereto I sent it.
(Isaiah 55:10-11)

His word is truth. When he sends his word, it will accomplish what it pleases, and it doesn't come back to him void. God had promised Abraham that Sarah would have a son, and God fulfilled that promise. Sarah had a son when she was ninety years old (her son was Jacob). God also hath promised to his people Israel that he would send a Savior. And that in the seed of Abraham will he call his son. And from Abraham begat Jacob, Isaac begat Jacob, and Jacob begat Joseph whose husband is Mary, of whom Jesus was born. And Jesus was promised to him so that there shall be no end. There are no more kings that will rise after Jesus, because he is the only begotten of the Father. Jesus Christ is the King of Kings and the Lord of Lords.

And God said, "Heaven and earth will pass away, but my word shall never pass away." And until to this day, God's word has reached my deepest heart through his son Jesus Christ, and it will reach to every nation, every kingdom, and every tribe and nation. And if this gospel of the kingdom shall be preached to all the nations, then the end will come.

This gospel has reached us, through the works of the apostles and prophets, who wrote the Bible by the inspiration of the Holy Ghost.

And this book is written to reach out to the lost, to let you know the love of God and to let you be ready in the second coming of our Lord Jesus Christ, the only begotten Son.

Chapter Twelve
Invest for Eternity

Lay not up for yourselves treasures upon earth, where moth and rust doth corrupt, and were thieves break through nor steal: But lay up for yourselves treasures in Heaven, whether neither moth nor rust doth corrupt, and where thieves do not break through nor steal: For where your treasure is, there will your heart be also.
(Matthew 5:19-20)

But thou, O man of God, flee these things; and follow after righteousness, godliness, faith, love, patience, meekness.
Fight the good fight faith, lay hold on eternal life.
(1 Timothy 6:11-12a)

The Rule of 72, Created by Albert Einstein

Divide 72 by the interest rate to estimate the number of years it takes for your money to double.

Let say at the age of 29 you invested $10,000 at a 12 percent interest rate. Here's how it works:

Age	12% Interest Rate
(Money doubles every six years)	
29	$10,000
35	$20,000

Age	12% Interest Rate
41	$40,000
47	$80,000
53	$160,000
59	$320,000
65	$640,000

Your money will double every six years. Let's say you live until 65. By then, your money will amount to $640,000.

You will have a very good retirement with $640,000, which is really good if you are living alone. Indeed, you won't even need life insurance if you accumulate this wealth.

Robert Kiyosoki , in his book *Rich Dad Poor Dad*, teaches you to invest in the stock market, GIC, or in real estate, because it's a real property. Some people invest in the stock market. If the market goes up, you can get a good reward. So investing is really good and you will reap good rewards, but it is very risky and not always a win/win situation.

In God's kingdom, we ought to invest for eternity.

These are the three Ts for investing in the Kingdom of God.

1. Your Time (Wisely)

When God created Heaven and earth and all things on the earth, he rested on the seventh day. God gave us six days to work and the Sabbath day to rest. The Seventh Day Adventists consider Saturday as their rest day because they count from Sunday to Friday, so Saturday is the seventh day when you look on their calendar.

Here, in North America, Sunday is the Sabbath. This is also true in Asian countries; there, we go to church on Sundays.

If ever you are working on Sunday, then go to Church on Saturday. Make sure to set aside time for God. The author of *A Purpose Driven Life* says, "The best gift you can ever give a person is not a diamond, but your time." When God finished his creation, he rested on the seventh day. "And God blessed the seventh day, and sanctified it: because that in it he had rested from all his work which God created and made." (Genesis 2:2-3)

In Exodus 23:12 the Lord also says, "Six days thou shalt do thy work, and on the seventh day thou shalt rest." Even God rested on the seventh day. He sanctified it, blessed it, and made it holy. The rest for Israel is that they don't work on Sundays, and that is also the same in my hometown in the Philippines. We go to church on Sunday, because it is the Lord's day. We go to church and worship God in spirit and in truth, through songs, and by hearing the word of God. We had to go to church to feed our souls through the word of God. God's word is the food for our spiritual maturity. So if you didn't go to church, you missed not only the word of God that you needed for that week, but also the blessings of God. I am not saying that if you don't go to church you don't have any blessings for that week. God is still going to bless you, but I find it more blessed for me, because God always refreshes me and blesses me when I go to church and have fellowship with other believers. Though our God is merciful and loving, the choice is still up to you if you want to go to church or not. He doesn't withhold his blessings upon you if you miss one Sunday because of illness or whatever reason. But as for me, Sunday is the most special day. It is when I can renew my strength and be able to give back my praise and gratefulness to the one who gave me life.

The best expression of your love to God is your time—loving God and giving our time by going to church and worshipping him with other believers. If you can give your time to other people that you really love, then I am sure that you can also give that time to our loving God, because he created you.

2. Your Tithes and Offerings

By giving your tithes and offerings to God. Malachi 3:10 says, **"Bring ye all the tithes in a store house, that there may be meat in my house, prove me now herewith, If I will not open the windows of Heaven and pour you about a blessing that there shall not be room enough to receive it."**

God actually says that. This is a command with a promise, a promise of God's blessings. If we give our tithes and offerings, we are not only giving back the tithes that belong to God, but we are also giving them as a sign of our love to God. And if we give to our church, we are supporting the pastors, the workers in our church, to fulfill their great commissions. The great commission is to preach the gospel to every creature, so that others might come to know God. Amen. Then our missionaries can go all around the world. Imagine where they might be able to go if there was no money coming in to support them. We are also helping the poor, the fatherless, the widows, and those people who are so unfortunate. We ought to show our love to God by giving the fruits of our labor. If you give your tithes, there's a promise attached to it—that God will open the windows of Heaven and pour out a blessing so that there will not be room enough to receive your abundant blessings. You might have to build another store house, right?

How Much Tithe Will I Give?

Every man according as he purposeth in his heart, so let him give; not grudgingly, or of necessity: for God loveth a cheerful giver.
(2 Corinthians 9:7)

174

A tithe is 10 percent of your gross income or net income, but we also give from our hearts, or according to our ability to give.

There was a story of a woman who gave her alms. There was a famine in the land and she had prepared her last meal for herself and her child, but the prophet Elijah asked her to give it to him. She willingly gave it to him. Then, a miracle happened; the woman never again ran out of food after that.

The key of blessings is that you don't give to expect a payback. You give because your heart was touched. You love God and you want to give in exchange for what God has done and has given to you.

And remember to give cheerfully and wholeheartedly, because God loves a cheerful giver.

3. Your Talents, Skills, or Gifts

What are you capable of doing? What are your skills? What are your gifts? If you can preach, or teach, or sing, use those talents for the glory of God, for the expansion of God's kingdom. "Offstage" are those working in the kitchen, when food is being served. They are those looking after the kids when parents are having worship services. They are the camera men. And so on. What do you have in your hand to be able to use for God's kingdom here on earth? Some people have the gift of giving. They give more than their tithes and offerings. What about you my friend? Remember the parable of the talents. Some were given five talents, some were given two talents, and some were given one talent. For one man, the five talents became ten talents because he kept on using it and wanted to have more. So he went on not only singing but also playing the piano or guitar and so on. The one given five talents hath gained another five talents more. (Matthew 25:21) **His Lord said unto him, "Well done, thou good** and faithful servant; thou hast been faithful over a few things, I will make thee ruler over many things: enter thou into the joy of thy lord."

The one who had only one talent didn't use it but buried it in the ground. When the master came back (verse 26), **His lord says unto him, "Thou wicked and slothful servant, thou knewest that I reap where I sow not, and gathered where I have not strayed; thou oughtest therefore to have put my money to the exchangers, and then at my coming, I should have received mine own usury. Take therefore the talent from him, and gave it unto him which hath ten talents."** (Matthew 25: 14-20)

God took the one talent and gave it to the one who had more talents, because he said, "For unto every one that hath shall be given, and he shall have abundance: but from him that hath not, shall be taken away even that which he hath. I assume that this man might have given salvation of his soul. Or it can be of anything that you are steward of it. And he never used his talent or never shared the love of God with others and did not live a life that was pleasing to the Lord." That's why the Lord took it away from him—even his very own salvation—because he was not faithful for this one talent. We can't lose our salvation by just taking it for granted. We may think we will go to Heaven because of grace alone; therefore, we continue and keep sinning because we think we are saved.

I believe that each child of God has been called for a purpose. That each of us had a measure of faith that God has given. We have differences of gifts, abilities, and skills, but we are accountable for each gift and talent God has given us. Some of us have been given talents for the expansion of the Kingdom of God. You can use your gift for the glory of God, or you can ignore it or bury it in the ground. But very soon when Jesus comes, we can either hear him say to us, "Well done, thou good and faithful servant, enter now into my kingdom." Or you can hear him say, "I never knew you, ye that doeth iniquity." This man has not only taken his salvation, but also was cast into the lake of fire. (Verse 30)

God has given us talents according to our ability and he has given us gifts.

And there are diversities of operations, but it is the same God which worketh all in all. But the manifestation of the Spirit is given to everyman to profit withal.
(1 Corinthians 12:6-10)

Some of the spiritual gifts are:

1. The word of wisdom;
2. The word of knowledge;
3. Faith
4. Gift of healing
5. Working of miracles
6. Prophecy
7. Discerning of spirits
8. Different kinds of tongues
9. Interpretation of tongues

There are few of us who have all nine gifts.

You don't have to worry if you don't have them all, because the Holy Spirit is the one who distributes them as he will (verse 11). If you have any of these gifts, then you better use them for the Kingdom of God and for the glory of God.

I have the gift of faith, which is the first gift I received. And then I received the word of knowledge and wisdom. And recently, God added the different kinds of tongues. I speak languages that I do not understand, but I know that I am talking to my Heavenly Father.

You have to know what God has given you and then use it for his glory.

Invest for Temporary Life Here on Earth	Invest for Eternal Life
• Go to see a movie • Buy a property • Have a luxury car • Have a vacation home • Invest for RRSP, GIC, etc. • Don't go to church • Have three or five wives • Be a millionaire or billionaire • Go travel around the world • Watch TV all day	• Go to church • Use your gifts and talents • Give to the poor • Choose to love • Choose to live a holy life • Pray for others • Involve yourself in a mission • Share your faith • Share your wealth • Fast and pray • Sing to the Lord • Live by faith • Repent • Give your tithes and offering • Volunteer in the church • Visit the sick • Volunteer in your community

These are just a few of these things; you can choose to invest in them or not.

If you invest for eternity, you reap eternal life. If you invest in temporary riches, you reap temporary riches here on earth but not riches toward Heaven.

Let's go back to the story of the rich man and the beggar, Lazarus.

Here's the example:

Temporary Riches	Eternal Riches in Heaven
Rich Man Has:	Lazarus (Beggar) Has:
Car	No Car
Mansion	No Mansion
$$$ Investment	No Investment
$$$ Money in the Bank	No Money at All
Religion:	Religion:
Atheist - Doesn't Believe in God	Believes in God
Date of Death: Unknown	Unknown
Destination:	Destionation:
Hell	Heaven or Paradise

Both of these men passed away, but they had different destinations.

If you take away your possessions like cars, mansions, and money, nothing is left behind except your life. When wild-fires struck in California, people lost houses and belongings. There was nothing left behind. The good thing is they still had their lives. Our lives are so precious. God could take away your life any moment from now. "God forbid." Where will your destination be if that happened? If you have not yet received the Lord Jesus in your heart, you have to seize the moment, for we know neither the time nor the hour God will take us home. Do you know where your soul is going? Your destination is final. The word of God is still the final judg-ment of your soul.

This is very important my dear friend; you can't be transported from hell to Heaven. This was shown when the rich man begged Father Abraham to send Lazarus to where he was, to dip his finger into the water to cool his tongue because it was so hot where he had gone. Note, this man was already dead, yet he still had his five senses. He could feel, see, talk, and hear. But the problem was there was a gap between them; neither one could cross over to the other side. This story tells us that our destiny is final.

So he pleaded again and said, "If that is so Father Abraham and please send Lazarus back to earth, because I have five more brothers." And Abraham told him they have Moses, the prophets, and the preachers.

In our generations today, we have television, internet, and radio programs like Praise 106.5 preaching the word of God five days a week. We also have Saturday and Sunday services. So you and I don't have any more excuses, because the Bible says in Isaiah 65:12, "Therefore will I number you to the sword and ye shall all bow down to the slaughter, **because when I called, ye didn't answer; when I speak, ye didn't hear**; but did evil before mine eyes and did choose that wherein I delighted not."

God is still calling his children to repent, but we rarely listen. He spoke through the Bible and through the mouths of the preachers, and writers like me, yet still we close our ears and do not want to hear or read anything about God. Will it be God's fault when we go to hell? No! Absolutely NOT! We choose not to hear and not to repent from our sins because we want our own way, not God's way. We want our own will and not God's will in our lives. So we choose our destiny by making our own choices to follow God or not.

It is only a matter of choice, to reject God's word or to receive it, to hear or not to hear, to obey or not obey, and to believe or not believe.

REPENTANCE

Behold, the LORD'S hand is not shortened, that it cannot save; neither his ear heavy, that it cannot hear:

*But your **iniquities have separated between you and your God**, and your sins have hid his face from you, that he will not hear.*
(Isaiah 59:1-2 Isaiah 50:1)

Remember what the Lord Jesus Christ said when he came to this earth. He said, "**REPENT, for the kingdom of Heaven is at hand.**"

The key word is to REPENT before this life is over.

Repentance means:

R - Return to God. By acknowledging that he is your creator and making him ruler over your careers, finances, marriage, and your life.

E - Enter into a new covenant with God, by obeying his word and following him all the days of your life.

P - Pray and confess all your sins before God and ask for forgiveness.

E - Enter into a new citizenship in Heaven by accepting the Lord Jesus Christ in your heart and making him your Lord and Savior.

N - No turning back from your sins or no compromise.

T - Thank God for your life and for giving his Son Jesus to die for your sins, and thank him for the eternal life through his Son and be grateful always.

If you feel the Holy Spirit is urging you to pray now, stop for a minute and PRAY... PRAY... PRAY...

Prayer of REPENTANCE

Oh God, I come before your throne. The throne of your grace, that I may obtain mercy and grace. Holy Father, I acknowledge my sins before you, and only you. Forgive me for all the sins I have committed, wash me with the precious blood of Jesus Christ. Cleanse me from all unrighteousness and make me whole and acceptable into your sight.

I now surrender my will to you. Let your will be done in my life from now on. I now accept you Jesus in my heart to be my LORD and Savior, please come into my heart. Thank you Father for forgiving my sins and for sending your only begotten Son to save me from my sins. Thank you for your grace and mercy. This I ask in the most precious name of our Lord and Savior Jesus Christ Amen.

If you follow this prayer, I now welcome you into the Kingdom of God.

Welcome to my world and to the world of our God and Savior, Jesus Christ.

The kingdom of God is our world, even though we are still in this world.

God knows who you are and where you are. He knows your thoughts, your actions, your past, and your future. He sees you when you pray.

God is calling you today at this very minute because he loves you and doesn't want anyone to perish. If you follow these small steps of repentance then God is going to walk with you, and he will be glorified in you. But if we choose to reject God's word, the very word of God will judge us in the last day. And John 12:48 says, "He that rejected me and receiveth not my word, hath one that judgeth him in the last days." The very words that I speak unto you will judge you in the last days."

Chapter Thirteen

Breaking Up Fallow Ground

Breakup your fallow ground: for it is time to seek the LORD, till he come and rain righteousness upon you.
(Hosea 10:12b)

The same day went Jesus out of the house, and sat by the sea side. And great multitudes were gather together unto him, so that he went into a ship, and sat; and the whole multitude stood on the shore. And he spake many things unto them in parables, saying , Behold, a sower went forth to sow; And when he sowed, some seeds fell by the way side, and the fowls came and devoured them up:

Some fell upon stony places, where they had not much earth: and forthwith they sprung up, because they had no deepness of earth:

And when the sun was up, they were scorched: and because they had no root, they withered away.

And some fell among thorns; and the thorns sprung up, and choked them:

But other fell into good ground, and brought forth fruit, some an hundredfold, some sixtyfold, some thirtyfold.

Who hath ears to hear, let him hear.
(Matthew 13:1-9, Mark 4:1-20)

This is the parable of the sower. The sowers are the preachers, evangelists, missionaries, or those who are doing the great commission to preach the gospel to the world and to the people around us.

In this parable, I found out that there are four types of ground, which symbolize the heart.

Four Types of Ground (Heart)

1. **Wayside heart** – They hear the word of God but understand it not, and the wicked one, which is Satan, catches away what was sown in their hearts.

2. **Stony heart** – They hear the word of God and receive the word of God with joy, but hath no root to themselves. So when persecution and tribulation come their way they are offended.

3. **Thorny heart** – They also hear the word of God, but because of the deceitfulness of riches, and the care of this world, they became unfruitful. These are the lovers of themselves, rather than lovers of God.

4. **Good heart** – They hear the word of God and understand it and beareth forth fruits, some hundredfold, sixtyfold, and thirtyfold.

In order for the word of God to penetrate into our hearts, we have to examine our hearts and cultivate what needs to be cultivated, what needs to break in us, so we can receive eternal life. Just like the rich man came to Jesus and asked, "Master, what can I do to inherit eternal life?" Jesus told him to follow the commandments, and the rich man said that he had been doing that since childhood.

So Jesus told him, "One thing you lack, go sell all your possessions and give the profits to the poor; then come and follow me." But the rich man was not happy because he had so many riches. He loved his riches rather than his soul, and rather than the word of God. Pray and ask God what the barriers are that are keeping you from accepting the word of God.

Breakup your fallow ground: for it is time to seek the LORD, till he come and rain righteousness upon you.
(Hosea 10:12b)

Don't worry. As long as you are willing, God can help you and ask the Holy Spirit to reveal it to you. Just remember that with God, all things are possible.

If you build a high tower, you have to first break up the soil or the sand to dig, sixty feet below the ground, in order for the tower to stand strong. It must have a sure, good, strong foundation so that the rain, the winds, and the storm can't shake it.

In North America, you can find all kinds of different houses, towers, townhouses, malls, and buildings. I've never seen any earthquake in this country these past thirteen years. But what I have seen so far, at least in the lives of families, is the earthquake of divorce.

Divorce is increasing so rapidly, one after another. And it breaks my heart so badly, and for sure, it also breaks God's heart. It's the kids who are more vulnerable to the pain, even more so than their parents who got divorced in the first place. And one thing the parents don't realize is they are passing this pattern to their children and their children's children.

One day, a friend of mine was discussing some business with me at a restaurant. I knew he never had time for his wife and his two kids. And all of a sudden, I felt that God was leading me to tell him about his love. I was talking to him with the guidance of the Holy Spirit. And one of my conversations with him was this:

I gave him two scenarios of what would happen if he continued along on his current path. I said, "There's a lot of business men and women out there who are very successful in their business, and yet not successful in their marriages."

Example:

1st Scenario	2nd Scenario	3rd Scenario
1. Business	1. Business	1. God
2. Business	2. Business	2. Family
3. Business	3. Business	3. Business/Job
4. Business	4. Business	4. Friends
5. Business	5. Business	5. Neighbors
6. Business	6. Business	
7. Business	7. Business	
8. Business	8. Business	
9. Business	9. Family	
10. Business	10. God	

In the first scenario, business is included as number one and continues all the way to number ten. Some will put their family last. Some will put their family first. Some don't even have God in their list and some put God first.

I told him, "Let's say you continue to keep working and working and will not have time for your wife and your children. You would probably become a millionaire and yet you do not have your wife and kids to love and treasure you—assuming you become a millionaire. What are you going to do with your million dollars? Money is not everything. You may lose it in a day or a month, and then what would you have?? You will end up with no money, no kids, no wife."

I continued, "Or would you rather put God first in your life and your marriage second and your business third? But still, in the end, you will be successful, and you still have your wife and your kids who love you and treasure you. What is more important to you?" Tears fell down his cheeks as he told me that I was right. He opened his heart to start fresh and accept the Lord Jesus as his Lord and Savior.

A few months after my conversation with him, he told me he started spending time with his family and reading the Bible to his kids before bedtime.

That was not part of my work; it was God's work at hand.

What about you my friend, if you are married, then treasure what God has given you. Start with a solid foundation, which is putting God first in your marriage and in your business and at your workplace. When God rules in your heart, you do what is pleasing to him. AND YOU WILL BUILD IN THE UNCONDITIONAL LOVE OF GOD. Let love grow from your heart, along with trust, love, faithfulness, respect, and the continuous essence of forgiveness. Forgive and always forget. This is your turning point in life—to live a legacy of love, faith, and hope.

Seek the LORD

Seek ye the LORD while he may be found, call ye upon him while he is near.
(Isaiah 55:6)

Wherefore (as the Holy Ghost saith, Today if ye will hear his voice, Harden not your heart, as in the provocation, in the day of temptation in the wilderness.
(Hebrews 3: 7-8)

Today is the day to seek the Lord, not tomorrow or any other day, because you do not hold your life or your tomorrow.

The life span of a man now is about seventy years. If you live more than that, then you have received a bonus already.

You can't say, "I have no time for God. I am busy with my business, I have business all over the world, and I have to attend to it. I have to build houses or I have to get my dreams fulfilled. I don't have time for God. I am studying and want to be a doctor; I don't have time for God."

My dear friend, I say it again: you do not hold your life. Even newborn babies or unborn babies will pass away. And they do not know when or how long they will live. Today is the day of salvation. If you hear God's voice, today is the day for you to seek him, for tomorrow it might be too late. God had promised, "Seek ye first the kingdom of God and his righteousness, and all this things shall be added unto you."

In Everything, There is a Season

"A time to be born and a time to die; a time to sow and a time to reap."

Now is the time to seek the Lord, because if we don't seek or answer his call, we cannot enter into his rest.
(Hebrews 3:19)

God's resting place is Heaven, and it is the promised resting place for everyone who believes in the Son of God. So I urge you today to enter into the perfect rest of God.

He says in Isaiah 55:7 "Let the wicked forsake his way, and the unrighteous man his thoughts: and let him return unto the Lord, and he will have mercy upon him; and to our God, for he will abundantly pardon. Wherefore do ye spend money for that which is not bread? And your labor for that which satisfied not? Hearken diligently unto me, and eat ye that which is good, and let your soul delight itself in fatness. (Isaiah 55:2)

The Jews require a sign; the Greeks seek after wisdom. So when we preach to the Jewish nation, they won't believe you if you don't have a sign, because they are used to that. God was with them, and they have the covenant, the tablet of stone, and the tabernacle of God. God has done many wonders among them and performed many miracles when they were still in Egypt and in the wilderness. Many of them had died in the wilderness because they were disobedient, and some of them were not able to enter into the Promised Land. They have experienced God's redemptive power and his mighty miracles. So that's why Jesus did so many miracles—he healed the sick, made the blind man see, raised Lazarus from the dead, cast out demons, fed the five thousand men with just two fishes and five loaves of bread, and turned the water into wine.

Jesus said, "I came to my own and my own receive me not."

One of the Pharisees came to him by night. Jesus said unto him, "Verily, verily, I say unto thee, except a man be born again, he cannot see the kingdom of God."

Nicodemus saith unto him, "How can a man be born when he is old? Can he enter the second time into his mother's womb, and be born?"

Jesus answered, "Verily, verily, I say unto thee, except a man be born of water and of the Spirit, he cannot enter into the kingdom of God." (John 3:1-5)

If you want to see the kingdom of God, you have to be born again. There are two kinds of born-again Christians nowadays. The ones that only sees the Kingdom believe and accept the Lord Jesus Christ as their Lord and Savior. They understand the will and plan of God, but they are still doing their own will, and they are not following God's will, nor are they living a life that is pleasing to God. They are not blind to the truth of faith and love. They know these things, but they don't live what they know or do what they say. They only see the Kingdom, yet they cannot enter into the Kingdom of God. When Jesus came to earth and preached repentance to all men, all of the people had seen the miracles he hath done, but only few people who had seen actually believed and followed him.

The second born-again Christian is the one who sees, understands, and accepts the Lord Jesus Christ as the one who can enter into God's Kingdom. Because he not only accepts Jesus as his Lord and Savior, but he also has the Holy Spirit and was baptized of the water and of the Holy Ghost. Therefore he lives a life that is pleasing to God. He doesn't only understand and know God, but he does the will of God. The Holy Spirit is the spirit of obedience that is dwelling in your heart when you truly repent of your sins and invite Jesus to come into your heart.

When Paul preached to the Jews, it was a stumbling block to them, and when he preached to the Greeks, it was foolishness to them. But to us who are called, whether we are Jews or Greeks, or Americans or Pilipinos, or Canadians or any nationality that is called, Jesus Christ is the power of God, and the wisdom of God.

But in him, are ye in Christ Jesus, who of God is made unto us wisdom, and righteousness, and sanctification, and redemption.
(1 Corinthians 1:24, 30)

If you are not a born-again Christian and I am speaking spiritual things to you, you cannot understand me. I will be foolish to your ear, and a stumbling block in your way. I pray that God will open your heart and that you will seek him with all your heart.

Indeed, For the sake of the chosen people Israel, the sign is that you will find a babe. And you will call him Jesus, because he will save his people from their sins. And in three days Jesus rose from death. And he is coming soon to take his own people. The salvation was first to the Jews, and by their stumbling, (Romans 11:15) we Gentiles are grafted into the vines. That is the plan of God. But Israel will be saved because they are the true branches of the Lord. A remnant will be saved and this remnant is saved by grace alone. There are a hundred and forty and four thousand of all the tribes of the children of Israel. A remnant shall be saved, from the tribes of Judah, Reuben, Gad Aser, Nepthalim, Manasses, Simeon, Levi, Issachar, Zabulon, and Joseph, all the way to the tribe of Benjamin. (Revelation 7:4-8)

When We Seek the Lord We Will Find Him

And ye shall seek me, and find me, when ye shall search me with all your heart. And I will be found of you, saith the LORD. (Jeremiah 29:13-14a)

If we seek the Lord our God, we can find him when we seek him with all our hearts. When we find the Lord, he will reveal himself to us and give us a heart to know him and his ways.

And I will give them and heart to know me, that I am the LORD: and they shall be my people, and I will be their God: for they shall return unto me with their whole heart. (Jeremiah 24:7)

And I will give them one heart, and one way that they may fear me forever, for the good of them, and of their children after them:

And I will make an everlasting covenant with them, that I will not turn away from them, to do them good; but I will put my fear in their hearts, that they shall not depart from me. (Jeremiah 32:39-40)

The problem in the Old Testament is that although they have the law, the prophets, who are the spokesmen of God to his people Israel, are still sometimes disobedient, even though they have seen the wonders of God's mighty hand. This is because they don't have the Holy Spirit that dwells in their hearts to fully obey God. That's why God says, "A new heart also will I give you, and a new spirit will I put within you: and I will take away the stony heart out of your flesh, and I will give you an heart of flesh."

And I will put my spirit within you, and caused you to walk in
my statutes, and ye shall keep my judgments, and do them.
(Ezekiel 36:26-27) (Hebrews 8:10)

When you accept and invite the Lord Jesus Christ into your heart, the Holy Spirit comes in and dwells there. You become a new creation. And whether you like it or not, if you have truly repented of your sins, you will definitely change into a brand new person. This has happened to me, which is why I can testify. You are aware of when you lie or commit sinful acts, because the Holy Spirit convicts you of your sinful actions.

This is the nature of a born-again Christian. When he was cleansed from all his past sins, he cannot sin because he becomes a new creature. The old self, which is of a sinful nature, is gone. That means that all his old sins were forgiven. For example, if he was a thief before, now he is not, because the Holy Spirit will dwell in him. So it is impossible for him to become a thief again. Our body is the temple of God. (1 Corinthians 7:31)

Therefore we cannot commit sin, but because we are still growing, it is impossible for us to become pure overnight. The cleansing of our spirit is a journey, until we become blameless, spotless, and not lacking anything.

Paul also mentioned that if I keep doing what I am not sup-posed to do, then it is not I who does it, but the sin living in me. So shall I continue in sinning that grace may abound? God forbids.

Apostle Paul saith to the church of Corinthians:

They were born-again Christians but it was reported to him that there was fornication among them. (1 Corinthians 5:1) And he told them that fornicators shall not inherit the king-dom of God. (1 Corinthians 6:9) He asked them to flee forni-cation, (6:18) because we are the temple of the Holy Ghost, and because we are bought with a price, which is the blood of Jesus Christ. Therefore we must glorify God in our body. (1 Corinthians 6:19-20)

If you are a born-again Christian and are participating in these sinful works of the flesh that I had mentioned, you will die spiritually. The spirit of the Lord that is living in you will leave, because God is holy and hates sin. The soul that sinneth it shall die. (Romans 8:13, Gal. 5:21.) Therefore you will lose your salvation if you don't go back to God and ask forgiveness for your sins. You become a backslider, someone who knows the truth and turns away from the truth.

Just as Paul instructed, I will tell you the same thing. Sex out-side marriage is a sin. But on the other hand, sex after mar-riage is not a sin. (1 Corinthians 7:3-4) So if you cannot con-tain or control yourself, it is better to marry and have your own husband and wife than to indulge yourselves with sin. God created man and a woman to be married; people created man-to-man and woman-to-woman marriages. We can't agree to the holiness of God and therefore we create our own rules and our own holiness to fulfill our own desires. This is not the will of God.

Freedom of Choice

Our God is a sovereign God and his wisdom is infinite. When he created us, he gave us the freedom of choice. And he cannot take that away from us. Although he is powerful, and he knows all things, he cannot mess up our choices. One time Ezra asked me why God created hell and sends people there. I told him, "He created hell for Satan and for those who follow Satan." He said, "Why can't God do something in order for people to go to Heaven. Like, the dog, if you tell the dog to come, he will come." I told him again, "God will never mess with our freedom of choice. If he does then we are like an animal and, like the dog, we won't have choices, which means we are no longer free, but slaves." Ezra said, "It is better to be like a dog going to Heaven."

God will never, ever touch your freedom of choice, because he is God. He only tells us what is right and wrong. That's why we have preachers of the word of God—they are everywhere. Churches are everywhere, to preach the good news to every human being. But still the choice is up to us. You cannot travel both roadways, the road to righteousness and the road to iniquities. You cannot serve two masters at the same time. Like the traveler, he chooses the less-traveled road, which I believe is actually the road to holiness and righteousness and the one that only a few find. *And that makes all the difference.* So whatever your choices, it will be your eternal destiny. And there's no more turning back when you close your eyes. Time is running out, so don't wait for tomorrow. Joshua says, "Choose now whom you will serve. Whether the God of our forefather or the god of the heathen, but as for me and my house, we will serve the Lord."

Since the day I accepted the Lord Jesus in my life, I made a commitment to follow him no matter what happened. And that commitment of mine has actually been tested through fire. I was able to come out of it without my faith being burned. But through that fire of testing, my faith and my love for God grew more and more each day. What about you my friend, will you declare it with me? *As for me and my house we will serve the Lord.* Amen.

Your Choices: Heaven or Hell

Enter ye in the straight gate: for wide is the gate and broad is the way that leadeth to destruction [Hell] and many there be which go in thereat: Because straight is the gate and narrow is the way [Heaven] which leadeth unto life, and few there be that find it.
(Matthew 7:13)

Two Roads

Straight Gate is a narrow gate but the destination is life. (Heaven)

Wide Gate and broad is the way but it leads to destruction. (Hell)

The wide road is the road most people choose, because it is the road of self-righteousness and doing your own will; injustice, unmerciful, and corruption. They are without love and without God in their hearts. The road is wide, because you can do your own will, and take your own way.

The other road is straight, but narrow is the way, and yet it leadeth unto life eternal, which is Heaven. This road is the road of righteousness, holiness, purity, obedience, faithfulness, love, and faith. It is very narrow, because you cannot do your own will (will of the flesh), or your own way, but only that which pleases God.

Jesus said, "Strive to enter in at the gate: for many, I say unto you, will seek to enter in, and shall not be able."

When once the master of the house is risen up, and hath shut to the door, and ye begin to stand without, and to knock at the door, saying, Lord, Lord open to us; and he shall answer and say unto you, I know you not whence ye are:

Then shall ye begin to say, we have eaten and drunk in thy presence, and thou hast taught in our streets.

But he shall say, I tell you, I know you not whence ye are; depart from me, all ye workers of iniquity.

There shall be weeping and gnashing of teeth, when ye shall see Abraham, and Isaac, and Jacob, and all the prophets, in the kingdom of God, and you yourself trust out.
(Luke 13:24-28)

One Minute to Live

Jesus Christ was crucified on the cross at Calvary with two thieves. One was on his left and the other was on his right side. The one on the right side said to Jesus, "Jesus remember me when you are already in paradise." And Jesus answered and said, "Today you will be with me in paradise."

This man recognized that he was a sinner, that he needed salvation, and that Jesus was the only way. At that moment the man repented of his sins by saying, "We deserve to suffer for what we have done. But Jesus didn't deserve to die because he is sinless." And by saying "remember me when you are already in paradise," it symbolizes repentance and a commitment to follow Jesus. He wanted to be with Jesus, wherever Jesus was going, he was determined to go with him if Jesus allowed it to be so.

And surely Jesus gave him the assurance that he would be with him today in paradise.

That hour and that day was the last chance for the man to repent for his sins, and he was forgiven and was saved. All

Glory to God in the highest! Even in the last minute of Jesus dying on the cross one man was saved and redeemed.

If you only have one minute to live, what would you do? Today is the day of salvation, tomorrow it might be too late. Today, if you hear God speaking to you, don't delay. Answer God's calling in your life right away, seize the time, for we know neither the day nor the hour God will call us home.

God is a God of mercy and grace, and one minute could account for everlasting life. But I am not telling you to wait for one minute before all is over. If you hear his voice then answer him and say, "Yes Lord, Yes Lord, I will follow you today."

What You Sow is What You Reap

(Consequences of our actions)

Sow to yourself in righteousness, reap in mercy; break up your fallow ground: for it is time to seek the LORD, till he come and rain righteousness upon you.
(Hosea 10:12)

For every sin that we commit to God, there's always a consequence for it.

For whatever we sow, good or bad, the fruit will soon unfold.

When David committed sin with Bathsheba, he killed Uriah, Bathsheba's husband. (2 Samuel 11:2-5 ,26-27; 12:9)

And the prophet Nathan came to tell him of his sins. And because of this sin his child had passed away.

Howbeit, because by this deed thou hast given great occasion to the enemies of the LORD to blaspheme, the child also that is born unto thee shall surely die.
(2 Samuel 12:14)

For every sin we commit there are always consequences, now or later. But David repented and asked God's forgiveness. He fasted and prayed all night that God would spare his child. (2 Samuel 12:16,22.)

No matter how ugly the sins we committed are, if we seek God's face and repent, we can be forgiven like David was. For the second time around that he was forgiven, God delighted in David and give him another child, which was King Solomon. (2 Samuel 12:24) The King who hath so much wisdom; and who hath build the house of God.

In 2003 I had fallen from God's grace. I had committed sin— fornication. In 2005, I got pregnant. Ezra wasn't ready for a commitment, and said he would never be ready to have a child. He asked me to abort the child. I told him this: "No! Even if you are going to leave me because of this child, I will keep it, and even if I will be miserable to raise it by myself, I will raise it." I know the word of God and understand it. So killing an innocent child in your womb is a sin. I told myself that I already committed a sinful act, which is fornication. Now I can't have a double sin by killing an innocent child in my womb. I prayed that God would give Ezra a heart to understand. So after a few weeks, he had started to accept it. He never missed any of my doctor appointments. He did the grocery shopping, because I couldn't carry heavy objects. When the baby was six weeks inside, I was home watching movies with Ezra. I began to bleed. I asked the Lord, "It is time now Lord?" Because prior to this pregnancy, more than a year before, God had revealed to me in a dream that I was going to be pregnant. And when I got pregnant, God again revealed to me in a dream that it would not come into being. In my dream, I saw Satan holding a baby in his hand. Satan said, "I will drop this baby." I answered and told him with anger, "No you can't drop this baby. Give me the baby." We were face-to-face talking and it was a huge warfare. Satan just dropped the baby and I woke up from that dream. I remembered this dream while we were still at home. I asked God, "Is this the time Lord?" So I was peaceful, and prayerfully talking to God with my spirit. I called my doctor and he told me to come to the hospital. On the way to the hospital, so much blood came out of me. But I asked the Lord, "If this is your will, you can preserve this child." But when we got to the hospital, the baby no longer had a heartbeat. I knew that God had taken it away for a good reason. I knew that this was the consequence of my sins, and I had to pay it. Although God had already paid my sins through the death of Jesus Christ, I still need to repent for every sin that I commit as long as I live. And surely God had promised forgiveness, healing, and restoration.

If my people who are called by my name, shall humble themselves, and pray, and seek my face, and turn from their wicked ways; then will I hear from Heaven, and will forgive their sins, and heal their land.
(2 Chronicles 7:14)

If these sins are not dealt with, it pays wages; sin doesn't evaporate. It will be passed on to the first and fourth generations.

God will visit with stripes, for the first and fourth generation of yours.

I wrote this poem after this loss.

GOD GIVETH, GOD TAKETH AWAY

Who lays the foundation of the earth that it cannot be moved?

Who commanded the moon to shine at night?

When the morning stars sung together

When the sun smiles at me in the morning.

Who divided the seas, lakes, and the spring water?

When it rains on the earth and satisfies the desolate ground, and food for the people.

Who provided food for the raven, the beast of the forest?

When the young ones cry unto God.

Who closes the womb and opens it in his time

Who giveth life for a moment and taketh it for a good reason?

Who can number the hairs of my head and count it when they fall

Who can number our days, can prolong them and shorten them.

Who can still the storm when the waves of the sea roar?

Who can see the future and know what is best for us

Who can understand the knowledge of God or his ways?

For his knowledge is too deep and wonderful

And his ways are higher than our ways,

Who giveth life to the lifeless and hope for the hopeless

Creator God who is Yahweh

The maker of Heaven and Earth

Things visible and invisible

The great I Am, the Holy One

The Alpha and the Omega

The beginning and the end.

Rebecca Daluddung Sept 30, 2005 4 a.m.

And this message will continue, until I see him face-to-face. Because I am a born-again Christian, people think that I am perfect. We are all in the process of purifying. Like the process of how gold was purified, and how the potter makes the clay. The gold has to be put into the fire, and the master doesn't leave this gold, because it cannot be either too hot or cold or have no heat at all. He makes sure that all the unwanted particles come out of that gold so that it will come out as pure gold.

This is the same process: all of the unwanted particles in our life should be burned by fire of testing and trials and temptation, so that we become as pure as gold, ready for use by the master. It is the same thing with the potter. If the potter marred the clay, it is because it has to be fashioned according to a vessel that we can actually use, not according to what we want. For God is the maker or the potter, I am the clay. He molded us make us a vessel of honor to his name. Some are made to honor or to dishonor. It is up to the master's hand. If we are obedient we can be a vessel ready to use for the master, for the salvation of many souls. The only thing you can do when God is going to put you through the fire of testing is to obey; the quicker you obey the quicker the process is done. If you have been victorious over something, God is going to use you to help others.

You are molded for a purpose. Find out how God is going to use you for the salvation of many souls.

As for me, I was broken, molded, and was put through the fire. Now I can say that I am a vessel of mercy ready to be used for the master's glory alone.

King David

King David was my favorite writer, and his writings, or Psalms, are my favorite. David walked before God, but he was not perfect; he did sin against God by going after another's wife. He committed sin with Bathsheba, which is called adultery. (2 Samuel 12: 9-10)

God sent the prophet Nathan to tell him that he sinned against God. And he humbled himself before God. And David said:

Have mercy upon me Oh God, according to thy loving kindness: according unto the multitude of thy tender mercies blot out my transgressions.

Wash me thoroughly from mine iniquity, and cleanse me from my sin.

For I acknowledge my transgressions: and my sins is ever before me.

Against thee, thee only have I sinned, and done this evil in thy sight: that thou mightiest me justified when thou speaketh, and be clear when thou judgest.
(Psalms 51:1-4)

This was my prayer when I fell into sin. (Fornication)

I even composed a song out of it.

Create in me a clean heart oh God
And renew a right spirit within me
Cleanse me with hyssop
That I may be whiter than snow
-Chorus-
Cast me not away (3X)
From your presence
Oh cast me not away (3X)
From your presence, your holy presence
Restore unto me the joy of your salvation
And renew a right spirit within me.
Pour a new anointing on my head
(Repeat chorus)

By Rebecca Daluddung 2006

And sure enough this song became a reality in my life. God had forgiven me, lifted me up, and pulled me out of the pit that I had fallen into. He cleansed me through his word (the Bible), restored my spirit, and poured a new anointing on my head. He restored my ministry by even a double portion of

204

the things I was doing before for the glory of God. And most of all, he never cast me away. I felt his presence every day, every moment. Even a double portion of his Holy presence and anointing. I have it because of his love for me, for his wonderful grace, and because I was willing to obey.

When we commit sin against God, the Holy Spirit quickens those sins in us. And we ask God for forgiveness.

He also uses people to tell us that we have sin. And God even uses our friends to tell us that we have sin against him. In the church, the preachers are responsible for one member if they commit a sin. They bring him before God, tell him what to do, and pray for him or her. If he doesn't listen, this results in dis-fellowhip from the Church.

And if we don't listen to others and especially to God, he then rejects us as his own people.

Not many that sayeth to me Lord, Lord shall enter into the kingdom of Heaven, but he that doeth the will of my Father which is in Heaven.
(Matthew 7:21)

God also sends trials (yet not all trials come from sins), and pain in our lives as a result of our sins and for us to come back to him. Yet if we don't listen, he also rejects us. Rejected silver or gold we will be called.

The bellows are burned, the lead is consumed of the fire; the founder melted in vain: for the wicked are not plucked away.

Reprobate silver shall men call them, because the Lord hath rejected them.
(Jeremiah 6:29-30)

We don't want to be called reprobate silver or gold because we didn't let the master mold us and take the things in our

205

lives that are not under his will. We want to be called the children of the most high God, refined by the fire, equipped for the work of God, ready to face Satan, watchman and woman of God for the glory of God who called us into his marvelous light.

Chapter Fourteen

HOPE

The Blessed HOPE

And now abideth faith, hope ...
(1 Corinthians 13:13a)

If ye continue in the faith grounded and settled, and be not moved away from the hope of the gospel, which ye have heard, and which was preached to every creature which is under heaven, whereof I Paul an made a minister.
(Colossians 1: 23)

For the Son of man shall come in the glory of his Father with his angels; and then he shall reward every man according to his works.
(Matthew 16:27)

Are you hopeless? Are you on a dead-end road? Are you all alone, unhappy, miserable, and wanting to end your life because you have no more joy, and life no longer seems to have meaning? You think that the world is turning you down and the only thing you can think of is to die?? Wait for a second my dear friend, hear me for a minute because I am about to tell you a very important message that could change your life forever. **There is hope for you!** Even in the midst of your suffering, hope is in the midst of trials, hope is in the midst of sickness, divorce, separation, loss of loved ones, loss of homes, and all the hopelessness you can imagine. Hope is here; the word of God is our hope.

The word of God is like a two-edged sword, piercing even to the point of dividing asunder the soul and spirit.

Fear thou not for I am with you, be not dismayed for I am thy God, I will strengthen thee, yea I will help thee and uphold thee with the right hand of my righteousness.
(Isaiah 41:10)

This was the word of the Lord when I was on my own dead end. I was hopeless. I had no joy in my heart, no meaning in life, and no reason to live after Ezra turned his back on me.

But glory be to the God that I am serving, he gave me life again—a second chance. That's why I am here now, writing this book to share to you that there is a God that loves you. He wants to give you life, more than you can imagine. There is always a new beginning, a new expectation, a new day. God has a wonderful plan in your life. But you cannot see and taste it if you want to die. God told me that if I commit suicide, I will go to hell. I know where my soul is going, so I didn't do it. When God spoke to me those words ... my life began to change. I was hopeful again and full of joy knowing that he has a marvelous plan for me, and I can see it through the eyes of my faith. Have faith in the word of God my dear friend. Go back and read about the faith I am talking about.

The God that I am serving is the God of Abraham, Isaac, and Jacob. He is the God that dried up the sea, so that the children of God could cross through it to go to the Promised Land. When they were in the wilderness, they desired meat, and God provided it to them in the form of manna from Heaven. He gave them water from the rock. God has never left them nor forsaken them.

If your trials are too great, then read the story of Job. He lost everything but God gave it back to him—twice as much as he had lost.

There is nothing impossible to God because all things are possible with him. You just need to have faith. If you have faith, you are hoping for the things that you have not yet seen. You are hoping that your marriage will be better, that you can have a better job, that you can have a better career or a better life. Don't hope for the better but for the best. Just pray and ask God to give you his best and hope that the best is yet to come.

What is the Foundation of Your Hope?

We live in a broken world, with broken laws, broken promises, broken homes, broken things, and broken lives. Some of us are broken in many ways. I have to be broken myself in order for God to use me as a vessel of honor into his name. But through my brokenness, God has shaped my life, restored me, equipped me, and used me. I was a broken vessel. I always wanted to be a virgin when I got married, but I have failed. First I broke my promise to myself, and I broke God's law through sinful acts. Now I can relay all this to you. I have been there my dear friend. So I know what I am talking about. The good news is you can be a secondary virgin for the glory of God.

A friend of mine is struggling with the lust of the flesh. He told me that this sin drains him down and makes him miserable. I shared to him my story and he felt he wasn't alone, he wasn't condemned, and he then felt accepted. He asked me if I could come over and pray for him. So I went to meet him at his place. I prayed for him, anointed his place, and sang some songs. That was a breakthrough for him. After one month I met him again. He was so full of joy. He learned how to fast and pray. He felt that he was guiltless. All I can hear every now and then while he was telling me his story is *Glory! Ohh...*

I told him, "This is the Lord's doing, it's not me, because you are willing and wanting to change, and that makes all the difference."

There is hope for you my friend. Jesus said in his word, "The thief cometh not, but to steal, and to kill, I have come, that they might have life, life more abundantly." This is the reason why Jesus came to earth, to give us hope in this life and the life to come. God's promise is true, but you have to find it yourself in the Bible. For every situation there are promises for you.

A Prayer for You

Father, I come before your throne. I stand in the gap of every person reading this book. (_____) right here right now at this moment oh God.

I ask you to please forgive their sins, Father have mercy and grace for them.

Father forgive the sins of your people, cleanse them with hyssop so that they maybe be whiter than snow. Touch every longing heart, every burden lift it up, every sickness, heal.... Heal every broken life, broken family, in the name of Jesus Christ of Nazareth.

Touch and reveal to your people that you love them and reveal your will into their life. Make them your people, chosen generations, that they should show forth your mighty works and declare your name on high.

Be lifted up in their trials, temptations, sickness, diseases, burdens, worries, fears. And give them hope to carry on in spite of what they are facing right now. Father be thou glorified in their life, be glorified in everything they do.

So that in your name they will put their trust in you all the days of their life.

Protect them with the evil one and give them your divine protection.

May they be a holy people, chosen generation, ready to be for the Master's use, until we see you face-to-face.

This I ask with your precious and mighty name Jesus Christ, Amen.

ACCOUNTABILITY

For I know their works and their thoughts; it shall come that I will gather all nations and tongues; and they shall come and see my glory.
(Isaiah 66:18)

For the Son of man shall come in the glory of his Father with his angels; and he shall reward everyman according to his works.
(Matthew 16:27)

And to you who are troubled rest with us, when the Lord Jesus will be revealed, from Heaven with his mighty angels,

In flaming fire taking vengeance on them that knows not God, and that obey not the gospel of our Lord Jesus Christ; Who shall be punished with everlasting destruction from the presence of the Lord, and from the glory of his power.

When Jesus shall come to be glorified in his saints, and to be admired in all them that believe (because our testimony among you was believed) in that day.
(2 Thessalonians 1:7-10)

Accountability – The demand that each individual takes full responsibility for his choices and actions; the willingness to accept the rewards or punishments that follow as natural consequences of his behavior or actions.

It is the glue that holds the society together. It is also a common agreement by the members of any society that they will be responsible in their dealings with one another.

The more one has, the greater his accountability.
(Luke 12:48)

To whom much is given, to whom much is required.

1. **Health (Health)**

2. **Intelligence (Skills or positions)**

3. **Wealth (Money)**

Accountability on Earth

The highest authority here on earth is the government. The president has the power to delegate work to the vice president, and so forth, going down to the other officers or rulers.

Let's first look at our society. If I kill someone unlawfully, I am not only accountable to myself for my actions, but I become accountable first to God, by violating his commandments. Then I am accountable to the family of the person whom I had killed. I am also accountable to the government—they are going to put me into jail.

Accountability also follows us when it comes to driving laws. I have a personal story in this area.

Since 2004, my routine has always been to start my day with a chai latte from Starbucks. To save time, I would sometimes stick my driver's license in my jacket pocket along with the money I would need for my drink. I did just that on a day that was going to be very crazy for me. I had three college applications to finish and drop off at their respective buildings. My plan was to reach the first college at 2:00 p.m., the second college at 3:00 p.m., and the third college at 4:00 p.m., to end my day at 5:00 p.m. When I reached the first college, they were already closed, and I felt my entire plan had failed. Luckily, a very nice woman, who was a coordinator at the school, saw me outside of the building and assured me that I would be called back the next week. I was of course very happy that I met her in time. I was so excited that I couldn't help but sing on the drive to the next school. In my eagerness to get to the next school combined with my giddy excitement, I ended up going 80 km/h in a 60 km/h zone. Suddenly I heard the Lord say to me, "Police." I said, "Lord not at this hour." But I still decided to hit my brake and there was indeed a police officer there. He asked me to pull over. I said to him, "I am so sorry sir, I was in a hurry. I have to be at a school and give them my application. They are going to close at 3:00 p.m." He told me to give him my driver's license. I looked and looked, but I could not find my license in my bag. He asked me if the car was actually mine, and made me give him my insurance papers to prove it. He then went to his car to check my paperwork while I continued to look for my license. Of course, at that moment I realized that my license was still in my jacket pocket at home! I forgot to remove it after my trip to Starbucks.

The officer came back to me and I told him what had happened with my license. To my surprise, he did not get angry, but only asked if I knew that he and I had the same birthday! He was very kind to me. He asked me if I knew how much a speeding ticket was. I didn't, and was told that it would be about $200. In my head, I was very upset, because I would much rather send $200 to my mom than spend it on a speeding ticket. The very kind officer then decided to give me a ticket for driving without a license instead of for speeding, which turned out to be only $56. He then wished me luck at my next college appointment and drove away.

That was quite an experience for me, but I had found favor in the sight of God and that policeman. All glory to God.

Imagine if we didn't have laws here on earth. People would be killing other people, and there would be no justice at all.

213

Imagine if we didn't have those police officers to make sure we have a safe place to live and to see who is speeding. I just can't imagine how this world would be without laws and justice. Thank God that this world is still in orderliness.

We are also accountable in our work. Whatever your position is—whether you're a manager or a president or you own a company—you are responsible for your employees. But you will be accountable for taxes if you don't abide in the law of how you manage your business and so forth.

And if you are an employee, you are accountable for your work to be done.

We are also accountable if we can't provide for our family. Here in Canada, if you are not a good provider or if you can't support your kids, your kids will be taken from you and will be handed over to the government. So if you have a family, you are accountable, not only to provide for their needs, but also to make sure you are a good example to them. There is a saying that goes like this: a good tree doesn't yield bad fruits, neither does a bad tree yield good fruits, because the root itself is the seed, so thus your offspring shall be. Likewise, the husband has to honor his wife and love his wife just as Christ died for the church; the same thing goes for the wife. So as his children honor their parents.

The next is the most important one. We are accountable to God because he is our creator. He has given us commandments, and we are given a free will to serve or not to serve, but we are accountable for our moral behavior and our actions. We face the consequences of our own actions, because we are directly answerable to God. So it is up to you to choose to obey or disobey or to use your freedom of choice wisely.

If we have been given wealth, we have a choice to use it or invest it for God's glory. And if we have talents or skills, we are also accountable to God if we don't use them properly.

Accountability in Heaven

1. **We are accountable for the gift** (gift of the Holy Spirit) of talents or skills that God has given us. The preachers of the word of God are responsible for what they preach, because God holds them accountable.

    The more one has, the greater his accountability.
    (Luke 12:48)

2. **To whom much is given, to whom much is required.** (Word of God) The more we hear the word of God, the more judgments come to us.

For I say, through the grace given unto me, to every man that is among you, not to think of himself more highly than he ought to think; but to think soberly, according as God hath dealt to every man the measure of faith.
(Romans 12:3)

3. **The way we live our lives here on earth.**

Know ye not, that to whom ye yield yourselves servants to obey, his servants ye are to whom ye obey; whether of sin unto death, or of obedience unto righteousness. But God be thanked, that ye were the servants of sin, but ye have obeyed from the heart that form of doctrine which was delivered to you.
(Romans 6:16-17)

Even though you are already a born-again Christian, you still have the choice to live according to God's word or not according to God's word. You can continue to serve Satan and live in sin, or continue to serve God and live a righteous life; to please others or to please God; to do your will or to do the will of God. But what I want to tell you is that not all the choices that you make will be beneficial to you. Yes, all things are permissible if you permit them to yourself and do your own will. But not all things are beneficial. Before you do something, you should ask yourself first, "Will this benefit me or benefit the one who saved me? What does the word of God say about this? If I do this, what will the consequences of my actions be?"

The life you have right now is not yours; it's just borrowed from God. He has given us life so we still can live, and still can breathe on this planet earth. But sooner or later, when he comes, whether you are alive or dead, you will go to face your own creator. Whatever you have done here on earth, you will give an account to God, whether it be of good or evil.

Is Your Name Written In the Book of Life?

And I saw a great white throne, and him that sat on it, from whose face the earth and Heaven fled away; and there was no place for them. And I saw the dead, small and great, stand before God; and the books were opened; and another book was opened, which is the book of life: and the dead were judged out of those things were written in the book according to their works. And the sea gave up the dead who were in it; and death and hell delivered up the dead which were in them: and they were judge every man according to their works. And death and hell were cast into the lake of fire. This is the second death. And whosoever was not found written in the book of life was cast into the lake of fire.
(Revelation 20:11-15)

The moment you came into this earth, you already had a book of your life and of your works. If God knows the number of your hairs, how much more must he know about your deeds? God has created the angels, and each person has a guardian angel assigned to him or her. They record your good deeds and bad deeds in the book of your life. So you are making your own true life story, which cannot be erased

216

in your book of life and works. And there is another book, which is not an ordinary book at all; it is called a Book of Life, or Lamb's Book of Life. And if your name is not written in the Book of Life, you will be cast into the lake of fire. This is your eternal destiny if you didn't believe in the name of Jesus Christ. It is called the second death; you will be forever away from God's presence or have eternal separation from God. (Hell)

The Book of Life is the Lamb's Book of Life. I believe that everyone who accepts Jesus Christ as their Lord and Savior will have their name written in the Book of Life. Revelation 3:5 says: "He that overcometh, the same shall be clothed in white raiment; and I will not blot out his name of the book of life, but I will confess his name before my Father, and before his angels." God is holy and just; that's why he needs to punish sin and lawlessness. Even though God is powerful, he doesn't force you to serve him. He is God and he has given us the freedom of choice. The choices we make are up to us. But they also bring consequences in our life, which can ultimately be eternal punishment in hell. That's why I urge you to believe now and accept him if you haven't received him in your heart.

The more one has, the greater his accountability.
(Luke 12:48)

Chapter Fifteen
There is Hope for You

What Are You Hoping For?

Are you are in a situation where you have no hope anymore? Then cheer up, my dear friend, it's not the end of the world. This hope that I am about to tell you is the hope of all the children of God. If you have been reading this book from the beginning, this is the highlight of your ministry: the receiving of rewards. But this is a reward of eternity that never ever fades away.

There are two very important things you should know about HOPE.

1. **Glorified body** – *But I would not have you to be ignorant, brethren, concerning them which are asleep, that ye sorrow not, even as others which have no hope. For if we believe that Jesus died and rose again, **even so them also which sleep in Jesus will God bring with him**. For this we say unto you by the word of the Lord, **that we which are alive and remain** unto the coming of the Lord shall not prevent them which are asleep. For the Lord himself shall descend from Heaven with a shout, with the voice of arch-angel, and with the trump of God: and **the dead in Christ shall rise first: Then we which are alive and remain shall be caught up together with them in the clouds, to meet the Lord in the air: and so shall we ever be with the Lord**. (1 Thessalonians 4:13-17)*

2. **You have a mansion in Heaven** – *Let not your heart be troubled: ye believe in God, believe also in me. In* ***my Father's house are many mansions;*** *if it were not so, I would have told you. I go to prepare a place for you. And if I go and prepare a place for you, I will come again, and* ***receive you unto myself; that where I am, there ye may be also.*** *(John 14:1-3)*

By faith he [Abraham] sojourned in the land of promise [Canaan], as in a strange country, dwelling in tabernacles with Isaac and Jacob, the heirs with him of the same promise: For he looked for a city which ***hath foundations, whose builder and maker is God.*** *(Hebrews 11:9-10)*

But now they desire a better country, which is Heavenly: *wherefore God is not ashamed to be called their God: for* ***he had prepared for them a city.*** *[New Jerusalem] (Hebrews 11:16)*

3. **Eternal life** – *For God so loved the world that he gave his only begotten son [Jesus Christ] that whosoever believeth on him should not perish but have everlasting life. (John 3:16)*

This eternal life that we are going to receive has no beginning and has no ending. This was the ultimate plan of God before the world began. But people are so wicked that they turned away from God. In the book of Genesis, Enoch never tasted death—he went to Heaven. (Hebrews 11:5) Then Elijah the prophet also went to Heaven. These two holy people walked with God and shunned evil. And the third who ascended to Heaven was Jesus Christ. He had to die for our sins to redeem us from the coming wrath. But he was raised from the dead. His body was changed from mortal to immortal, from visible to invisible. His body is already glorified. That means it will never taste death or sickness ever again. It became a body that will be with every believer of Christ. The bodies of those who reject God and his plan of salvation will also be eternal, but they will spend eternity in torment in hell.

This is the good news! That one day, we can have this glorified body like Jesus had, and that we have a place in New Jerusalem and that we will live forever and ever. If I think of the word *eternity*, I can't comprehend how much and how long it is. Then I begin to think that God is eternal, and if I live a hundred years here on earth, I would have lived just a minute with the Lord, because one day with the Lord is like a thousand years. But the second piece of good news is that there is life after death. Jesus is the evidence of life eternal and we can have that as well, if we keep on serving and following God. For those of you who are already born again and walking in the truth, I will urge you brethren to keep your life spotless and blameless until you see Jesus.

*Nevertheless we, according to his promise, look for new Heavens and new earth, wherein dwelleth righteousness. Wherefore my beloved, seeing that ye look for such things, be diligent that ye may be found of him in peace, **without spot and blameless.***
(2 Peter 3:13&14)

If you are reading this book, it is because of God's love for you. The things I have written are not my own words. If you reject my words, you are not rejecting me, but the one who says those words. I love you my friend, I want to pass on to you what God has taught me all these years. And I want you to receive this eternal life that only God can give you, if you believe in his son Jesus Christ. And if you have friends, family, or neighbors that have not known Jesus Christ, I can only have one wish for you: please share with them this book. Time is running out. We know neither the time nor the hour when Jesus will come again. But what matters most is that we have eternal life and we have this assurance that we have the salvation of our soul.

The Seal Which is the Holy Spirit

*In whom ye also trusted, after that ye heard the word of truth, the gospel of your salvation: in whom also after that ye believed, **ye were sealed** with that **Holy Spirit of promise**,*

Which is the earnest of our inheritance until the redemption of the purchased possession, unto the praise of his glory?
(Colossians 1:13-14)

When you purchase a property, you need a contract stating that the property belongs to you. It is called the title deed, and is made official with your name and your signature. When we accept Jesus into our hearts, he promises that he will send his Holy Spirit, just like a title deed promises you your property.

*For John truly baptized with water; but ye shall be baptized with the **Holy Ghost** not many days hence.*
(Acts 1:5)

*But ye shall receive power, after the **Holy Ghost** is come upon you: and ye shall be **witnesses** unto me both in Jerusalem, and in all Judea, and in Samaria, and unto the uttermost part of the earth.*
(Acts 1:8)

*And when the day of Pentecost was fully come, they were all with one accord in one place. And suddenly there came a sound from Heaven as of a rushing mighty wind, and it filled all the house where they were sitting. And there appeared unto them cloven tongues like as of fire, and it sat upon each of them. And they **were all filled with the Holy Ghost**, and begun to **speak with other tongues, as the Spirit gave them utterance**.*
(Acts 2:1-4)

When the day of Pentecost comes, all of them were filled with the Holy Ghost, and began to speak in tongues.

When I had been a born-again Christian for twenty years, I had still never spoken in tongues. God had taught me about faith—how to operate and walk by it—as well as how to forgive, how to love, etc. I knew that I had the gifts of faith, love, discernment, teaching, and evangelism, but not the gift of speaking in tongues.

An ex-boyfriend of mine, whom I will call Choice, was also my brother in Christ. I recall one day I spent with him, when we were fasting on the last day of the month. I didn't believe that I could go without eating until midnight, so around 3:00 p.m., he asked me to read Acts 2:1–5. He told me that on that day, I would begin speaking in tongues. So I spoke to God with my spirit and said, "Lord I already have the best gift, which is the gift of love. If you add another gift, it is just a bonus to me." So we started praying, Choice put his hands on my head a few times. I fell on the floor a few times. And then I felt the mighty presence of God. I began speaking in a language that I didn't understand. I felt like I was home ... Home sweet home ... that I was speaking with my Heavenly Father in languages that I didn't understand. I was crying out to him, as if he was right there in front of me. I was crying, and worshipping God on another level of the Spirit. I can't explain the joy and the beauty of his presence; it was more than I had experienced before. It was true when King David said, "In your presence, there is fullness of joy, and there are pleasures forever more." What a mighty God we serve.

And this Spirit is our seal even unto the Day of Judgment.
(Revelation 7:2)

A New Jerusalem or New Heaven

A New Jerusalem The city of the living God
But ye are come unto mount Zion, and unto the city of the living God, the Heavenly Jerusalem, and to the innumerable

company of angels, to the general assembly and church of the first born, (Jesus Christ) which are written in Heaven, and to God the Judge of all, and to the spirits of just men made perfect.
(Hebrews 12:22-23)

*And **I saw a new Heaven and earth**: for the first Heaven and the first earth were passed away; and there were no more sea.*

*And I John saw the **holy city, New Jerusalem**, coming down from God out of Heaven, prepared as a bride adorned for her husband.*

*And I heard a great voice out of Heaven saying, **Behold, the tabernacle of God is with men, and he will dwell with them, and they shall be his people, and God himself shall be with them, and be their God.***

*And God shall wipe away all tears from their eyes; and there shall be no **more death**, (Glorified body) neither sorrow, nor crying, neither shall there be any more pain for the former things passed away.*
(Revelation 21:1-4)

This is the promise that every believer in Christ Jesus is waiting for. Abraham and the patriarch are looking for this city— a city that is not made with the hands of men but by God. We are waiting for the second coming of Jesus Christ. It's a pity that his chosen Israel, his own people, receive him not. Some are still waiting for the coming messiah. They stumble to this stone, a precious cornerstone that is Jesus Christ. But through their unbelief, we were grafted into the vine. Israel are the true vine; though they stumble, God is able to graft them in, when the fullness of the Gentiles comes.

We Gentiles are so blessed to believe it, even though we hadn't touched him or seen him. When Jesus comes again, he

224

doesn't come again as love, but he will come to take his own people, those who follow him, and this is the joy of his coming. But to the unbelieving people, he will come as a judge, to judge the ungodly and those whose names are not written in the Lamb's Book of Life.

Jerusalem's God is the master builder

*By faith, Abraham, when he was called, went into the place which he should have received for an inheritance. He obeyed, and he went out, not knowing whither he went... **For he looked for a city which hath foundations, whose builder and maker is God.***
(Hebrews 11:8&10)

These all died in faith, not having received the promises, but having seen them far off. They were persuaded of them, and they embraced them, and they confessed that they were strangers and pilgrims on the earth.

But now they desire a better country, that is, an Heavenly wherefore God is not ashamed to be called they God. For he hath prepared for them a city.
(Hebrews 11: 13&16)

Holy City/New Jerusalem
Book of Revelation
The New Jerusalem is the New Heaven that Jesus hath promised before he left. I go to prepare a place for you, to where I am there you may be also.

It was **made by the hand of God**. It was a **great Holy City of Holy Jerusalem**. Having the glory of God: and her light was like unto a stone most precious, even like jasper stone, clear as crystal. Revelations verse 11

Jerusalem had Twelve Gates
And had a wall great and high, and had twelve gates, and at the gates twelve angels, and names written thereon, which

are the names of the twelve tribes of the children of Israel: And on the east three gates; on the north three gates; on the south three gates; and on the west three gates.

Twelve Foundations which names of the twelve Apostles were written on it.

And the wall of the city had twelve foundations, and in them the names of the twelve apostles of the Lamb. Verses 12–14

Violence shall no more be heard in thy land, nor wasting nor destruction within thy borders; but thou shalt call thy walls Salvation, and thy gates Praise.
(Isaiah 60:18)

Jerusalem's Wall was PURE Gold
And the building of the wall of it was a jasper: and the city was pure gold, like unto clear glass.

And the foundation of the wall of the city were garnished with all manner of precious stones.
(Revelation 21-18-20)

1. Jasper	7. Chrysolyte
2. Sapphire	8. Beryl
3. Chalcedony	9. Topaz
4. Emerald	10. Chrysoprasus
5. Sardonyx	11. Jacinth
6. Sardius	12. Amethyst

Jerusalem is The LORD GOD Almighty/LAMB Jesus Christ Temple
The twelve gates were twelve pearls; every several gate was of one pearl: and the street of the city was pure gold, as it were transparent glass.

And I saw no temple therein: for the Lord God Almighty and the Lamb are the temple of it.

Jerusalem's Glory of God and The Lambs is the Light
And the city had no need of the sun, neither of the moon, to shine in it: for the glory of God did lighten it, and the lamb is the light thereof.

Jerusalem's People: Only those whose name are written in the Lamb's Book of Life, can walk and enter in.

And the nations of them which are saved shall walk in the light of it: and the kings of the earth do bring their glory and honour unto it.

And the gate shall not be shut all by day: for there shall be no more night there.

And there shall in no wise enter into it anything that defileth, neither whatsoever worketh abomination, or maketh a lie: but they which are written in the Lamb's Book of Life.

Jerusalem's Pure River of Water
And he showed me a pure river of water of life, clear as crystal, proceeding out of the throne of God and of the Lamb. (Revelation 22:1-5)

Jerusalem's Tree of Life
And the midst of the street of it, and on either side of the river, was the tree of life, which bare twelve manner of fruits, and yielded her fruit every month; and the leaves of the tree were for the healing of the nations.

Jerusalem's No More Curse
And there shall be no more curse: but the throne of God and the Lamb shall be in it; and his servants shall serve him: Verse 3

Jerusalem's Will See Jesus Face-to-Face
And they shall see his face; and his name shall be on their foreheads. Verse 4

Jerusalem's We Shall Reign With Him Forever
And there shall be no night there; and they no need candle, neither light of the sun; for the LORD GOD giveth them light: and they shall reign for ever and ever.
(Revelation 22:5)

The Reward of the Overcomer

*And behold, I come quickly; and **my reward is with me, to give everyman, according to his work shall be**. I am the Alpha and the Omega, the beginning and the end, the first and the last. Blessed are they that do his commandments that they may have the right to the tree of life, and may enter in through the gates into the city. [New Jerusalem]*
(Revelation 22:12-14)

The Reward of the Overcomer
1. **God's children.**

He that overcometh shall inherit all things, and I will be his God, and he shall be my son. (Revelation 21:7)

2. **We may be able to eat from the tree of life.** Enter through the gate of New Jerusalem. (Revelation 22:12-14)

....to him that overcometh will I give to eat of the tree of life, which is in the midst of the paradise of God.
(Revelation 2:7)

3. **Give us a crown of life.**

....be thou faithful unto death, and I will give thee a crown of life.
(Revelation 2:10)

228

4. Right to eat hidden manna, white stone with a new name written on it.

To him that overcometh will I give to eat of the hidden manna, and will give him a white stone, and in the stone a new name written, which no man knoweth saying he that receiveth it.
(Revelation 2:17)

5. Make us rule over the nations.

And he that overcometh, and keepeth my works, unto the end, to him will I give power over the nations: And he shall rule them with a rod of iron; as the vessels of a potter shall they be broken to shivers: even as I received of my Father. And I will give him the morning star.
(Revelation 2:26-29)

6. We will be clothed with white raiment; will not blot out our name from the Lamb's Book of Life.

He that overcometh, the same shall be clothed in white raiment; and I will not blot out his name out of the book of life, but I will confess his name before my Father, and before his angels.
(Revelation 3:5-6)

7. Give us his new name.

Him that overcometh will I make a pillar in the temple of my God, and he shall go no more out: and I will write upon him the name of my God, and the name of the city of my God, which is new Jerusalem, which cometh down out of Heaven from my God: and I will write upon him my new name.
(Revelation 3: 12-13)

8. Seed and your name will remain.

For as the new Heavens and the new earth, which I will make, shall remain before me, saith the LORD, so shall your seed and your name remain.
(Isaiah 66:22)

9. Grant us to sit in his throne.

To him that over cometh will I grant to sit with me in my throne, even as I also overcame, and am set down with my Fathers in his throne.
(Revelation 3:21-22)

10. We shall shine like the sun.

Then shall the righteous shine forth as the sun in the kingdom of their Father.
(Matthew 13:43, Matthew 13:50)

11. Will not taste the second death (Hell).

He that hath an ear, let him hear what the spirit saith unto the churches; He that overcometh shall not be hurt of the second death.
(Revelation 2:11)

The Hope of My Calling (New Jerusalem)

I heard you call my name
I hear your voice
You said, "I Love you"
You said no greater love than this
That a man lay down his life for his friends
You didn't call me servant but friend
And you told me all the secrets in Heaven.
You said your love is greater than anyone

You took my place, the price I have to pay
You said, "I Love You"
There's no greater love than this.

I was changed, never be the same again
From glory to glory never ceasing changed
Until one day I will see you face-to-face.

This is my Hope of my calling
A life everlasting, no beginning and no ending,
A body changed from glory to glory;
From mortal to immortality;
A glorified body like yours,
I would be transformed and fully changed.

When I see you face-to-face,
Beholding your throne, your beauty
And you stand before me; before the angels in Heaven
That I am yours because I answered your call;
To hear you will say to me,
"Well done! Thou good and faithful beloved of mine
Enter now into my kingdom".

And in thy presence, there is fullness of Joy
A voice of gladness and rejoicing and praising
Glorifying your name, for thou alone is exalted above all.
There be no more night and sickness and mourning will flee.
For in thy presence, there are pleasures forever more.

I will be clothed in white robe, like the angels in Heaven,
Singing Praise and glory to your name;
I will bow down and worship thee;
And declare the greatness of your love and Mercy.

Then I will drink of that living water clear as crystal
That never runs out dry, and I will never be thirsty again,
Eat from the manna of Heaven, and never be hungry again
And when I walked, on those streets of gold
That are not made in the hands of men, but God

How beautiful, how magnificent, how awesome are thy creations OH LORD!
My eyes could see and behold and understand your plans for me.

The New Jerusalem is where I belong,
I am only a pilgrim and orphan in this world.
A mansion made of pure gold, and all the kinds of precious stone.
Where I lay my head.
And in the corner of Eden,
Where I eat all the kinds of fruits and never grow old.

This is my comfort in serving you, and in my affliction,
To be with you OH God in the time comes,
I am waiting, and all your children are waiting,
Come Oh LORD JESUS Come!

By Rebecca Daluddung 2004

Chapter Sixteen
Prayer is Healing

Prayer is Healing

*If my people, which are called by my name, shall **humble** themselves, and **pray,** and **seek** my face, and turned from their wicked ways; then will I **hear** from Heaven, and will forgive their sin, and will **heal** their land.*
(2 Chronicles 7:14)

Prayer is to humble ourselves before God and acknowledge him—that he is above all things and that we can't do anything without him.

✟ It is also about seeking God's face, his ways, and his will in our life, and circumstances we are facing.

✟ It is also turning away from our sins or repenting of our sins and turning our will in accordance to his will, as well as God's standard of holiness and righteousness.

God's promise: God will hear from Heaven, will forgive our sins, and will heal our land.

He also promised in Jeremiah 33:3, "Call unto me and I will answer thee; and show the great things which thou knoweth not."

Prayer is the most powerful weapon you can have in your life.

My life is a life of three *P's*, which are **Prayer**, **Praise**, and **Petition**. I just can't go on with my life without prayer. It's like the air that we breathe in and we breathe out. Praise is likely the same thing. When I wake up in the morning, I usually have a song in my head that the Holy Spirit gave me; the song stays in my head throughout the day. From God came all the achievements I have, and everything that I went through in life—whether it be difficulties, trials, or sufferings. I couldn't bear or be able to go on without prayer and praise and petition our Heavenly Father for what he had promised.

It's my way of talking to my God; to communicate with him when I am in good times or bad times. I pray and sing when I am sad, I pray when I am happy, I pray when I am in trouble, etc.

I pray for my needs and for the needs of my family.

How to Pray

I sing in the choir at Willingdon Church, but I also pray for other people when they come to the altar and ask for prayers. I pray for the people who need prayer and the people around me—they knocked on my doors and asked me to pray for them.

One Sunday morning, a fellow choir member sat beside me and asked, "You always pray, don't you?" I told her yes, I love to pray. She replied that she didn't know how to pray. Whenever she tried, she would just fall asleep. I couldn't help but smile.

"Can you teach me how to pray?" she asked. My advice to her was to learn from the ACTS of the apostles.

Jesus Taught Us How to Pray

After this manner therefore pray ye: Our Father which art in Heaven, Hallowed be thy Name.

Thy kingdom come. Thy will be done in earth, as it is in Heaven.

Give us this day our daily bread.

And forgive us our debts, as we forgive our debtors.

And lead us not into temptation, but deliver us from the evil: For thine is the kingdom, and the power, and the glory, for ever. Amen.
(Matthew 6:9-13)

ACTS of the Apostles

A   Adoration – You have to adore God for who he is. Because he made the Heaven and earth and everything. (Psalm 99:9) Exalt the LORD our God, and worship at his Holy hill, for the LORD our God is holy.

Hallowed be thy name. (Matthew 6:9) He is our creator, salvation, provider, healer, etc.

C   Confession – Confess you sins before God, because God is holy and he hates sins. For I acknowledge my transgressions: and my sin is ever before me. Against thee, thee only have I sinned, and done this evil in thy sight: that thou mightiest be justified when thou speakest, and be clear when thou judgest. (Psalm 51:3-4) Thy kingdom come, thy will be done or earth as it is in Heaven. The angels in Heaven, all they do is the will of God. When we do the will of God in our life, then his kingdom comes in our midst and in our lives, because the Bible says: the kingdom is within you.

If you offend anyone, you have to ask for their forgiveness before you come to God. Then you confess your sins before God, and ask for his forgiveness as you forgive those who trespass against you. (Matthew 6:14)

T   Thanks giving – Thank God every day for the blessings he has given you. Our God is full of surprises. He always blesses us and answers our prayers. (Psalm 100:4) Enter into his gates with thanksgiving, and into his courts with praise: be thankful unto him, and bless his name. Thank God, for his provision and for all the blessings you receive. Thank him by faith that you had received just what you had asked for. (Mark 11:24)

S   Supplication – You ask God for the things you want in your life, because the Bible said, Ask and it shall be given you, seek and ye shall find; knock, and it shall be opened unto you. For everyone that asketh receiveth; and he that seeketh findeth; and to him that knocketh it shall be opened.(Matthew 7;7-8) Give us this day our daily bread, lead us not unto temptation. You ask God to supply all your needs according to his riches and glory, through Christ Jesus our Lord. (Matthew 7:7-8)

Then you thank God for the answer and end your prayers in the name of the Lord Jesus. For God hath promised: "If ye then being evil, know how to give good gifts unto your children, how much more shall your Father in Heaven give good things to those who ask him?" (Matthew 7:11)

Pray Without Ceasing

Confess your faults one to another, and pray for one another, that ye may be healed, The effectual fervent prayer of a righteous man availeth much.
(James 5:16)

My sister Virgie taught me how to pray. I just added a few things that God taught me over the years.

The Five Things We Need to Pray

1. Pray for your family, loved ones, and friends.
2. Pray for the teachers, preachers, and missionaries.
3. Pray for the president of Canada, the U.S., Philippines, Israel, and all countries.
4. Pray for your friends (weak and sick).
5. Pray for your personal needs.

What to pray for:

- Family's divine protection
- Family's desire and dream fulfillment
- Healing for sickness
- Comfort for the grieving spirit
- Financial providence for the missionaries
- Wisdom to preach the gospel and boldness
- Safety when traveling
- Wisdom in governing our country
- Salvation of the soul for the lost
- Physical and spiritual health

When I pray, I always pray for Ezra's safety. One day he told me he was in an accident. Nothing happened to him and his car, but the car that hit him was smashed. He couldn't believe how he was not hurt. I said, "What a powerful angel." I knew then that God sent his powerful angels to protect him from harm, and I give all the glory and honor to God.

Chapter Seventeen
Testimonies of Prayer

Confess your faults one to another, and pray for one another, that ye may be healed, The effectual fervent prayer of a righteous man availeth much.
(James 5:16)

Ryan Struggles With the Lust of the Flesh

One day Ryan (not his real name) called me and shared with me that he had a problem with lust of the flesh. He didn't even love the woman in question. The Spirit of God was so strong in him that he told me, "This can't be, I am a Christian and why is it that I am living with this kind of sin?" I didn't ask him how long this had been going on, but I believe it was a large part of why he suffered from depression. He asked me to come to his home and see him. So I went to see him and prayed for him. I lay my hands on him. I asked God to forgive him and cleanse him from his sin. Then I asked Ryan to confess his sins and ask for God's forgiveness. And Ryan repented from his sins and asked God's forgiveness.

After the prayer, God spoke with a small voice to me and told me to tell Ryan these words. "Tell Ryan that I LOVE him, and that his sin is forgiven." Ryan said, "Yes, I feel that this is the turning point in my life."

And just after the prayer, the Holy Spirit commanded me to dedicate and anoint his place. I prayed for God's cleansing over the place to make it holy. And then we sprinkled anointing oil over each room. Ryan has an anointing also on his hand that I gave him and taught him to say in Jesus's name.

After that, we sang some songs and then I left to go home.

After a month, we met again at Starbucks and he told me what the Lord is doing in his life. He started to fast. He felt the presence of God and declared that he felt that he was guiltless. He was so excited and kept saying Hallelujah... I told him that it is not I who is doing this for him, but it is the Lord. The Lord is the only one who can change people.

The third time Ryan and I met, we were at my home. We prayed together and, for the very first time, he felt God's presence so strongly. He also prayed in a strong manner.

God was so good to him; I rejoice for what the Lord is doing in his life.

Not long after, Ryan found a woman that he really loves and he was truly amazed at how God loved him, that he has given him another chance to love again. All glory to the King of Kings and the Lord of Lords King Jesus our Lord and King.

Woman Who Had a Manifestation of a Demon

Cita (not her real name) has been a Christian for many years. She goes to church every Sunday, reads lots of Christian books, volunteers in the Church, etc.

One day, Cita called me, saying that she was distressed and needs to be prayed for because of her friend.

When I reached her place, she began telling me why she was upset. She was crying while telling me the story. I just listened to her with compassion and didn't say a word.

After that, I told her that I would pray for her. As soon as I put anointing oil on her head and lay my hand on her, she was praising God and giving him adoration. After a few seconds, she burst out; a voice came out of her and said something I didn't even understand. It was an angry, wailing voice.

So I rebuked that devil right away to leave, with a strong, powerful voice and authority. I was praying beside Cita, and she reached out and held my hands. She sounded as if she was in pain.

She was panicking and called her counselor and put her on the speaker phone. Her counselor told her that it was because of the presence of God that this was happening. I wanted to pray for her, but she was on the phone and I didn't have the opportunity to do so. When I came home, the Lord told me to fast and pray. So I called her early the next morning and told her that we need to fast and pray for three days.

I was filled with so much compassion for her that I declared I would fast and pray for three days. On the day of our fast, I told her what the Lord wanted us to do.

She needed to repent and confess her sins before God, and she needed to ask the Lord Jesus to be her Lord and Savior. She had been attending one of the deliverance ministries in Vancouver. She asked me to be her sponsor, but I told the Lord that I would not start ministering to her, not unless she gave her life completely to Jesus. So the second time we met, I asked her again if she did what I told her on the phone. She said yes, and she took out her little notebook and read to me what she wrote that day. I was listening very intently, and when I heard those words, that she was giving her life to Jesus, I began to weep and cry for joy because the Lord hath done something on our fasting. Although she had given her life to the Lord before, I knew that this was a re-commitment to love and seek the Lord in a deeper form of relationship.

241

While I ministered to her, the devil sometimes blocked her mind with darkness and she felt uncomfortable. So when she decided to make Jesus her Lord and Savior, she told me, "I hear them saying [the devil], 'If you leave us now, your life will never be the same again. We have been your friend for a long time.'"

The third time we met, she told me her story when she was young. She also mentioned that one day she attended a crusade and she just yelled out loud in the middle of the congregation. And another time, her body was so stiff that you could lay her in two chairs and she would never fall. These are just the manifestations that she had a devil or was possessed with a devil.

A lot of times, when Satan wants to strike, I have had to rebuke it with authority to leave. And we have always been victorious.

Somehow, she graduated from that School of Deliverance and I see her now, growing. The enemy can't do anything. She loves God even more and she has a very compassionate heart to the poor. She often gives lots of clothes to be shipped to the poor. And she is continuing in the faith and still growing spiritually. What a wonderful God we serve.

I still continue to see her and pray with her.

A Little Boy Was Healed From Cold and Ear Infection

Henry (not his real name) was sixteen months old. He was a very active and strong little boy. He had been sick for three days and his Mom brought him to the hospital because his eyes started to roll. On the third day of his sickness, they called the ambulance because he fell and couldn't stand properly. He had an ear infection and he was sleepy because of medication. He had been sleeping all day.

I was babysitting, and Henry's mom told me to watch over him, to make sure he was breathing right. At 8:45 p.m. I put his sister to bed, and I went to check on Henry to give him medicine. I took him out of the crib and put him on my lap. His eyes were closed, and I gave him the medicine. He was too weak, and his body was like a cooked vegetable. I felt compassion on him and asked the Father to please heal him. I put my hand on his head, and I blew seven times on his ear and on his tummy. While I was blowing, he started to laugh, and kept on laughing with his eyes closed. I gently touched his chest, confirming to him that he would be ok and that Jesus loves him. He was still laughing so hard that he coughed. Suddenly, he sat on my lap, opened his eyes, and looked around. I brought him upstairs and gave him macaroni and cheese; he was so hungry. I was rejoicing with tears for what happened. Somehow, I felt the presence of the Lord while praying.

So when Henry's parents arrived, I told them the story and showed them a photo of Henry eating. And Henry's mother was so happy; she hugged me so tight and said thank you. His mother said to us, "I guess I have to start praying myself." Henry's dad hugged me and said thank you before I left. I told him to thank Jesus, and he showed me his necklace with a cross on it.

I felt so happy and strong even though I myself had a cold from running around and working too much.

On Monday I came back to the house for our regular cleaning. Henry's mom following Henry to say hi to us. I saw that he was so happy and healed. His mom said, "Thank God Rebecca channels Jesus."

A Man With Grief

A friend of mine came to my place one Saturday evening. He was about to go out, when I asked him about what happened with his wife. He told me that his wife had passed away a week after their baby was born. He had a six-year-old daughter. As soon as I learned that it had been six years, I was totally mad. I was filled with the presence of God. I shared my anger with my friend. My friend then became totally mad at me. He said, "I just want to let you know that the way you talk to me right now, it kills me. This is the reason why I never talk about it with other believers."

I told him that I didn't care what he thought about me. I asked him to just let me pray for him, and he agreed. I took his hand and started to pray. This time, my prayer became stronger and stronger, and then it was so intense. I was crying out to God. And for the very first time, I felt his grief, very deep, even deeper than the seas. I was filled with intense anguish, sorrow, and mourning.

It was the most beautiful prayer I had ever entered through on behalf of my brother. I was on my knees, pleading, and before I knew it… my friend was crying with me. Then, it was time for him to pray. He said, "Father, thank you for the privilege to be in your presence. Please forgive me for saying something to Becky a while ago. Becky please forgive me, Father please forgive me."… After our prayer, he was totally thrilled. He asked me, "Does this happen to you often??" I said, "Yes, when you can tap into the power of God, Heaven is open and your prayers will never be the same again." On that very night, he wept until 3:00 a.m. He had been grieving for a long time. It even crippled him to do anything when the trauma would strike him. Thank God, now he is better and better every day. He took a counseling course and now he's waiting for his certificate. Jesus came to set the captives free.

A Woman With So Many Problems

I attended a one-day course for how to write your book in 40 days by Bob. There, I met a woman. We got to know each other so quickly in that little time we were together. I gave her a ride home because she lived just next to the street I lived on. I prayed for her before we split up. She wanted to have a prayer with me again but somehow she forgot about it.

After two months, I met her in our building and I found out that she just moved a week before. She just finished her course as a massage therapist. And because of the economy's downturn, her husband was not making enough money. They didn't have a choice but to separate for a while because of financial problems. She was previously not working and also had kidney stones. We were very happy at that point to have run into each other. I told her to come and see me anytime I was home so I could pray for her.

One day, I was feeling so tired, so I was looking for someone who would give me a massage. I called everyone I knew but somehow, everyone I knew was busy. Then suddenly I remembered her, and called her. She came and give me a massage and after that I prayed for her. She was crying and felt the presence of God and she told me, "Thank you sister, God was really on you."

After three days she came again and asked me to pray for her. I started with a song. I was singing together with my computer on YouTube. While I was singing, she already started crying and felt the presence of God.

After a couple of songs I came near her and lay my hands upon her hand and prayed for her. She was just crying all the time.

I knew that God had answered my prayer and her cry of plea. After a month, she came and knocked on my door at 9:00 p.m. on a Sunday. She told me that she just started a job, that day, and that the Lord healed her. She was so happy and just came to thank me. I told her "Thank Jesus."

Friend Asking for Prayer With Her Three Children

I am always busy with my business. My life was totally transformed and is very different than before. Starting a business
is really very challenging. I don't have so much time for talking to other friends anymore, except for someone who is in
need of prayer. One friend called me on a Thursday about ten
times, but I didn't answer because I was talking to another
person. On Friday she called me at 9:00 a.m., so I kind of
wondered what was the matter. So I called her back. She said,
"I want you to pray for me. Will it be possible to come over
tonight and just pray with you?" But I said, "The Lord wants
us to pray now." So I just prayed. After the prayer, I told her
that God was trying to give her something. I told her to put
her right hand on the phone, and say "I receive it Lord." She
said it a couple of times and all I could hear is "I receive it
Lord, I receive it Lord." She was crying also because of the
presence of God. What an amazing God we serve. That evening, I went to pray for her and her three kids. We had an
amazing hour with the Lord. I lay hands on each and every
one of them. While her eyes closed, the Lord opened her
spiritual eyes; suddenly she could see me wearing a white
suit, like a gown. Glory to God! Somehow she could also see
visions regarding each of her children. We intercede also
with her husband who is not active anymore.

Lady Who Was Stressed and Couldn't Sleep

A friend of mine once called me and asked me to pray for her.

I asked her what was wrong, and she told me that she had
been stressed out and couldn't even sleep. I told her that she
was too young to be so stressed.

So I took my Bible and began to share the word of God to her.
I asked her the following questions. Do you pray every night?

Do you confess your sins before God? I read to her 1 John 1:9. She then asked me, "What's the use of confessing your sins if you keep doing the same thing over and over again?"

I explained to her the difference between confession and repentance. Repentance is turning away from your sins 360 degrees. Confession is asking God to forgive your sins daily. I asked her if she usually showers. She smiled and said yes, so I continued and asked, "If you take a shower today and tomorrow you're going to take a shower again when you get dirty right?" And she answered yes. I explained to her the difference between a person who hears the word of God and does it, and the person who hears the word of God and never does it.

She had accepted Jesus in her heart before but she had never repented. I asked her if she wanted to have a prayer for repentance and she said yes. I lead a prayer of repentance and also prayed for her. The next morning, I saw her and she told me that she slept really well the previous night—and she looked well rested. All glory to Jesus.

A Woman Who Wants to Meet Her Soul Mate

In 2009, I met a woman at one of the churches I attended. We both speak in tongues so we decided to set up a time that she could come to my place so we could pray together. The only prayer she told me (as much as I can remember) was that she wanted to be married again. So I prayed for her and asked God to send the right man into her life. She also prayed for me, and she told me that God is going to use me.

After a few months, she got a boyfriend. To make the story short, she just got married this year and now is pregnant and very happily married.

God had answered our prayer together. What an amazing God we serve.

A Man With a Marital Problem

I met this brother in Starbucks. He goes to the same church I attend.

He called me one day to take a look at his place for cleaning.

I went to see the place and at the same time, I prayed for him after he told me that his wife didn't want to come to Canada to stay, because she loved her work so much.

He told me that his wife had been away for five years, and they kept visiting each other, but he wants God's will to be done in his life. He didn't want to have a divorce, because he knew the will of God. The following month he came to my home and I prayed for him for the second time. He said that I am a godly woman. After three months he went to visit his wife and asked me to pray for him again for the third time. When I went to see him in Starbucks, we went to his car and prayed for him again. After he came back for a few weeks, he called me and told me that his wife was coming to Canada and that this had never happened before. He told me thank you for my prayer. So to make the story short, the wife came to Canada and he was so happy. Praise God, he made a way for them to be together. I was praying to God to let the wife come here and that God would make a way to preserve their marriage. All glory to the living God we serve.

Bear Each Other's Burden

Bear ye another's burdens, and so fulfill the law of Christ.
(Galatians 6:2)

I can tell you all the countless blessings I have but they would be too numerous to write. God has changed my heart totally. I may not have a luxury car or a massive home. But I have a loving God who, whenever I will come to him in prayer or praise, always gives me the answer to everything I need. I have a best friend; she wasn't a born-again Christian. I will name her Rose (not her real name). I have known her for twelve years. I was in financial trouble in 2004 and had lots of debts, so she told me to cancel all my credit cards and we just consolidated and paid it all down. I had just one credit card left. However, after we paid it all, I blew that credit card again. I did not do it purposely, but because I didn't have a job and I had to use it. My heart has changed and I don't like to use credit cards anymore. I have been strictly using cash since then. I buy when I have the money and I will borrow money if I have unexpected expenses. I have lots of friends; however, I can only approach someone whom God put in my heart. Rose is the one I go to when I am in financial trouble. Rose is not just a friend to me; she is like my sister. She scolds me when I need it, she tells me when I am wrong, and with her loving heart she rescues me when I am in trouble financially. I just love her as she is. For example, I owed her some money, and one day she called me and said, "Don't pay me anymore ok? I will just give it to you as a gift." Guess what? I had tears of joy, knowing that God had touched her heart.

Food Poisoning that Leads to a Blessing

September 18, 2010, I got sick because of food poisoning, and following that I got bacteria in my stomach. I was on medication for a week, and I had suffered so much physically that I couldn't sleep in the night, so I had to call Choice to pray for me. Choice came and visited. He drove me to the doctor's office, and took care of me. May and Sister Rosa, my roommate, cooked for me and washed my dishes. Sister Rosa helped wash my clothes. Shahin, my brother in Christ and a church mate, came and bought some groceries for me and he didn't ask for money. I wasn't working for four weeks because I was so weak and got physically exhausted all the time. I had missed my piano lessons and choir practices. One thing

I didn't miss, though, was the regular schedule of cleaning because God had provided people to work in my business.

During my sickness, I didn't perform any transactions at the bank. My money was late and, because of that, my car insurance payment had bounced twice. My insurance company then canceled the monthly pre-authorized payment plan.

I needed the car so I had to pay the remaining $1,000.00 for the insurance of the remaining nine months. I wasn't working for three weeks by then, so all the money kept going out. The next week, I was feeling a little bit better. I woke up one day, about to go to work, when Loti saw that my car and the car next to it had been vandalized during the night. The front glass was broken and the tires had been poked.

I called Shahin and just said, "I need your help!" And I told him what happened. So he said, "Ok you can use my car, I have two cars, I will come and pick you up in thirty minutes." I waited for an hour for him and we still were able to go to work on that day even though we were two hours late. The truth is, I didn't know that Shahin had two cars. I just called him because I saw a missed call from him from the night before my car was vandalized. The reason he was calling me was to have his home cleaned. When I called him in the morning, I didn't even ask him anything. All I said was, "I need help." That's all that came out of my mouth. Surely the Lord knows all things. So I used his car for a week until my car had finished being repaired.

Blessings Money from Heaven

Now the second blessing after my car was vandalized started from my not having enough money to pay the insurance company. I told Choice about my situation—that I needed money to pay the car insurance. Sister Rosa overheard it and asked me what the problem was. So I told her about the situation.

She wanted to help me, but couldn't because she was not working. She then borrowed $300.00 from her friend's Visa just to help me. I also asked a friend of mine, Rock, and he loaned me about $487.00. I asked Shahin, and he gave me $800.00. I told him, "I owe you $800.00 now and will pay you later." But Shahin said, "No! You don't owe me anything. I give this to you because the Bible said that if your brother comes to you and needs something, give it to him and don't expect payment. So I am giving you this money and will forget about it. Just do to others the same thing." (Matthew 5:42)

So I told him, "Thank you so much, you are a blessing." And he answered and said, "You are a blessing too." Those few days, all I did was sing praises to God. I wept and felt so humbled in the presence of God and how he does these things in my life. I had learned that God is awesome, that he can produce something out of nothing. Again he reminded me that all things are possible for him. Glory!! I had paid the insurance and $300.00 for the car repair. I pray that there will be more Shahins in this world.

That we may be the children of your Father in Heaven: for he maketh his sun to rise on the evil and on the good, and sendeth rain on the just and on the unjust. (Matthew 5:45) The food poisoning had actually become a blessing to me. I had a healing miracle and a financial miracle at the same time. Glory to the living God we serve.

I may not have a million dollars in the bank, but I do have a heart of compassion, the agape love. If my friends need help, I always help them, pray for them, and go the extra mile for them without even asking them to pay me. In return, God had given back to me even more than I can do for others.

This is not my own strength, but God's love and spirit within me that does the works.

Great Blessings

April 27, 2011

It's been fifteen days, while Rebecca, the editor, is editing my book. I just signed with Expert Author Publishing for a five-year contract to sell my book. I have to give them another half payment for the remainder for the book. I need $1,100 for that book. I met a lady who really needs a cleaning for her three-story house, which is brand new. I accepted the offer even though it is very low pay for a big job like this ... but I am desperately needing to do some jobs for my book. So I decided to go and clean for myself for a few days, and on other days, I brought one or two people with me. It took me one week to finish the cleaning and I overestimated the cost ... I had worked long hours ... And I got sick after this ... So I went for a massage, and I was crying because every time that Mom Lordes touched me was so painful. So the following week, it was time to give the remaining $1,100 to the company. I only had $700. And it wasn't enough to cover he amount and I still owed $300 for my rent. So I texted Bernice and asked if she could give me the $100 dollars that she promised to give on top of the $2,000 she's been contributing to the book. She answered and said, "Only $100?" I said , "To be honest, there's $1,100 remaining. My friend who said he would help me couldn't do it because something happened to his business. He is not making enough money." So Bernice texted me again, and asked me to get it from Carol Ann, her sister. I was at the Staples to buy some office supplies, when she texted me this ... I couldn't help but cry in the corner of the Staples, because there I was trying to kill myself working, and I even got sick so I could get money to pay for the book.

And there I was; I felt like heaven was open to just pour me the blessings without even doing anything.

I felt so blessed. The book was finally paid for. What a blessing. Bernice and Stephen had paid for all of it. I contributed only $44 dollars. How would you like to write a book and someone would be financing it? There is really nothing impossible for God, is there?

Car from Heaven

May 2, 2011

I was visiting Lyn Valley Church again ... I love Pastor Owen's preaching and the young people's music.

Bernice and Stephen go to this Church and I visit once a month when we are not singing in the choir. I saw Bernice and Stephen this morning. I invited Mark to the Church and Victoria was with me.

After church Victoria and I went to a Chinese restaurant for lunch. While eating at the restaurant, Bernice called me and said, "Stephen and I are worried about you driving your car here and there, so we want to give you my mom and dad's car. What do you say?" I said, "You mean, you want to give me your mom and dad's car without me paying for it?" In my head I repeated what she said just to make sure I heard her correctly. And Bernice said yes ... I continued and said, "What can I say???" Bernice said, "Just say yes." I said YES. I was so happy to hear that I am going to have a new car.

June 18, 2011

I was ready to pick up the car, so I told Shahin to drive me to North Vancouver. But he couldn't make it because we miscommunicated. He then drove me at 1:30 to pick up the car after our lunch together.

I got home at 3:00 p.m. and was in the parking lot. I was listening to the PRAISE 106.5 music when the LORD spoke to me again through the song. I begin to cry and feel his presence and was speaking in heavenly languages. I am so grateful and so thankful in my spirit for this car. I am thankful to God and to Bernice and Stephen for blessing me. My car name is still Beulah, which means "the married one," and "the Lord delights in you." My car is a part of my everyday life and whether it be a Toyota Camry or a Mercedez Benz or BMW, my car will still be named Beulah. To God be the glory for the things he has done and for the things he is going to do. I know that God is going to do even greater things.

And that's how I got my car today. I have been driving this car for four days now. It was a Toyota Camry year 2000 and it was in the best condition. I told Robert about the car blessing and he couldn't believe it. He was more thrilled than I ever was, because he even Googled how much this car was worth and it is about $4,000 to $7,000. That's how much this blessing is worth. Well, I am more humble than what you think. I never expected a new car without paying for it.... I feel so blessed to have Bernice and Stephen in my life. My car, which is a 1991 Toyota Corolla, is still alive actually, except now it has an oil leak and the car shoes have problems and the muffler has a hole in it. It may cost $150 to fix the muffler. I drive it every day to North Van and West Vancouver. The back was opened, the gas tank cover is broken, and one door is broken. Rock used to joke with my friends when they had a ride with me saying, "Beulah wants to retire and already has arthritis," so everybody was laughing about it. I was content having this car for ten years without complaints. The insurance is due on June 22, 2011, and it needs an air car before you can insure again. It was five days before the car insurance finished and it was just the right timing for me to get rid of the car. I gave it as a gift to a friend of Robert's.

Truly, the God we are serving is amazing and full of surprises. This car was a huge surprise to me. I had spent $10,000 for the first car I ever bought, which is Beulah. After ten years, you have to pay for the insurance every year and maintenance and repairs. I guess if I saved all my money for that car, and invested it, maybe I would be a millionaire now.

God had given me this verse regarding my blessings.

For the LORD God is a sun and shield: the LORD will give grace and glory, no good thing will he with-hold from them that walk uprightly.
(Psalms 84:11)

The Power of PRAISE and WORSHIP

*O **sing** unto the Lord a **new song**: sing unto the LORD all the earth.*

*Sing unto the LORD, **bless his name; shew forth** his salvation from day to day. **Declare his glory** among the heathen, **his wonders** among all people.*

*Give unto the LORD glory due unto his name: bring an offering, and come into his courts. **O worship the LORD** in the beauty of his holiness: fear before him all the earth.*
(Psalm 96:1-9)

When we come into the throne of God, we acknowledge that he is our God and that he is our creator. He made the heaven, earth and everything you see and do not see. We come to him with a humble and contrite heart and we boldly approach his throne, because of the blood of Jesus that had shed on our behalf.

We come before him and sing a new song to him; blessing his name for he is great and greatly to be praised. We declared his wondrous works in our lives and sing of his great goodness, faithfulness, and loving kindness toward us. We give him the glory due his name. We are his children washed by the blood of the lamb. He created the Heaven and earth and on the seventh day he rested and made it holy. Sunday for us is a day of rest; we enter into the rest of God when we drop everything on Sunday and come before him. We come together to worship God on Saturday and Sunday. We sing and we listen to the preaching of the word of God which is our daily bread, the food of our soul. (Matthew 4:4)

When we sing to God, we are offering to him the fruits of our lips, and it goes up to him like an incense toward Heaven.

Honor and majesty belong to God and we find strength and beauty in his sanctuary. We come out strengthened, in our inner person. Because while we worship at his foot stool, he gives strength, healing comfort, and answers to our every need. We don't come out empty, but full in the presence of the almighty God.

I learned the power of praise when I was in Hong Kong. I would sing and give my testimonies every now and then. Whenever I had a need, and that need was not met immediately, I would take the cup of worship and praise God. A lot of times I would have my answers very quickly. I learned that at the heart of worship, God dwells in our midst and inhabits the praises of his people. Sometimes I don't even have to do anything when I have a need. He just gives it to me before I can ask him, or sometimes people will call me and ask if I needed this or that. God will even put into my heart who the people are that I can approach. And I don't have to beg, because God has already touched their hearts. Sometimes I don't even have to ask God for my needs. All I need to do is sing and worship at his feet and he takes care of the rest. Just like the story of Jehoshaphat. (2 Chronicles 20) They were afraid of their enemies. So they fasted first and approached the throne of God (verse 3). And the LORD hath promised in verse 17: Ye shall not need to fight in this battle: set yourselves, stand ye still, and see the salvation of the LORD with you. O Judah and Jerusalem: fear not, nor be dismayed; tomorrow go out against them; for the LORD will be with you.

Jehoshaphat appointed singers to praise the beauty of holiness and to praise the LORD. And when they began to sing and praise, the LORD set ambushes against the children of Ammon, Moab, and Mount Seir, and they were smitten. (2 Chronicles 20:21-22) All of their enemies died and none escaped. That's the power of worship and praise. Sometimes we don't have to do anything. Just PRAISE!!! And God will do the rest; that's a miracle of praise. If faith can move mountains, praise can move the hand of God. Because the God we are serving is a powerful God. He knows all things; he knows what's best for us; he knows what we need and when we need it. He is ever present, and he knows what's in our hearts and minds. So when you have a need, if faith doesn't do anything, try the power of praise. Close the door of your room, sing a song to God for an hour, and just praise and give thanks into his name.

Dreams Do Come True

In 2009, on the 23rd day of January, God had given me this verse in the Bible.

Is not this the fast that I have chosen? To loose the bands of wickedness, to undo the heavy burdens, and to let the oppressed go free, and that ye break every yoke? Is it not to deal thy bread to the hungry, and that thou bring the poor that are cast out to thy house? When thou seest the naked, that thou cover him, and that thou hide not thyself from thine own flesh?
(Isaiah 58:6-7)

And from this verse God had spoken to me in the form of a DREAM and a vision. This vision is going to be a charity for the missionaries, for the poor and the needy. It will be called Charis Now Foundation ("Charis" means GRACE), so that I will always remember the grace of God in my life. Charis Now Foundation's mission is to provide financial assistance for the missionaries; it will provide food, shelter, and clothing for the poor and the needy.

In November 2009, I applied for a Charity Corporation Society for this dream. It took ten business days to get the Charity Certificate of Corporation. I was so blown away by how quickly I was able to get it and rejoiced with the Lord for that. The next step would be to obtain the Business License for the charity so that we could issue an official receipt for tax purposes. Ray, one of the directors I chose, suggested that we don't do any charitable work outside of Canada because it may take too much time and too much work. We also needed a lawyer to write the agreement between the charity and the church. But I insisted on doing it even though it might have cost me time and money, because that was the dream God gave me.

Bernice had referred a lawyer, but he charged $1,500 for reviewing the charity application for CRA and for writing the agreement letter. I know God is able to provide but this was in a different way. I met another lawyer in April and I told him that I needed his services. Stephen Miller, the lawyer, was kind enough to offer an hour and a half free for his services and I met him in May 2011. He suggested that I make an agreement by myself by giving me a copy of a contractor agreement (Real Estate), and he would give me more time to look at it.

I made one agreement from another sample I found on the internet, according to what the Charity needs. I went to see the lawyer again and he told me that I did a great job. He just made a few amendments.

I submitted the application on July 11, 2011, and it was received by July 13th. It took one month to process the Charity License. I finally got the Business License for Charity on August 15, 2011. I can't explain how happy and grateful I am for what the Lord is doing in my life. Indeed, he is still the God for whom NOTHING is IMPOSSIBLE. All Glory to the living God we serve. Holy, awesome, and great is he!

Donate today and call Charis Now Foundation at **604 719-4187**.

When you dream, go for it: Dream BIG, not small. How many ripples are your dream? Take action to pursue it. Then you can have it. Knowing that God is with you. He will help you through. Know that your dreams really do come true.

By Rebecca Daluddung - August 16, 2011

Chapter Eighteen
Jesus is Coming Again

*And then shall appear the sign of the Son of man in Heaven: and then shall all the tribes of the earth mourn, and they shall **see the Son of man coming** in the clouds of Heaven with **power** and **great glory**.*

*And he shall send his angels with a great sound of trumpet, and they shall **gather together his elect**, from the four winds, from one end of Heaven to the other.*
(Matthew 24:30-31)

*For the **Son of man shall come** in the glory of his Father with his angels; and then **he shall reward every man according to his works**.*
(Matthew 16:27)

Parable of the Ten Virgins

*Then shall the kingdom of Heaven be likened unto ten virgins, which took their lamps, and **took no oil** with them: But the **wise took oil** in their vessels with their lamps. While the bridegroom tarried, they all slumbered and slept. And at **midnight there was a cry made, Behold, the bridegroom cometh; go ye out to meet him**. Then all the virgins arose, and trimmed their lamps. And the foolish said unto the wise, Give us of your oil; for our lamps are gone out. But the wise answered, saying Not so; lest there be not enough for us and you: but go ye rather to them that sell, and buy for yourselves.*

259

*And **while they went to buy, the bridegroom came**; and
they that were **ready went with him to the marriage**: and
the **door was shut**. After came also the other virgins, saying,
Lord, Lord, open to us. But he answered and said, **Verily I say
unto you, I know you not.***

*Watch therefore, for ye know neither the day nor the hour
wherein the Son of man cometh.
(Matthew 25:1-13)*

We are now at the age of waiting for our bridegroom, Jesus
Christ.

This is actually the highlight of our ministry, the end of all
times, but it is also the birth of a new life that will never end.
We are called for this purpose, to be with the Lord Jesus;
where he is, there we will be also.

The parable of the ten virgins is a shadow of things to come,
for the Kingdom of Heaven or Kingdom of God. Jesus will
come and return, because he is our bridegroom. And all the
children of God will be the bride. The marriage supper is
when we will all drink with him at the supper table. "But I say
unto you, I will not drink henceforth of this fruit of the vine,
until that day when I drink it new with you in my Fathers
kingdom". (Matthew 26:29)

FIVE WISE VIRGINS	FIVE FOOLISH VIRGINS
Repent of Their Sins	No Repentance
Accept Jesus as Lord and Savior	Accept Jesus as Lord and Savior
Receive the Baptism of Water	Baptism of Water
Receive the Baptism of Holy Ghost	No Baptism of Holy Ghost
Live a Holy Life - Word of God	Live According to the World

260

The parable of the ten virgins is happening right here in front of our very eyes and is a shadow of what is going to happen when Jesus comes. The five were foolish and the other five were wise. The five wise virgins were the people who have really been born again in the spirit and live a life in complete obedience to the will of God, never compromising in that respect. The five foolish virgins have been born again but they deny the power of the Holy Spirit; they still live a disobedient life, and compromise to the likeness of this world. The wise virgins were loyal, faithful, knowing, understanding, and obedient to the will of God. And when Jesus comes, they are ready to meet him. The oil represents the Holy Spirit that lives in every believer's heart. So long as you are an obedient child of God, the Holy Spirit dwells in you. But if you defile the temple of the Holy Ghost that is your body, then he has to leave, because he is holy.

I met a brother from Calgary in a business meeting I attended. I went to meet him at Starbucks. While he finished presenting his business idea, I gave him a magazine Bible as a gift for his birthday. He then told me that he is also a born-again Christian and he always carries and reads his Bible. And he added, "You know, I am going to work seven years and then I will retire and do whatever I want to do." I told him, "You know, I was also like that before, but over the years, I learned something. For example: Jesus is coming back three years from now, and your plan is seven years. Yes, you have money, but when you stand before God one day he will ask you, 'What have you done for my kingdom?' You may have money but what have you done for the kingdom of God? That means we have to live a holy life to God. We continue to do our work and also work for God's kingdom here on earth. We live as if it is today—Jesus is coming today. In that case, we have to give our best for today."

And he was speechless somehow after that. For I know that he learned something from me. And the good news is I learned something from him too.

I told him that I go to this Starbucks every morning and get a chai latte. He asked me, "You mean you never give it up?" I said yes, and he continued and said, "They said that you have to give up something that you love before Easter, just like Jesus had to fast for forty days." I said, "Oh really? Well Easter is already finished. But starting tomorrow, I will have my forty-day fast for my chai latte." And to make the story short, I was able to complete the fast for forty days. I didn't crave the chai for that forty days. Glory to Jesus! Since then, I HAVE TO FAST FOR FORTY DAYS FOR CHAI LATTE EVERY YEAR.

We all can learn from each other. There is something you know that I never knew, and there is something I know that you also never knew or heard before. God even taught me that I can learn from a child.

Back to the parables again, notice in verse 6, there was a cry made, **behold the bridegroom cometh, go ye out to meet him.**

So the wise virgins were ready and went with him, to the marriage: and the door was shut. Verse 10

Only those wise children of God who are filled with the Holy Spirit will be able to come in, because they are ready and they have been waiting for him. But the foolish virgins will not be able to get in, although they are invited because the Lord said, "Verily I say unto you, I know you not."

Not every one that saith unto me Lord, Lord, shall enter into the kingdom of Heaven; but he that doeth the will of my Father [God] which is in Heaven.

Many will say to me in that day [Judgment day], Lord, Lord have we not prophesied in thy name? and in thy name have cast out devils? And in thy name dome many wonderful works?

And then will I profess unto them, I never knew you: depart from me, ye that work iniquity. (Matthew 7:21-22)

The Judgment Day is the day of the LORD. It's the end of all things, but also the new beginning of a life everlasting. It's when Jesus comes back and takes his bride as his own—to punish the unjust and receiving of rewards of the child of God. It's also the eternal separation between the child of God and the child of the devil. It is like the last hearing in court, that you will be declared guilty or not guilty. Because on this judgment day, there will be no more mercy or grace. On the final day of the judgment, there will be no lawyers who will plead your case. You will be standing alone. In Heaven there are two sets of books: the books of works and the books of life. If your name is not written in the Book of Life, you will be cast into the lake of fire.

How will we know that we can enter into the Kingdom of God, or Kingdom of Heaven?

Jesus talks about it in John 3:3, That except a man be born again, he cannot see the kingdom of God.

In order for you to see the Kingdom of God, the requirement is you have to be born again. How can you be born again? What Jesus was trying to explain to Nicodemus is that one must be born again. When Adam and Eve committed sin at the Garden of Eden, we died spiritually. We fell from the grace of God through their sinful acts. We had inherited that sin even from birth. Therefore, we died spiritually; we lost our connection to God. It is much like not paying your electricity bill and having your power cut off.

How can we be re-born or be born again when we are already old and gray? How can one enter into her mother's womb and be born? That's exactly what Nicodemus was curious about when he asked Jesus. And Jesus answered and said to him:

John 3:5 - That except a man **be born of water** and of **the Spirit**, he **cannot enter into the kingdom of God**.

Second Requirements In Order to Enter Into the Kingdom of God

We must be born again in **water and of the Spirit**. Water baptism is your public confession in your faith. Born again in Spirit means your old spirit must be born again. The sinful old spirit, which is the disobedient spirit, must be born again into a spirit of obedience.

And it shall come to pass afterward, that I will pour out my spirit upon all flesh; and your sons and your daughter shall prophesy, your old men shall dream dreams, your young men shall see visions: And also upon the servants and upon the handmaids in those days will I pour out my spirit.
(Joel 2:28-29)

You must have a new heart and a new spirit that comes from God. When you repent and accept Jesus as your Lord and Savior then you become a child of God. You receive the Holy Spirit that comes from God so you become born again in Spirit, through the incorruptible word of God.

A lot of people have seen the Kingdom of God. They know the Bible—they even memorize it from Genesis to Revelation. They know God and know God's word, but they only see it from a distance. They can't enter into it, because they don't live what they know. It's not about how much you know. It's about how little you know about God's word and how you obey it. The key word is obedience. The real born-again child of God is the one who knows the word of God and obeys God's words. It is he who will be the one who can enter into the Kingdom of God.

That's why Jesus said, not everyone who will call on the name of the Lord ... Many people are calling upon God but they are still living in sin; they can't leave their sin behind. That's why God will tell them, "I never knew you, ye that doeth iniquity." Even if you had the gift of prophesy, it doesn't qualify you to go to Heaven. You must repent and do the will of God. The only thing that will see us through the judgment day is not who we are or what we did, but what Jesus did for us. (See Jesus Is Life)

Jesus said:

> *Therefore whosoever heareth these sayings of mine, and doeth them, I will liken him unto a wise man, which build upon the rock:*
>
> *And the rain descended, and the floods came, and the winds blew, and beat upon that house; and it fell not: for it was founded upon the rock.*
>
> *And every one that heareth these saying of mine, and doeth them not, shall be likened unto a foolish man, which build his house upon the sand: And the rain descended, and the floods came, and the wind blew, and beat upon that house, and it fell: and great was the fall of it.*
> *(Matthew 7:24-27)*

This is like the parable of the wise virgins. The wise virgin builds her house upon the rock, which is Jesus Christ. The sure foundation is obedience to the will of God. The wise virgin is the wise builder. Even if persecution, trial, temptation, financial crisis, nakedness, homelessness, or sickness comes, not even angels can separate her from God. She is determined and persistent, knowing the day is coming that her LORD (Groom) will arrive, and she will be accountable for every action and decision she has made. She knows the will of God and obeys it. She was a testimony in life, in word, and in deed. The foolish virgin was the opposite; she heard the word of God and knew it, but never obeyed it. She kept procrastinating until the judgment day, so she ran out of oil.

She wanted to be part of the wedding day, but the door was shut; the groom said, "I never knew you." How would you react in the first place? The bridegroom doesn't know you at all. The Bible says,

Not everyone that saith unto me Lord, Lord, shall enter into the kingdom of Heaven; but he that doeth the will of my Father which is in Heaven.
(Matthew 7:21)

The five foolish virgins thought that they could go to the banqueting table, but they can't. Jesus Christ is the bridegroom, and we are the bride of Christ. The five foolish virgins were hearers of the word only and not doers. When trials, persecutions, and temptations came, the foundation she lays, it fell, and great was the fall of it, because she wasn't a doer of the word of God. How would we know?

Jesus said:

A good tree cannot bring forth evil fruit, neither can a corrupt tree bring forth good fruit. Wherefore by their fruits ye shall know them.
(Matthew 7:18, 20)

The Eternal Separation

When the Son of man [Jesus Christ] shall come in his glory, and all the holy angels with him, then shall he sit upon the throne of his glory: and before him shall be gathered all nations: and he shall separate them one from another, as a shepherd divideth his sheep from the goats: And he shall set the sheep on his right hand, but the goats on the left. Then shall the King say unto them on his right hand, Come, ye, blessed of my Father, inherit the kingdom prepared for you from the foundation of the world.

For I was hungered, and ye gave me meat:

I was thirsty, and ye gave me drink:

I was stranger, and ye took me in:

Naked, and ye clothed me:

I was sick, and ye visited me:

I was in prison, and ye came unto me.

Then shall the righteous answer him, saying, Lord, when saw we thee an hungered, and fed thee? Or thirsty, and gave thee drink? When saw we thee stranger, and took thee in? Or naked, and clothed thee? Or when saw we thee sick, or in prison, and came to thee? And the King shall answer and say unto them, Verily I say unto you, Inasmuch as ye have done it unto one of the least of these my brethren, ye have done it unto me.
(Matthew 25:31-40)

Then shall he say unto them on the left hand, Depart from me, ye that accursed, into everlasting fire, prepared for the devil and his angels:

For I was hungered, and ye gave me no meat:

I was thirsty, and ye gave me no drink:

I was stranger, and ye took me not in:

Naked, and ye clothed me not:

I was sick, and in prison ye visited me not:

And these shall go into everlasting punishment: but the righteous into life eternal.
(Matthew 25:34-46)

This is the eternal separation between the child of God and the child of the devil. This is the harvest time where the angels will gather the children of God. This is the worst thing that can happen to a believer, to be separated from God forever. Do you want to be with God forever in Heaven? Or do you want to be with Satan and his angels in the eternal lake of fire? The choice is yours. As for me and my house we will serve the LORD. This is when I want to hear God saying to me: Well done, thou good and faithful servant: thou hast been faithful over a few things, I will make thee ruler over many things: enter thou into the joy of thy Lord. (Matthew 25:21)

Who then is a faithful and wise servant, whom his lord hath made ruler over his household, to give them meat in due season?

Blessed is the servant, whom his lord when he cometh shall find so doing. Verily I say unto you, that he shall make him rule over all his goods.
(Matthew 24: 45-47)

Jesus Will Come As a Judge

And it is appointed unto men once to die, but after this the judgment.

So Christ was once offered to bear the sins of many: and unto them that look for him shall he appear the second time without sin unto salvation.
(Hebrews 9:27&28)

And I saw Heaven opened, and behold a white horse, and he that sat upon him was called Faithful and True, and in righteousness he doth judge and make war. And he was clothed with vesture dipped in blood: and his name is called The Word of God.

And out of his mouth goeth a sharp sword, that with it he should smite the nations: and he shall rule them with a rod of iron: and he treadeth the winepress of the fierceness and wrath of Almighty God.

And hath on his vesture and on his thigh a name written, KING OF KINGS, AND LORD OF LORDS.
(Revelation 19:11,13,15,16)

Jesus Will Come As a Judge and Will Also Be Called the Lamb of God

These shall make war with the Lamb, and the Lamb shall over come them: for he is Lord of lords and king of kings: and they that are with him are called, and chosen and faithful.
(Revelation 17:14)

Jesus Christ is the king of Kings and the Lord of Lords. He has given a name that is above every name and that every tongues shall confess that Jesus is Lord for the glory of God the Father.
(Philippians 2:9-12)

Thou shalt suck the milk of the Gentiles, and shall suck the breast of kings:

and thou shalt know that I the Lord am thy Savior and thy Redeemer, the mighty One of Jacob.
(Isaiah 60:17)

And I saw thrones, and they sat upon them, and judgment was give unto them: and I saw the souls of them that were beheaded for the witness of Jesus, and for the word of God, and which hath not worshipped the beast neither his image, neither hath received his marked upon their foreheads, or in their hands; and they lived and reigned with Christ a thousand years.
(Revelation 20:4)

I Jesus have sent mine angel to testify unto you these things in the churches. I am the root and the offspring of David, and the bight and morning star.

And the Spirit and the bride say Come. And let him that heareth say Come. And let him that athirst come. And whosoever will, let him take the water of life freely.
(Revelation 22:16-17)

The Everlasting Punishment

Therefore will I number you to the sword, and ye shall all bow down to the slaughter: because when I called, ye did not answer; when I speak, ye didn't hear; but did evil before mine eyes, and did choose that which I delighted not.
(Isaiah 65: 12)

And they shall go forth, and looked upon the carcasses of the men that have transgressed against me: for their worm shall not die, neither shall their fire be quenched; and they shall be an abhorring unto all flesh.
(Isaiah 66:24)

The enemy that sowed them is the devil; the harvest is the end of the world; and the reapers are the angels.

As therefore the tares are gathered and burned in the fire; so shall it be in the end of this world.

The Son of man shall send forth his angels, and they shall gather out of his kingdom all things that offend, and them which do iniquity;

And shall cast them into a furnace of fire: there shall be wailing and gnashing of teeth.
(Matthew 13:39-42)

This is what is going to happen with those people who didn't believe in God. They will be cast into a furnace of fire,

270

where there is wailing and gnashing of teeth—the eternal condemnation.

Our God is the God of mercy and grace. He is the God of Abraham, Isaac, and Jacob, who spoke to them and called them to serve him. He also has spoken through the prophets in the Old Testament. In the New Testament God has spoken to us through his Son Jesus Christ and the disciples of Jesus. And this is through the holy word the Bible.

God is still calling each individual today to repent of their sins. He does this through the pastors in churches today, and he is also calling us through our friends that have come to know the Lord Jesus Christ. God loves you so much and he wants you to come to know him. Accept his invitation, not just to serve him but also to receive his perfect plan of eternal salvation for your soul.

If you have a friend that is really a born-again Christian and keeps asking you to come to church with them, he or she is not the one who is calling you to come to church. Your friend is only an instrument for God to call you.

One day, you can't reason out to God, because if you didn't answer his calling or hear him when he spoke, you have no one to blame but yourself alone.

From the Bible, the pastors, your friends, the radio stations like PRAISE 106.5, and some televisions and internet programs—God's word is still calling every individual because he doesn't want anyone to perish.

I will also choose their delusions, and will bring their fears upon them, because when I called, none did answer, when I speak, they did not hear: but they did evil before mine eyes, and choose that in which I delighted not.
(Isaiah 66:4)

The Reward of Satan - Wicked (Hell)
Hell - Worm and Fire Will Not Die Nor Be Quenched

And they shall go forth, and look upon the carcasses of the
men that have transgressed against me: for their worm shall
not die, neither shall their fire be quenched; and they shall be
an abhorring unto all flesh.
(Isaiah 66:24)

In order to understand hell, let me first talk about Satan. Lucifer (Satan) is the anointed cherub.

Thou sealest the sum, full of wisdom, and perfect in beauty;
Thou hast been in Eden the garden of God; Thou art anointed
cherub that covereth: and I have set thee so thou wast upon
the holy mountain of God; thou hast walked up and down in
the midst of the stones of fire. Thou was perfect in thy ways
from the day that thou was created, till iniquity was found in
thee. By the multitude of thy merchandise they have filled the
midst of thee with violence, and thou hast sinned: therefore
I will cast thee as profane out of the mountain of God: and
I will destroy thee, o covering cherub, from the midst of
the stone of fire Thine **heart was lifted up** *because of thy*
beauty, **thou has corrupted thy wisdom** *by reason of thy*
brightness: I will cast thee to the ground, I will lay thee before
kings, that they may behold thee.
(Ezekiel 28:12-17)

Lucifer was perfect in beauty and full of wisdom, but he corrupted the wisdom that God gave him. He was so full of pride and beauty that his heart became evil and he wanted to be god himself, rather than bowing to God who created him. God didn't create hell for human beings. He had created hell for Lucifer the fallen angel and for those who serve and follow Satan.

*And the **devil that deceived them was cast into the lake of fire and brimstone, where the beast and the false prophet are, and shall be tormented day and night forever and ever**.*
(Revelation 20:10)

The devil, who is Lucifer, the father of all lies, first deceived Adam and Eve, and is still deceiving other people today and sending his false prophets or false pastors. These false prophets and pastors will all have their own destination, which is hell or the lake of fire. You must understand that hell is created only for Satan and those who choose to follow Satan and do his evil ways.

The Reward of Backsliding

For if we sin willfully after that we have received the knowledge of the truth, there remaineth no more sacrifice for sins, But a certain fearful looking for of judgment and fiery indignation, which shall devour the adversaries. He that despised Moses' law died without mercy under two or three witnesses: Of how much more punishment, suppose ye, shall he be thought worthy, who hath trodden under foot the Son of God, and hath counted the blood of the covenant, wherewith he was sanctified, an unholy thing, and hath done despite unto the Spirit of grace? For we know him that hath said, Vengeance belongeth unto me, I will recompense, saith the Lord. And again, The LORD shall judge his people.

It is a fearful thing to fall into the hands of the living God.
(Hebrew 10:26-31)

The Reward of the Fearful and Unbelieving and the Evil Doers

But the fearful, and unbelieving, the abominable, and murderers, and whoremongers, and sorcerers, and idolaters,

*and all liars, shall have **their part in the lake which burneth with fire and brimstone: which is the second death** [Hell].*
(Revelation 21:8)

Warning Against False Prophets, False Doctrine

For many deceivers are entered into the world, who confess not that Jesus Christ is come in the flesh. This is a deceiver and an antichrist.

Whoever transgresseth, and abideth not in the doctrine of Christ, hath not God. He that abideth in the doctrine of Christ, he hath both the Father and the Son.

If there come any unto you, and bring not this doctrine, receive him not into your house, nether bid him God speed:

For he that biddeth him God speed is partaker of his evil deeds.
(2 John 7:9-11)

Warning Against False Prophets - They Do Miracles and Wonders

For there shall arise false Christ, false prophets and shall show great signs and wonders; insomuch that, if it were possible, they shall deceive the very elect.
(Matthew 24:24)

Warning Against the Anti Christ and the Mark of the Beast

I have not written unto you because ye know not the truth, but because ye know it, and that no lie is of the truth.

Who is a liar but he that denieth that Jesus is the Christ? He is antichrist, that denieth the Father [God] and the Son. [Jesus Christ].
(1 John 2:21-22)

Whole Duty of Man

Let us hear the conclusion of the whole matter: Fear God, and keep his commandments: for this is the whole duty of a man.
(Ecclesiastes 12:13)

The fear of the LORD is the beginning of wisdom: but fools despise wisdom and instruction.
(Proverbs 1:7)

For the LORD giveth wisdom: out of his mouth cometh knowledge and understanding.
(Proverbs 2:6)

Get wisdom, get understanding; forget it not; neither decline from the words of my mouth. Forsake her not, and she shall preserve thee: love her, and she shall keep thee.

Wisdom is the principal thing; therefore get wisdom; and with all thy getting get understanding.

Exalt her, and she shall promote thee: she shall bring thee to honour, when thou dost embrace her, She shall give to thine head an ornament of grace: a crown of glory shall she deliver to thee.
(Proverbs 3:5-9)

Why Choose Wisdom?

Receive my instruction and not silver, and knowledge rather than choice gold. For wisdom is better than rubies; and all the things that may be desired are not to be compared to it. I wisdom dwell with prudence, and find out knowledge of witty inventions.

The fear of the Lord is to hate evil, pride, and arrogancy, and the evil way, and the forward mouth, do I hate. Counsel is mine, and sound wisdom: I am understanding; I have strength. By me king reign, and nobles decree justice. By me princes rule, and nobles, even all the judges of the earth. I love them that love me, and those that seek me early shall find me.

Riches and honour are with me; yea durable riches and righteousness. My fruit are better than gold; yea than fine gold; and my revenues than choice silver. I lead in the way of righteousness, in the midst of the paths of judgment: That I may cause those that love me to inherit substance; and I will fill their treasures.
(Proverbs 8:10-20)

For the wisdom of this world is foolishness with God: for it is written, He taketh the wise in their own craftiness
(1 Corinthians 3:19)

Why Do We Need to Fear God?

*And fear not them which kill the body, but are not able to kill the soul, but **rather fear him (God) which is able to destroy both soul and body in hell.***
(Matthew 10:28; Luke 12:4-5)

And he said unto them, Take heed, and beware of the covetousness: for a man's life consisteth not in the abundance of the things which he possesseth.

And he spake a parable unto them, saying, The ground of a certain rich man brought forth plentifully: And he thought within himself, saying, What shall I do, because I have no room where to bestow my fruits?

And he said, This will I do: I will pull down my barns, and build greater; and there will I bestow all my fruits and my goods.

And I will say to my soul, Soul, thou hast much goods laid up for many years; take thine ease, eat drink, and be merry.

But God said unto him Thou fool, this night thy soul shall be required of thee: then whose shall those things be, which thou hast provided?

So is he that layeth up treasure for himself, and is not rich toward God.
(Luke 12:15-21)

Fear - Reverential fear means fear of God, as a controlling motive of the life, in matters spiritual and moral, not a mere "fear" of his power and righteousness retribution, but a wholesome dread of displeasing him. (*Vines Complete Expository Dictionary*, pp230)

The story of the rich man is very dreadful in the end. He had enjoyed life with financial and material abundance, but he was poor in riches of God.

The rich man forgets that he has a Creator, that God created him, and that God gave him a soul—not just a body. He forgets that if God took away that life, which is his very soul, he can no longer enjoy life, both here on earth and in the life to come. He invested his whole life by getting so much wealth, and he forgot that God is also just and holy. The accumulation of wealth without God is evil, and there's an eternal consequence that Jesus talks about in verse 21. That whoever stored wealth without God is vanity of vanities and eternal damnation.

I have seen the wicked in great power, and spreading himself like a green bay tree. Yet he passed away, and lo, he was not; I sought him but he couldn't be found. Mark the perfect man, and behold the upright: for the end of that man is peace. (Psalms 37:35-36) Riches in this earth but poor toward God.

TOTAL COMMITMENT COVENANT

I the LORD have called thee in righteousness and will hold

thing hand and will keep thee and give thee a covenant of the people, for a light to the Gentiles.
(Isaiah 42:6)

Heavenly Father, I hereby am on obedience to your call to serve you with all my heart, mind, and soul, to fulfill my covenant with you as I have promised you since then.

I ask you then to make my life holy and acceptable to you. Use me mightily and be a light to the Gentiles and to everyone.

I now commit myself unto thee, with all my heart, with all my mind, and with all my soul, to love and serve you all the days of my life, until you come. Sealed with your mighty and most precious name JESUS CHRIST, amen.

Yours truly,

Rebecca Daluddung

November 12, 1996

When I look back on what the Lord hath done in my life, there are too many blessings to write of. God is so faithful to me. I had made a total commitment to God—to follow, love, and serve him all the days of my life. So when uncertainty comes my way, I don't have to worry about it. The God that I am serving is able to deliver me, even in my sinful acts. He is able to lift me up, heal me, rescue me, build me up, and equip me for his glory.

So if you have not make a commitment to God as of today, make one, sign it, and date it. I made a commitment to follow the Lord for whatever it cost me to follow him, even if I have to eat grass. That's my commitment. I thank God I didn't eat grass the time I passed through the fire of testing and trials.

My friend, make a commitment today.

TOTAL COMMITMENT

DATE: _____

Dear God,

I come before your throne today. Please forgive me for all the sins that I have committed unto you. Wash me from all unrighteousness and cover me with the precious blood of your Son Jesus Christ who died for my sins.

I now commit my life today, at this very moment, to follow and obey you all the days of my life. Help me to live a life that is pleasing unto you and prepare me for the second coming of my Lord and Savior Jesus.

This I ask in Jesus's mighty name, amen.

Yours Forever,

_____

(Sign Your Name)

Beauty and the Beast

The story of "Beauty and the Beast," which is widely known, is only a tale, but it has a very remarkable meaning for me.

The beast loved the beauty, but the beauty didn't like the beast because he was too ugly. But on the other hand, the beast was gentle and patient. He kept asking the beauty, "Will you marry me?" The beast planned to ask her over and over until she said yes. The beauty missed her family, and although he did not want to let her go, the beast loved her so much that he gave her a mirror to see him with, a horse to ride on, a key to his home and treasures, and gloves to make her invisible. While she was away, she unexpectedly missed the beast. Through the mirror, she could see that he was dying from missing her so much. She realized that he loved her, and that she loved him.

The story of the "Beauty and the Beast" has a lot to offer for me, if I put it this way: The beauty is me, and the Lord is the beast. The Lord Jesus gave me:

1. **Mirror – represent the word of God (Bible)**

2. **Horse – represents our Faith**

3. **Key – represents our Repentance**

4. **Gloves – represents the Holy Spirit**

The Lord Jesus is so holy, righteous, and without sin. He loved me while I was a sinner. He saved my life and said, "I love you my daughter, I will die for you, and I will take your place." Jesus saves me from my sin and from the power of hell. God has given me the mirror, which is the word of God, to know the truth that sets me free, to learn of his love for me, and to know all the answers in this life I'm living. It was given to me so that I may know God's way, knowledge, wisdom, and standard of righteousness, and walk according to them.

So that I shall not fall into the trap of this world—the vanities of life—God has given me Faith, to believe unceasingly and wholeheartedly in every word he said is true. I believe all of his words pertaining to this life here on earth and the life to come. Faith is the love of God and the hope of the second coming of our Lord and Savior Jesus Christ. Faith makes me believe in the judgment day and the receiving of rewards. I believe that the word of God stands forever and that what God said he will do will come to pass. I have Faith that I can move mountains, and that I can ride in the highs and lows of the uncertain roads I am traveling in life. I have Faith that I will be able to stand in the trials and temptations and whatever happens in my life.

The key is my Repentance. By turning away from wickedness to holiness and by turning away from my sin and doing his own will, I glorify the name of God. I choose to leave the darkness and live in a perfect shining light of Jesus Christ as an example in my life.

And most of all I have the gloves, which are the Holy Spirit that is within me as a seal that I am his daughter. They are a sign that I will live a life that is pleasing to him, to have the fruits of love, joy, peace, patience, and suffering with him. The Holy Spirit is the power that makes me obey God's will, and it makes me live in holiness and purity for his glory alone. It separates me from the world, but also helps me.

In my life, I have been the Beauty, which the world will attribute to sinful acts (fornication). Because I inherited these sinful acts through Adam, I deserve to die, because the wages of sin is death. But God so loved me that he sent Jesus Christ (Beast) to save me from my sin. He was no Beauty—he suffered because of me just like Isaiah said:

He was oppressed, and he was afflicted, yet he opened not his mouth: he is brought as a lamb to the slaughter, and as sheep before her shearers is dumb, so he openeth not his mouth. He was taken from prison and from judgment: who shall declare his generations? For he was cut off out of the land of the living: for the transgression of my people was he stricken. And he made his grave with the wicked, and with the rich in his death; because he had done no violence, neither was any deceit in his mouth. Yet it pleased the LORD to bruise him; he hath put him to grief: when thou shalt make his soul an offering for sin, he shall see his seed, he shall prolong his days, and the pleasure of the LORD shall prosper in his hand. He shall see of the travail of his soul, and shall be satisfied: by his knowledge shall my righteous servant justify many; for he shall bear their iniquities.
(Isaiah 53: 7-11)

This is the Beauty of the Lord Jesus. You can have this too. When you are caught up in the vanities of this world, remember the mirror (Word of God), the horse (Faith), the key (Repentance), and the gloves (Holy Spirit). They are available for you any time.

The Invitation for the Marriage

And behold, I come quickly; and my reward is with me, to give every man according as his work shall be. I am the Alpha and Omega, the beginning and the end, the first and the last,

I Jesus have sent mine angel to testify unto you these things in the churches. I am the root and the offspring of David, and the bright and morning star.

And the Spirit and bride say Come. And let him that heareth say, Come. And let him that is athirst come. And whosoever will, let him take the water of life freely.
(Revelation 22:12-13,16-17.)

282

While we are still living here on earth, we have the chance to undo our ways. We have all the time to repent and come before God. Now is the time to repent—not tomorrow, not next week, not next year. Today is the day of salvation, tomorrow would be too late. If you hear the word of God today, if you are reading this book today, today is the day of your salvation. Return to God so that you can also have a part in the marriage supper of the Lamb.

Let us be glad and rejoice, and give honour to him, for the marriage of the Lamb is come, and his wife hath made herself ready. And to her was granted that she should be arrayed in fine linen, clean and white: for the fine linen is the righteousness of saints. And he saith unto me, Write, Blessed are they which are called unto the marriage supper of the Lamb. And he saith unto me, These are the true sayings of God.
(Revelation 19:7-9)

If you hear God calling you to come, don't delay. Pray this prayer with me.

Heavenly Father, I come before you today. I believe in your words, that you sent Jesus Christ to die for my sins. I acknowledge that I need salvation and that only Jesus is the way that you had provided. I ask you to forgive all my sins. And cleanse me from all unrighteousness. I invite you to come into my heart and be my Lord and Savior. This I ask in Jesus's mighty name, amen.

Watch and Pray - Jesus Is Coming Soon

Take ye heed, watch and pray: for ye know not when the time is.

Watch ye therefore: for ye know not when the master of the house cometh, at even, or at midnight, or at the cockcrowing, or in the morning.

Lest coming suddenly he find you sleeping.

And what I say unto you I say unto all, Watch.
(Matthew 13:33,35-37)

How do we watch? We must watch for the days that are evil. We have to make sure that our garments are always white, meaning that we don't participate in the works of the flesh or a sinful nature. We have to obey God's word and not compromise to the likeness of this world. We have to be filled with the Holy Spirit and pray always. We have to keep our lights burning, and always be a shining light.

Share the Love of God "The Great Commission"

Go through, go through the gates; prepare ye the way of the
people; cast up, cast up the highway; gather out the stones;
lift up a standard for the people. And they shall call them,
a holy people, the redeemed of the LORD; and thou shall be
called, sought out, a city not forsaken.
(Isaiah 62: 10,12)

And he said unto them, Go ye into all the world, and preach
the gospel to every creature.
(Mark 16:16)

Are you a follower of Christ? If the answer is YES! I have good news for you. You have a mission to obey. We are given this command to go and make disciples to all nations, to teach them what God had commanded them. You and I have a great MISSION to accomplish. To share God's love for mankind, so that people you know—your loved ones, friends, neighbors, and the people around you—will come to know the Lord Jesus as their Lord and Savior.

This is the reason why this book is written. You and I are witnesses that there is a loving God who is mighty to save. And your life and the evidence in your life show that God is in you and still working in you.

If you can't write, then tell your testimony and give a book to someone else. I want you to share this book with people. If you have received one copy of this book for free, I would urge you to give one free copy to another friend in return.

On New Year's Day in 2008, I was with my friends Ruby and Aleta. We went to Vandussen Park to see the Christmas lights.

While I was at the park I was adoring all the different kinds of lights in color. God had spoken to my heart, "If only each of the tiny lights out here is a child of God, it would be trillions of lights shining in the dark." And it was really true; we can be a shining light to shine on others who are in darkness. We can either turn on these lights or turn off the lights. We can do this not only in times of darkness, but also in the day, to show God's love in your life.

Be a shining light like the stars above, so that people look up to you and say that God is really in you.

Ye are the light of the world. A city that is not set on a hill cannot be hid. Neither do men light a candle and put it under a bushel, but on a candle stick; and it giveth light unto all that are in the house.

Let your light so shine before men, that they may see your good works, and glorify your Father which is in Heaven. (Matthew 5:14-16)

Your life is a testimony, a witness to the people around you. As born-again Christians, we are a living letter, read by everybody. The way we live our lives now is the way you live a legacy of your life.

I want to live this legacy for my children, these REAL RICHES, which are the salvation of my soul that will last forever and ever. Where no thief can take it away from me. They may take my money, my car, and my house, but they can't take away the salvation of my soul. It is the riches where it doesn't go rotten, like the things you see with your eyes—like houses, cars, etc. It is seal forever by the blood of Jesus. I want to live this legacy of Love, Faith, and Hope. I want to share it with you, this legacy, and most of all the real riches that you can have forever. You cannot buy these real riches in the market or in the shopping mall. They are the real riches that only God can give you, if you are willing to receive them, keep them, and treasure them. It is priceless, yet it is a free gift. No treasure on earth can ever be likened to it. So when God gives it to you, keep it and treasure it and use it for the glory of God.

You Are Chosen Generations of Royal Priesthood

But ye are a chosen generation, a royal priesthood, an holy nation, a peculiar people; that ye should show forth the praises of him who called you out of darkness into his marvelous light.
(1 Peter 2:9)

I will GO

Go through the gates of Heaven;

Prepare ye the way of the people;

Share the love of God to every man.

Preach repentance and salvation of souls through every nation.

Cast up! Cast up, the net of salvation;

Go into the highways and byways and valleys and to the mountains.

Gather all the children of God, the chosen people.

And lift up a standard for the people.

That we might be called;

A chosen people, royal priesthood, holy nations.

The redeemed of the Lord,

Wash and bought by the blood of the lamb.

Show forth his love and his glorious works and wonders in our life.

And his marvelous works, and mighty things God has done in our life.

In response to your call Oh Lord,

I will answer, Yes Lord, I will go.

By Rebecca Daluddung

A Lady Who Accepted the Lord Jesus Christ

I had been sick because of the food poisoning I mentioned earlier. It was the second week of my illness, and both of the people working for me were not available. I had to look for someone to fill their place to go and clean houses. I had just interviewed Imelda four days prior. She started Monday and I asked her to come again Tuesday. On Tuesday morning, she came at 7:30 a.m. I was praying in the car before we left. While I was driving, I was sharing with her the love of God and the importance of the soul, about the rich man and Lazarus, about repentance (Acts 2:38), and about Revelation. I shared with her that there are books of works, and books of life. That whosoever's name was not written in the book of life will be cast into the lake of fire. So I had been talking all the way to pick up another lady. And while I parked the car, I showed her the verses in the Bible explaining the things I had just told her.

After a few minutes the Lord told me to stop talking and "close it," almost like closing a business deal. I needed to make sure she understood so that she could make a decision. So I asked Imelda, "Would you want to accept the Lord Jesus Christ today as your Lord and Savior?" And she said, "Yes sister." So I told her, "When we get to the place where we are going, I will lead you in prayer." So when we arrived there, I led her in prayer of repentance and acceptance. I asked her to follow what I said. After I prayed and I prayed again, I told her that I saw the light ... The sun just suddenly shined on us. And I just felt the presence of God and I was crying, and she was crying. I told her that right then, all the angels of Heaven were rejoicing for one person who repents of her sin.

It was a very special day for her and for me. God really does love her. I asked her how she felt after our prayer. She said, "I felt something on my spirit when the sun shined on us. I felt something and I was crying." I told her, "That was the power of God." And she said yes.

I wasn't feeling great physically, but my spirit was so strong. She was one of the fruits of why I got sick. If I wasn't sick, I wouldn't need help with the cleaning. So my sickness brought God's glory. All the glory and honor to the living God we serve. On the way home, I told her that the angels in Heaven were having a party for her. "Likewise I say unto you, there is joy in the presence of the angels of God over one sinner that repenteth." (Luke 15:10)

God knows that her timing was just right. I had the boldness to open my mouth and preach to her about salvation. Truly the word of God said, "Who ever has an ear let him hear ... And today is the day of salvation, tomorrow will be too late."

Pass It On

Have you ever seen a very good movie and you tell your friends about it?

You can't wait to tell them, so you call them right away and tell them that they need to see this movie right away. Well my friend, this is not a movie, this is the book of salvation. This is the most important message they need to hear. What does it profit a man if he gains the whole world, yet loses his own soul? Nothing will he gain. So I urge you to give them a copy of my book. If you don't know how to share your testimony, give them my book and let God work through you. Pass it on after you read it; don't display it on your shelf. Ok, my dear friend? Pass it on my dear brother and sister in Christ.

Pull Them Out of the Pit

While this book was in the process of being editing, Rebecca, who was my editor (by the way, I love her name because, of course, it is my name), communicated with me constantly.

Just in the month of May 2011, I met Honey (not his real name) a month before. I call him Honey because he is a very sweet guy. I had met a lot of people before. Some guys were business men who were very successful and handsome, and even a millionaire got interested in me, but I wasn't interested in any of them as a boyfriend. However, this Honey is one of a kind. He is sweet and his kisses are sweet because I agree to let him kiss me, of course. I actually like him ... I know for sure that I am a very perfectionist type of woman. I like everything to be perfect. So if I am going to date a man, he should first of all meet all the three important qualifications I am looking for:

1. He must be born-again Christian.

2. He must love GOD first, and then love me unconditionally.

3. He must be single.

So this guy meets the first two qualifications, but the third one is the issue. Please pardon me for saying this, but I don't

289

date married men, or divorced men. So it makes me think over and over again of what is happening with me. Why did I come to like Honey? Why is it that of all the men in the world, I came to like him? I keep asking God. The fact that I like him makes me crazy. I constantly think of it and often cannot sleep because of those thoughts. All this time, I avoided the guys who are divorced; I don't want to be with them because they might do the same thing with me. That's been in my mind all these years. So dating a guy who had kids and is divorced is not on my list.

One day, the Lord spoke to me in a small, still voice because of all the questions on my mind for the previous two weeks. The Lord said, "When you see Honey, you should see how I love you." Then I answered the LORD and said, "You are right Lord, I am no different than Honey. The fact that he has been married twice and got divorced doesn't make me more righteous than him. I am also a sinner, bought by the blood of the lamb. If I was perfect, and everybody is perfect, then we don't need a Savior, we don't need a Redeemer. You shouldn't have come to save us." Indeed, I realized that I too had failed once and for all with Ezra. Through Honey, I had learned that no one is perfect in the eyes of God, and that everyone needs a second chance, and that they should not be cast away. I learned that you have to accept them for who they are, and even for their past.

And that was the end of my crazy question, "Why him, why Honey?" God had answered my questions.

After I had been dating Honey for two weeks, he wasn't happy that I called and left a message for his mom.

He came and told me that he was not happy about that. So I said to him, "You want to make your own rules, so I will make my own rules. If you don't want my rules, and I don't want your rules, you walk away, and I walk away."

He told me that he is doesn't like me to be friends with his mom. And I told him that I only have one rule. No sex before marriage. He was surprised and asked me if I can do it. I told him that, yes, I can do it.

Following this, I still continue to see Honey and I enjoy his company a lot. But I was afraid that the passion between me and him would be crazy enough to consume me and, again, I would fail to be pure before marriage. I told Rock about my fear. There's only one thing I fear, and it is that I will fail again, and be lost forever from God's presence. So after another week, I decided to run away from him. Because I don't want to fail and I don't want to go down to that pit where I had fallen in 2003.

I went to visit Lyn Valley Church on June 12, 2011. I invited Mike to come with me for the third time.

We went for lunch after church and Mike was telling me how God is changing him in so many ways. He bought a new car and he wants to quit smoking. After I talked to Mike, we went our separate ways. I decided to go to Fell Ave beach, which is one of my favorite places to go. I was talking to God through my spirit and was amazed at what God is doing in Mike's life.

On the way home, I was making a left turn on the marine drive from Fell Ave. Then I saw a woman in a wheel chair, and the wheel was stuck on the edge of the pavement. She couldn't move the wheel chair. And I said, "Oh my God she needs help." So I prayed and asked in a loud voice, "Lord, could you send someone else to help her please?" And the Lord said, "Why don't you go and help her, you are the one who first saw her." I answered again and said, "With my high heel LORD, Do you think I can pull her out with my high heel?" (I love wearing high heels to go out, especially to church and business occasion.) "Ok Lord I will go.... "So I quickly turned and went back and parked my car in the parking lot beside the woman. As soon as I parked, another car parked beside me. I waved at him and I got out of the car. He asked me, "Are you going to help her?" I said, "Yes, but maybe you can help me because you are stronger than I." So we went to help her, and the lady was so thankful. I told the guy that he was a Godsend, because I was praying a while ago that God would send help to her, so he smiled and drove away.

The moment I drove out and made a left turn … I was thankful that I came back and rescued her to make sure she was safe from that pit she was stuck in. Then the LORD spoke to me again in a small voice, "Isn't that what you are doing?" I answered and said, "Yes LORD," and I was suddenly crying while driving in my car. "That's what I have been doing ever since you raised me up. And I see that with Mike and Mark's life and other people's lives." The powerful emotional picture of this woman and the event convinced me not to run away from Honey, but to help him out of the pit where he had fallen. And as Peter denied Jesus Christ in the first place, the second time around Peter died for Jesus, because he then had the power, which is the Holy Spirit that makes him invincible. That was God's revelation to me on that Saturday night at Willingdon Church. So I don't have to fear anymore and God gave me the anointing and the power to overcome like Peter.

I know that it wasn't only me doing the work that God had called us to do. We all have calling, different callings, different ministries, different offices or gifts. Let us use them for the glory of God. By pulling out someone from the pit, or giving money to the poor, or praying for the sick and visiting them, you will make a big difference in our lives here on earth and it is all for the glory of God.

292

TO THE GREAT I AM

Father in Heaven,

I am so grateful for you making all things possible. Truly you are the God of all possible and the impossible things. You have proven to me over and over again that you can do all things. I worship you in the beauty of your holiness and for your great wisdom, unfailing love, and faithfulness in my life.

I love you, Father, with all my heart, and I will serve you all the days of my life. Use me for your glory, use this book to reach out to the lost and to bring back all of your children that have fallen astray. I pray that all who read this book will come to know, love, and serve you until we see you face-to-face. Thank you for this life you've given me, use me for your glory. Here am I Lord, send me. Thank you for Bernice and Stephen and others who helped make this book into **REALITY**. You are my **Real Riches**, a treasure beyond compare that will never be lost or stolen. Thank you for giving me the Real Riches, the seed you have given me. Now I will sow for the glory of your name. I give you back all the glory and honor and power forever and ever. Amen.

Yours Forever,

Rebecca Daluddung

CPSIA information can be obtained at www.ICGtesting.com
Printed in the USA
LVOW120724131011

250245LV00003B/3/P